# HOW

# TO

# LOVE

# A

# NICE

# GUY

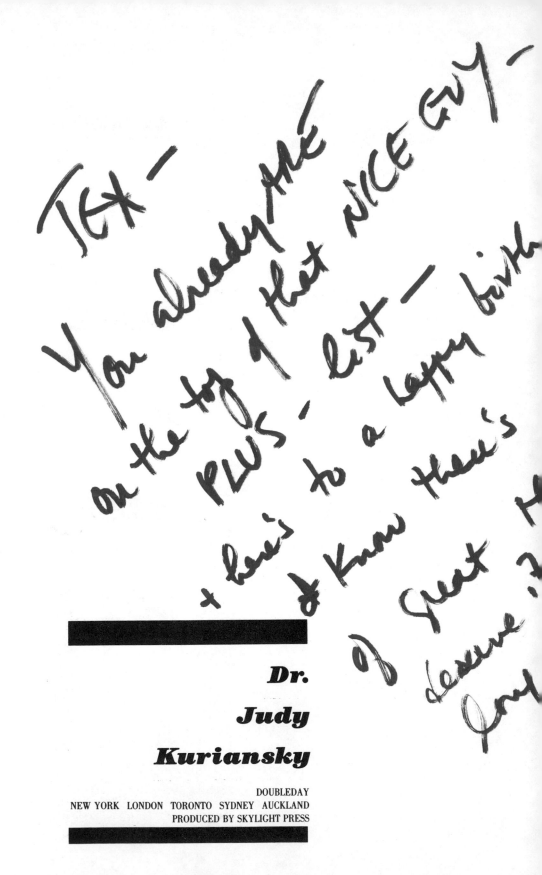

TEX —
You already ARE
on the top of that NICE GUY —
PLUS, list —
there's to a happy birth
+ here's I know there's
of great th
deserve ?
guy

**Dr.**

**Judy**

**Kuriansky**

DOUBLEDAY
NEW YORK  LONDON  TORONTO  SYDNEY  AUCKLAND
PRODUCED BY SKYLIGHT PRESS

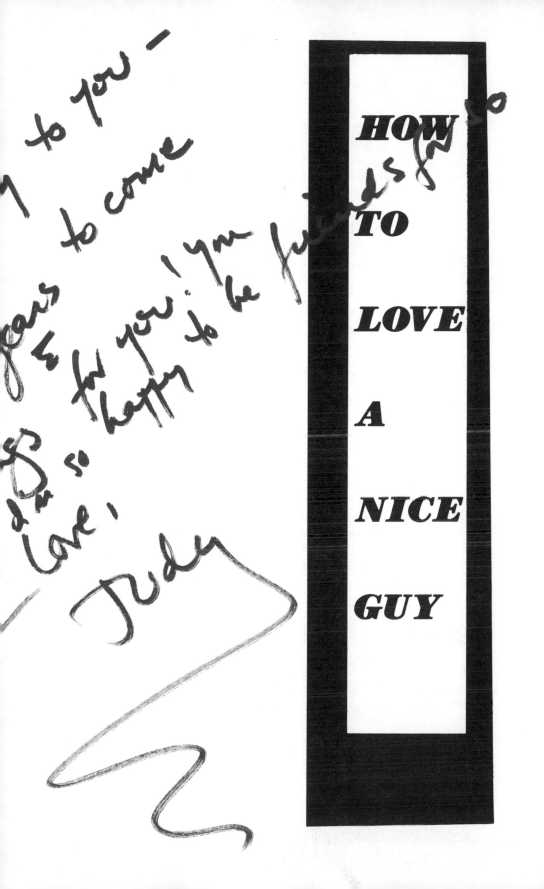

# HOW TO LOVE A NICE GUY

PUBLISHED BY DOUBLEDAY
a division of Bantam Doubleday Dell Publishing Group, Inc.
666 Fifth Avenue, New York, New York 10103

DOUBLEDAY and the portrayal of an anchor
with a dolphin are trademarks of Doubleday,
a division of Bantam Doubleday Dell
Publishing Group, Inc.

Published by arrangement with:
Skylight Press
166 East 56th Street, 3-C
New York, New York 10022

Library of Congress Cataloging-in-Publication Data

Kuriansky, Judith.
How to love a nice guy/
by Judith Kuriansky.—1st ed.
p.     cm.
1. Mate selection—United States.    2. Interpersonal
relations.    3. Women—United States—Attitudes.
I. Title.
HQ801.K87    1990
646.7′7—dc20                                        89-37105
CIP

ISBN 0-385-24869-5

TO NEW LOVERS
IN THE NINETIES,

TO ALL THE
NICE GUYS
WHO
FINISH FIRST
AND THE WOMEN
WHO SEE THAT
WHAT DOES NOT
GLITTER
MAY STILL BE GOLD

# ACKNOWLEDGMENTS

When I read this book, I beam, and thank Lynn Sonberg and Meg Schneider, who had the vision and the pragmatism to get it all going and see it through—to keep an eye on the forest and a hand on the trees. And Guy Kettelhack for his literary skill and soul. With a combination of talent and caring, literature and love come alive.

Thanks, too, to Carol Hill, who helped shape this book, as only an eleven-mile-high dancer can do. And on that journey, warm cheers to my editor, Casey Fuetsch, for her valuable inspiration and dedication, and the staff at Doubleday, including Jill Roberts and Jennifer Rogers, for their wonderful positiveness and valued support.

To my family, friends and colleagues, who contribute so profoundly to my growth and my happiness and my experience of so many facets of love . . .

And to all the women and men over the years across the country in so many walks of life who have shared their hearts so profoundly with me . . .

The cases in this book are based on real people I have come across in my practice, lecturing, media appearances, teaching and life experiences. All the names and identifying details have been changed, while maintaining the integrity of the example. In some cases, stories have been put together as composites to protect an individual's identity and to more clearly present a point.

# CONTENTS

# HOW

# TO

# LOVE

# A

# NICE

# GUY

Listen in on a lunch meeting at an elegant restaurant—a late lunch where the waiters are discreetly clearing up and hoping their two last customers, two women who've been talking to each other for hours, might soon be ready to leave.

"But you can't *marry* him!" Pam leans over the table, sharing this urgent appeal with Marian in a hushed voice. "What would people think?"

"Look," Marian says, with more bravado than she really feels, "I *know* I make more than he does, and I know we come from different backgrounds. But I don't care. I love him and he loves me and we're going to make it work."

Not every woman in Marian's situation would have the courage to consider marriage: prejudice that a man isn't rich or educated or "suitable" enough often gets in the way. But the dilemma couldn't be more common. There are thousands of women who, like Marian, made all the right moves, but still find themselves alone. They are wonderful, bright, charming, interesting women who feel battered by love wars they never bargained for.

Or maybe they *were* successful in entering a long-term relationship, but found that so many of those relationships never worked out—the "right" man so often turned out to be anything but.

What this book will do is give you the best chance of finding that right man—not the man you think

# New Love Choices and Why You Need to Make Them: Your Ten-Step Program for Change

you *ought* to love, but the man you really *will* love and, perhaps more important, who will love *you*. He may turn out to be a plumber. Or a nuclear physicist! Whatever you may find him to be, I guarantee that you'll benefit from the journey to get clear about what you're *really* after in a man—a journey into your own true self. A journey that will involve sharing between two people rather than two professional profiles, two souls rather than two status symbols.

For years I have been on the radio, taking calls and giving advice to thousands of women and men—five nights a week, three hours a night. I've received letters from women across the country in response to my national columns in women's magazines and newspapers. I have talked to thousands of people on television programs I've done in cities across the country and on shows like Oprah, Donahue, Sally, Larry King and Geraldo. I see scores of patients in private practice—and thousands more people when I lecture around the country, from health spas to advertising clubs to universities. When the topic is "love," as it usually is—whether sex, marriage or the desire for a long-term relationship—there isn't much I haven't heard!

And what have I heard most strongly? You not only *want* "love" (whatever your definition of that slippery concept is), you *depend* on it for happiness. Enough energy is expended in the pursuit of love —or fantasizing about it, bemoaning the lack of it, or berating yourself (or your partner) for not being able to find and sustain the "right" kind of it—to send our planet into a new orbit. We're beleaguered by our own urgent doubts and dreams and requirements, along with enough "scientific" data to depress us for decades (like the now famous Harvard–Yale study that left shock waves by its suggestion that any woman over thirty who wants to get married has as much chance of that as winning the lottery).

With all these obstacles, our determination to find love can seem poignant, if not downright tragic. We are so muddled by love messages, some of them broadcast by society, some internalized from our own early conditioning in the family (much of which isn't even conscious), and by our own fumbling experience of wrong man after wrong man, that we're understandably confused about how to bring "love" into our lives. We're not even sure what it *means* anymore.

## REDEFINING HAPPINESS

Here's where I come in. This book will help you to clarify, step by step, exactly what love means—not to your mother; not to your last lover, boyfriend or spouse; not to your best friend; and not to a glib quiz in a glossy women's magazine—but to *you*. Once you've defined love for yourself, you'll be miles ahead, with the *realistic* prospect of bringing love into your life.

Prepare to be surprised. In addition to all of the forces operating on you from the outside—your parents' effect on you, society's impact, the way Sam or John or Pete used to treat you—you've got a much more formidable enemy: yourself. The primary source of obstacles to love isn't, in fact, any of the things you may think "victimize" you from the outside. It isn't what statistics or your mother tells you. It's the deep, inner message about what you "deserve" that you tell *yourself.*

If I were writing this book a decade ago, I'd have a much harder time getting this message across. In fact, if women have made any "inner" strides at all in the past couple of decades, it's that we've grown to see ourselves less as the hapless victims of Fate than as masters of our own lives. Thank heavens for this trend—the strongest one I've clocked in the two decades I've spent talking and listening to thousands of people as a psychologist. It's clear that more and more women are already waking up to the fact that *they* hold the reins to their lives—that they're responsible for their own actions.

The problem is that it can be hard to apply this positive sense of responsibility to love: somehow, in love, everything we "know" goes out the window. We're usually in such a terrible muddle of half-understood motivations, jealousy, fear, envy and fiercely held opinions about what is "right" and "wrong" for us that we can't get the *clarity* to see what, if anything, we can do about it.

I want you to see you've got the same power to choose what you want in your love life as you're learning you have in other areas of your life. The clarity women have gained in their social, professional and financial lives can be had in love, too. "Love" doesn't have to torture you. It can be something you happily, willingly, carefully make part of your life—with your eyes open all the way.

But, again: prepare to be surprised. As you undertake this journey and discover that the mystery of love isn't *quite* so mysterious (at least not in the ways you may have thought it was), I make you two promises.

First, you'll discover that what you *thought* you wanted in a man may not have much to do with what you *really* want. As a result, you may find love in some pretty unexpected places. As you'll see shortly, many women find themselves redefining their ideal man from the ground up when they waken to their real needs and desires.

Which brings me to the second promise. Not only will I help you define what love means to you, but—with the help of numerous women who've done it—I'll show you *how* to find that love and make that "unconventional" match work in the real world.

True satisfaction with a man *is* possible: it just starts with asking yourself some questions you may never have dared—or known—to ask yourself before.

When asking yourself these questions, you'll probably discover that you have many conscious and unconscious emotional prejudices about love. No matter what a woman's own accomplishments are, she may feel nagging certainty (for example) that the only man she could possibly love must be smarter, more powerful, more aggressive, and must make more money than she does. She is, after all, still "only a woman." This is an especially terrible self-view because it's so common. It also allows for a strong double standard: you often hear of the doctor marrying his receptionist, a lawyer marrying his secretary, but haven't "doctor" and "lawyer" always implied "man"? Until now, we've had a hard time imagining the reverse—that a highly accomplished *woman* might choose a man of "lesser" achievement or station.

And this is where we get to that painful, condescending-sounding phrase "marrying down." The traditional idea has always been for a woman to "marry up"—marry a man who would increase her status and take care of her for the rest of her life. Marrying a man "less successful" than you has always been referred to as "marrying down."

What a self-defeating way of looking at marriage—or any relationship! A woman who is afraid of "marrying down" implicitly feels that her own stature—her very worth—is dependent on the status of the man she loves. Assuming this, she erases any of her *own* accomplishments, the self she is no matter *whom* she gets involved with. It's also, obviously, a damaging and demeaning way of looking at another human being—judging him solely by his status in the world. Furthermore, it's a limited definition of "success" in terms of money, power or status, as opposed to emotional maturity, personal fulfillment or spirituality.

Worse yet, defining love in terms of who's "up" or "down" is a prejudice that keeps men and women apart who might find deep happiness together. Indeed men and women should strive to be "peers"—equals on any number of levels. When you're equal in your love for each other, your self-confidence, your ambitions to grow and live productive lives, your ability to care for and give strength to each other, you're talking about the kind of equality that makes a relationship work. This has nothing to do with who's on top, or money or—in the status sense we've grown to think of it—"power."

Why is this type of relationship possible now? Because more women are fulfilling their potential, getting ahead in their careers, earning substantial salaries and leading the life that they used to wait for a man to give them. I prefer to eliminate the concept of direction—the idea that you might be marrying "up" or "down"— entirely. Instead, I want you to start focusing on the dynamics that go on between you and your lover, on what you're each doing for and with the other, independently of whatever the "World Out There" thinks. When you do this, you start to examine your relationship productively.

Of course, it's not that the World Out There doesn't count. As you'll see in a moment, we'll devote a good portion of this book to the problems of adjusting to outside pressures, which may be especially severe when you find yourself loving someone who has a different background from your own. But you can't *start* with that worry. Not, anyway, if you want to give yourself the chance you deserve— to find love in the right place for *you*. Again, that love may turn out to be a very different experience than you expected. And a far more satisfying one.

Learning all this sounds like a tall order. How will we go about it?

## TEN STEPS TO FINDING LOVE WHERE YOU LEAST EXPECT IT

First of all, this book is a *program for change*. Each chapter is a step—and each step leads to the next. So, by the end of our journey, you'll have gotten a whole new—and more accurate—sense of who you are, what will make you happy, and what kind of man you're really looking for. To reach these broad horizons, we'll start with what goes on in you from the moment you "fall" for a man.

## STEP 1: DEMYSTIFY ATTRACTION: THE "SOMEHOW YOU KNOW" SYNDROME

There's a lot less mystery to attraction than you may think. The first step allows you to see what is going on when your knees get weak and you're stunned once again by the power of attraction—when what I call your love antennae whir wildly and you've zapped into your romantic fantasy. (You'll hear the term "love antennae" a lot in this book. It's a metaphor for the "sensors" that take in and send out love messages and let us—and the man we've zeroed in on—know we're "receptive.") In fact, what you're feeling is not all, or even primarily, "magic." The forces you're responding to are easier to delineate than you may realize. It's also a relief to name and acknowledge them: you'll see that you're actually *choosing* to be attracted to the men you "fall" for, and recognizing that gives you the first real glimmer that you can choose *not* to rise to the bait.

## STEP 2: DETERMINE YOUR CHECKLIST

Here we will explore what I call your checklist. Your checklist is a rich source of clues to who you are and what you want. It's the inner "eligibility test" to which you subject every man you meet. Usually more unconscious than conscious, it tells you with lightning speed whether "he" is measuring up, whether "he" is the One. You'll discover that your responses form patterns, even if you don't think you're attracted to any one "type" of man. This step will show you what you're working with when your inner console lights up and tells you "Get him!" or "Get away!" It will also show you what you may want to change.

### Step 3: Confront Your Dream Lovers

The third step brings you into one of the deepest and most intimate areas of love: your fantasies. By taking a close look at your "dream lovers"—the men, or ideals of men, you truly believe could satisfy you (but often elude you or let you down)—you come face to face with your deep beliefs about yourself and what you want in a man. And then you'll see how some of these beliefs may be steering you way off course from your goal of happiness. Falling in love with a human being is different from falling in love with an idea. This chapter will help you wake up to that difference, so that you won't be as prone to falling into a relationship that fits your fantasy but makes you miserable, or to vaulting out of a relationship that could turn out much better than you think—even if he's not your dream lover.

### Step 4: Wake Up to Emotional Traps

Here we go a bit deeper, seeing what underlies our choice of dream lovers, what we *assume* when we make the attraction choices we do. You'll recognize that what *looks* like sabotage ("Why do I keep getting into these self-destructive relationships?" or any other variation of "Why can't I learn . . . ?") is in fact the result of your responding unconsciously to what I call emotional traps—inner messages that tell you to behave in certain ways because you're unconsciously convinced you *have* to. (For example, the need to be loved combined with the fear of being abandoned leads to a fear of attachment. That "fear of attachment" is an emotional trap.) You'll see how other women have faced a variety of emotional traps—and learned to escape them.

### Step 5: Recognize Family Dramas and Scripts: How to Stop Reenacting the Ones That Don't Work

Here we'll come to an understanding of the family "dramas" and "scripts" you continue to play, usually unconsciously. These inter-actions with our parents we had as children—and those we observed between our parents and among other family members—all have a profound effect on how we behave now. Waking up to that effect means seeing which scripts we're continuing to follow and thus which scripts unnecessarily bind us and hold us back. Becoming conscious of your scripts will help you choose the ones you'd rather follow and refuse the opportunity to star in the ones that don't work anymore.

## STEP 6: CHANGE YOUR CHECKLIST

After the adventure of this inner housework, you'll learn how to change your checklist—how to dig in your heels when you feel a rush of old, inappropriate messages threatening to sweep you away toward the same old destructive ends. ("I know he's wrong for me, but I can't help myself!" doesn't have to be your motto.) You'll reconstruct a new checklist that will contain traits you truly *do* want in a man and in a relationship. This is a cleansing process, and a freeing one, with a wonderful outcome: to how you how much *power* you have over what once may have seemed like Fate or being at the mercy of men. Your power will grow from the first step to the last—to the point where you've got a whole new sense of Mr. Right; how to find him and how to grow in the relationship; and, even more important, a new sense of *you.*

## STEP 7: DISCOVER A NEW VIEW OF SEX

The sexual "cues" we've learned to respond to can sometimes get us into trouble. Money, power and the primitive animal are just a few of those turn-ons—and we often find our fantasies don't prepare us for real life and real love. The good news is that it's possible to develop new cues, to resist the knee-jerk reaction of acting on your first sexual impulse and to give yourself time to respond to other, more subtle ones. You can also learn to weave sexual fantasy into your life so it doesn't disrupt what you do *out* of bed. This is particularly crucial because, as many women know, if a man doesn't feel "dominant" in financial or social terms, it can translate into disaster in the bedroom—if he feels he's "not man enough." Similarly, a woman's relative position of "dominance" as chief breadwinner or greater professional success can wreak havoc with her own expectations and feelings of sexual adequacy. There *are* solutions to the sexual dilemmas you face in "new partnerships." You'll explore them here.

### STEP 8: LISTEN TO HIM: WHAT MEN ARE THINKING

This is largely a book about and for women, but getting realistic about your chances in love also means finding out about *men*—in their own words. You'll learn to view men not as some alien race, but through mirrors similar to those in which you see yourself. They come from just as rich a family tapestry as you do; they must deal in equally painful ways with the expectations of "society" (and their families, co-workers and friends)—not to mention the women they've been involved with. You'll see how and why it's sometimes difficult for a man to accept the "new partnering" I'm talking about—and how to navigate through his reaction to not playing a traditional role. You'll see how his checklist, family scripts and past experiences help you gain essential appreciation for what *he* brings to the love equation and how his love antennae work.

### STEP 9: NAVIGATE THROUGH REAL LIFE

Here's the real scoop on what to do now that you've made the choice. Is everything perfect? No. The world around you may appear to be out of sync in any number of ways. Now we'll look at how to cope with the concrete problems you'll face. What problems? Family disapproval; pressure and lack of support from friends; problems in the social and job arenas (introducing him to your boss, colleagues, clients; mixing different pleasures, like football and the ballet); money problems about running the household and taking vacations; and dealing with your *own* occasional misgivings. Learning to draw on what's really important to you—your love for each other—is especially important when you come up against these inevitable blocks. And in this chapter, you'll be armed with *practical* solutions!

### STEP 10: LEARN FROM SUCCESS STORIES

Nothing is more persuasive or inspiring than success. You'll meet a number of men and women who picked partners who seemed to their families, friends and the rest of the World Out There very unlikely candidates for romance and marriage. However, because they have learned to listen to *themselves*, and because they're operating from an honest assessment of what each truly is seeking in relationships and in life, they've found and are building lasting love. You'll recognize many issues at work here that we'll have explored throughout the book: dealing with different backgrounds, unequal incomes, age differences and differences in ambition. Everything you may have thought had to be a "problem" can be dealt with much more positively than you probably suspect. Success stories here will offer proof.

When I call these ten steps a program for change, I don't mean a program for changing the world. It's a program for changing your approach to love. Women who've undergone this change of attitude, who've learned to open up to new ideas about love and to men they'd previously never dreamed they'd meet, much less love, all experience a kind of breakthrough, a moment where something *releases* in them, and they see the range of choices we've been talking about as real. You'll see what I mean when you meet the following two women: Audrey and Carol.

### AUDREY

One look at her and you know Audrey works in the world of fashion. She is not only pretty and well-dressed, but she has a talent for "putting it all together" that makes you notice her when she walks into the room. Her innate sense of style has in no small way contributed to her success as a fashion editor at a major women's magazine. However, while her profession might seem predictable, her love life has been anything but.

Audrey is married to Alex, a building contractor who, as you might expect, is more familiar with brick than chic. In fact, Alex still kids Audrey about her "profession"—he can't understand how she can make so much money talking about hemlines. Not so secretly, he's also very proud of her. He knows she's a very special lady, and he can't believe he found her. Audrey sometimes has a hard time believing it, too.

"The magazine was moving to a new building," she says about the time she first met Alex, "and it was a *mess*. Half the walls hadn't been put up between the new offices, and there were plaster and dirt and gaping holes everywhere. In the middle of it all, this guy, covered in white dust in the grimiest overalls it's ever been my misfortune to

see—the contractor responsible for the renovation *and* the mess—
is sitting on top of my new desk, eating his lunch. Needless to say,
I was not pleased. I asked him what the hell he was doing here and
wasn't all this supposed to be *finished* by now? He blinked contentedly
at me—he's got the damnedest way of *never* getting upset over
anything—and laughed. 'You ever hear of a building finished on
time?' he said. 'This is New York, lady.' He also informed me I
didn't look half-bad for a magazine editor. He'd always thought editors
looked like small-town librarians with thick glasses and thin hair.

"I'd like to say the rest is history," Audrey continues, "but if
it was, it was pretty strange history! Alex had to spend the next four
days finishing up in our offices, and I had to spend the same four
days trying to make sure that files and desks and chairs were put
where I wanted them. We bumped into each other a lot. We laughed
a lot. We got to like each other a lot. Then he asked me if I liked
football. I said no. He said maybe I'd learn to like it if I went with
him to a game that Saturday."

Audrey smiles, remembering his audacity.

"I'd never met anyone like him. I mean, sure, I'd dated plenty
of men—lawyers, stockbrokers, doctors and even an occasional
athlete—you get to meet a lot of people in the magazine business.
But I never thought I'd fall in love with, let alone marry, a man who
didn't own a suit!"

Audrey remembers her parents were "less than thrilled" when
she brought Alex to meet them. Alex couldn't hide the fact (and didn't
try to) that he hadn't gone to Harvard or Yale. "Did you ever hear a
Catholic mother suggest to her daughter, 'Why don't you live with
him for a while?' " Announcing to her parents that this was the man
she wanted to marry did not gladden their hearts.

But Audrey knew Alex was the right man once she got over her
*own* trepidation. "Frankly, I wasn't sure at first that the problems
caused by our different interests and backgrounds were surmountable.
I made myself go out with another guy when I first met and started
going out with Alex—I wanted to be sure I wasn't just temporarily
swept away by how *different* he was from every other man I knew.
So this other guy, Mr. Corporate Executive, took me out to dinner
one Friday night, and I was curious to see what it would be like after
so many beer and pretzel evenings with Alex. The first thing I noticed
on my fancy dinner date is that I didn't laugh once. Alex and I
laughed all the time. He'd grown on me, I guess. I missed him. I

knew he was for me. He may not have owned a suit, but he sure wasn't an 'empty suit' like all the other men I'd dated."

Sometimes love can come through the back door. You can be surprised, as Audrey was, into the revelation that you're enjoying something or someone you never expected you could! Audrey and Alex were able to deepen their initial flirtation into love. Certainly it took more steps and time (don't worry—you'll hear about them later!), but the point is that Audrey's breakthrough happened almost in spite of herself. By allowing her heart to open on its own, she found someone she would never have consciously chosen. And, with her real feelings as her guide, she made the right choice.

"Allowing" your heart to open isn't always, or even commonly, easy, however. It often takes time and help to see how your options can open up and how much greater your opportunities for love are than you think. The following story is a typical example of struggles many women face in overcoming prejudices about men and love. The point is, there's a "breakthrough" waiting on the other side—even if sometimes it takes work to get to it.

### CAROL

Carol had made great strides professionally. It had taken several years, but she'd turned a dead-end office job at a company that produced humorous cards and calendars into a position that allowed her to get paid for what she'd always loved doing: cartooning. She had always loved to doodle for friends, but it had taken her a long while to take her talent seriously.

Carol's increasing professional success did not, unfortunately, herald a new era in her personal relationships. A pretty woman, Carol always felt men were attracted to her for superficial reasons. She had had such a low opinion of herself for so long that despite the fact she was now extremely well-regarded professionally, she still gravitated toward self-absorbed men whose attention she had to struggle to get. She kept wondering why she kept meeting so many "unreliable" men, until increasing insight in therapy led her to understand she was their accomplice in depriving her of what she thought she wanted. Striving for but not getting what she wanted, she played the part of a lovely companion they could flaunt, rather than a woman with whom to share deep feelings, and struggled always to win their approval to *prove* her self-worth.

With insight into these dynamics, Carol's self-confidence grew, and she began to find the flashy, driven, narcissistic men she had surrounded herself with less appealing. This change allowed her love antennae to pick up James.

Carol met James in a studio drawing class he had taken—not to pursue any great talent, but to help him in the art therapy degree he was working toward. Right away she was drawn to his warmth and liked him as a friend. "He's the first man who's ever asked me about myself. He's the first guy I've ever shown my drawings to!" Carol was elated that she'd found a man with whom she could share more than a superficial date and started to wonder if he could be more than a friend—until the day James asked her up for coffee at his place.

"If I had a fantasy about James," Carol says, "it ended when I walked into his apartment. It was a mess! Small, stuffy, with books and papers piled up on the floor and in every corner—unopened mail lying all over the place, clothes dropped on tables and chairs." Carol came to a dead halt. "I know I don't live like royalty," she says, "but I was so used to going out with guys for whom appearances counted *first*. They all had terrific, glamorous bachelor pads, and I had to confront the fact that I'd always expected to hook up with a man who would make my life better—*materially* better. There didn't seem much chance of that with James!"

Carol was troubled with ambivalence. She loved being with James—wasn't that love?—but he wasn't her "picture" of the man she thought she should be with. Even so, she couldn't just suddenly write him off because he didn't offer what other men she knew had. He offered her so much else—so much of what she really needed from a man, but had never had the self-esteem to believe she really deserved.

Slowly, through therapy, and through her continuing delight in the things she *did* love about James, Carol was able to question her assumptions about who she "had" to be within a relationship—and began to see that she was being driven by deep fears that she wasn't "adequate." This led her to get involved with men whose *appearances* were so successful that she felt they lent her worth. As her own sense of self-worth grew, bolstered by James's continuing delight in who she was, not just what she looked like or what she did, a new picture of possibility began to occur to her.

"It's not that I like messy apartments any better than I used to!" Carol laughs. "But where James lives and how modest his aspirations are don't stop me from loving him. I know he's developing in his own ways, just as I am in mine. And now I feel, for the first time in my life, I've found a man I can really grow with—not just acquire as some badge to prove my 'worth.' "

Carol's story is inspiring because it shows how facing some hidden, unconscious truths about *herself* brought her happiness. As you'll soon see, it's your assumptions about who you are and what you deserve that often get in the way of seeing all the options you have. You'll learn ways to uncover those assumptions so you can get clearer about what you truly want—not what you're driven out of old fears to think you have to settle for.

But let's pause a moment to see what Audrey and Carol, different as their stories are, have in common. Each of them came to see the differences between what she thought she must have in a man and what it was she actually wanted and needed. Each came to realize that her initial criteria for selecting a man—what I refer to as a checklist for determining a partner's eligibility—did not, in the end, bring her the right man.

Throughout this book, I'll be referring to the idea that we all carry around a mental checklist of desirable traits in men and that we're (sometimes consciously, sometimes unconsciously) *always* ticking off items on this list, every time we think of or meet a man. To make sure your checklist works for you—by enhancing your chance of meeting the right man instead of hindering it—you may have to do the work that Carol learned to do: become *conscious* of assumptions and hidden fears that are holding you back.

And, since you picked up this book, you're more than likely conscious of being "held back." Perhaps you've just broken up yet another relationship. "Another disaster! Why couldn't I see it coming?" you ask. "I must be jinxed!" Well, the truth is, it wasn't an unforeseeable "disaster." It was the inevitable result of working with the wrong checklist.

The men we choose almost always reflect our inner conflicts

about who we really are, or our dreams and fantasies about what we want to be. The major conflict we feel within ourselves is the struggle between a preconceived idea ("I should marry a rich, successful, accomplished man because that's what I'm supposed to do") and what may be a very different genuine desire ("I want a man with whom I can be intimate and share my life fully"). When you're conflicted in this way, your checklist is bound to steer you wrong. Either it urges you to seek a man you really don't want (and so you're always disappointed when you find him), or you seem to sabotage yourself by being attracted to someone you "know" isn't right for you but reinforces some secret, negative view of yourself ("He gives me what I really deserve—nothing").

Many a woman's conscious *and* unconscious desires coalesce into a desire that sounds simple on the face of it: to "marry well." What does "well" mean to her? It can vary from an intellectual man, to someone who cuts a dashing figure in work or social circles, to someone of whom her mother would heartily approve. He can be a man at the top of the corporate or artistic ladder, or a guy her friends would "die" for. Unfortunately, even if the woman does find this version of her ideal man, she often finds she's picking a man who is more right for her friend, her mother or her boss than for herself. She may be stuck in a painful, stagnant relationship—or suffer a bitter breakup, never quite knowing what went wrong.

Let me say at this point, I am *not* telling you to settle—but to *select*. And to make this selection on the basis of a wider variety of factors, mostly based on who a man is and how he treats you rather than how he looks or what he does.

An important point about occupation: there's nothing wrong with asking someone what he "does." As long as it doesn't automatically mean you're consciously or unconsciously getting ready to "rate" a man according to someone else's standards. Information about a man's job, background or lifestyle serves as a point of reference—an objective, verifiable fact that places him in the world—and may indicate his interests as well as his means of earning a living. But women need to be aware of the amazing number of presumptions and prejudices, some of them highly misleading, that they may bring to his answer about what he does. He says, "I'm an attorney," "I'm a college professor," "I'm a journalist," "I'm a plumber," and a woman will almost certainly jump to major conclusions about his education, social status and earning capacity—and therefore his suitability as a mate.

A big problem with these prejudices isn't only that they're so often wrong, but that they urge you to act on them quickly, before you've given yourself a chance to figure out what it is you *really* think or want.

I offer that the process of selection we all use when we decide who's right and who's wrong for us has to be *slowed down*. When we look at the women who've been successful in seeing the real love options open to them—high-fashion Audrey with down-to-earth Alex, increasingly secure Carol with her sensitive James—we see, in each case, that they've taken time. Time to allow the relationship to unfold at its own pace. Time to get to know someone for who he is and not for what he looks like or what he does for a living. Time to explore their *own* feelings about what they want in a relationship or out of life. Time to experience how their partners make them feel about themselves.

It's not easy to get past the first knee-jerk reactions we feel when the unconscious items on our checklists send out bulletins. ("He's a doctor—I must get to know him!" "God, he's so gorgeous—just what I like!" "Just listen to those polysyllabic words—this is the brilliant guy I've been waiting for!") But it's extremely important that you start paying attention to *what you actually let in*, as opposed to what you're striving to see in a man out of your own urgent needs. In fact, understanding that difference is critical. And the first step in understanding that difference is to pull back on the reins—give yourself *time* to see if *you're* painting the picture or if the picture is unfolding as it is. Your own needs can be so urgent that, instinctively, you may resist taking time to be more objective. But if happiness is your goal, the "wait" is worth it.

Learning to wait and watch—and to investigate your own true feelings during that time—is what this program will teach you. Once you've taken the time to explore the inner you, the picture of what makes you happy will almost always be different from what you imagine now.

One thing I can guarantee about "happiness" right now: it means more than landing a man! A fundamental issue for women has to do with the strong, misbegotten belief that you've got to look to a *man* for total happiness, as if he somehow "completes" you. But you'll never find happiness if you're convinced you're less than "whole"! I'll help you dig inside yourself and come up with the inner strength and power that will make you realize you're complete—and "enough."

It's time to take stock—to gently unravel and critically examine the standards by which you accept or reject a possible mate, to look at the real motivations for your choices. And to adopt some *new* ones that will bring you happiness. Bear in mind that this must be done thoughtfully and carefully, with full respect for the power these standards still hold for you and for the fact that they do retain a certain validity even today. There is much truth in the fact that a woman's life is immeasurably enriched by the love of a good man. The question is what *constitutes* a "good man." The answer will be different for everyone. Each union involves elements of surrender and vulnerability. Letting someone into your life at the most intimate levels is an enormous risk. You need to bring as much wisdom to the process as you can. I'll help you do that, by helping you understand what is going on inside you. Awareness is half the battle: then change can happen.

From the bedroom to the boardroom, there are a lot of problems to face. I'll show you how women have overcome a variety of common hurdles, with a wonderful result: a love that's stronger for the difficulties it's had to weather. A love based on something far less ephemeral than status or what "they" think is right for you. A love based on the real delight a woman and man can take in each other, a delight that comes from within each of them—and lingers in the loving space between them.

That's what we're after as we begin our ten steps. That's, after all, the gift we're striving for: a love *you* can live with and grow with. Come with me and find that love for yourself.

What is attraction?

Given how you usually experience it—in one sudden jolt—attraction seems to defy analysis. You *feel* it, spontaneously, like a sudden flame rising up. You don't "think" about it—at least not at the moment it's happening. What drives the bee to the flower (or the moth to the flame) seems mysterious, magical, and—depending on whether your own experiences *after* attraction have been positive or negative—"wonderful" or "tragic." What it almost always feels like is larger than life—the old "stranger across the crowded room" phenomenon, where you see "him" and you're swept away. It could be his eyes, his build, the way he gestures when he speaks, the way he stretches out his legs in a chair—some overwhelming sense that *he's* the one. "And somehow you know," as the song goes. You may not be able to put it into words, but you know the *tug*.

Call it chemistry. Call it animal instinct. Fate. That "special something." It's sweeping and unmistakable. And, if you're like some women, you don't especially *want* to know why you're drawn to a man, because you worry that would take the magic away—ruin things. You'd rather just enjoy it—not figure it out. That's how many women feel at the moment of attraction, or when the attraction is reciprocated and they're in the first, elated throes we call "falling in love." Who wants to dissect that?

However, if "some enchanted

# *Demystify Attraction: The "Somehow You Know" Syndrome*

evening" has a habit of turning into "a hard day's night"—if the honey you're attracted to always turns sour—you may well be curious about what that tug you feel is all about, and why you're so often pulled in the wrong direction.

Don't worry, looking deeper doesn't mean the "magic" will vanish. It just increases the chance that the man you fall in love with will be the right man for you! That will make the magic even *more* wonderful—and the love between you greater.

## HOW YOU DECIDE TO BE ATTRACTED

Why are you attracted to one type or a limited number of types of men? Or, if you resist this idea ("After all," I can hear some of you say, "I've gone out with lots of men and they've all been different"), what accounts for all the men you *don't* have a desire to meet? We all have some ballpark idea of what kind of man attracts us—and perhaps a more vivid idea of the kind of man who doesn't. These are usually such "givens" that it probably hasn't occurred to you to figure out exactly why you've got them. You simply "know" who's right and who isn't. Again, you may resist the idea of finding out *why* you know this—but your very resistance can be a clue that you need to take a look inside. And, if you're not happy with the men you've found so far, you've got much inducement to take that look. Don't be afraid!

In fact, when you declare that the reason you're attracted to one type and not another is "chemistry" ("and that's all there is to it"), you're refusing to see the *whole* story. What you're covering up is the *decision* you've made to go with one type and not another. That's an extremely important and complex decision, made as much unconsciously as consciously. When you "decide" to be attracted, you're acting on certain factors and according to certain qualifications: what I call needs. When you've decided on the "right" man, what you're doing is choosing someone you believe will meet those needs. Your needs direct you to pick X, not Y (or Sam, not Peter), and you do.

Where do all these complex needs come from? A variety of sources: brain chemistry, which is the only factor over which you don't have control (but it makes up the smallest percentage of what urges you to be attracted to a man); cultural stereotypes that surround us, including what the media reinforces as the right "love choice";

early conditioning (from childhood as well as our early dating experiences); and family relationships—especially the "scripts" we follow based on what we learned from our parents and siblings. Of these four factors, we'll be concentrating on the last three throughout this book—because they're the three we can *do* something about!

Most of us aren't conscious of these forces, but it's richly rewarding to *become* conscious of them. Why? Because by awakening to the fact that you're not a slave to "mysterious" forces over which you've got no control, you discover a whole new world of *choice*. You *do* have control over old patterns of behavior that don't work anymore—you *can* change them for the better.

So let's see what is really going on when "somehow you know . . ."

## THE FOUR ATTRACTION FACTORS—AND THE NEEDS THAT FUEL THEM

Deep inside our psyches—the "first cause" behind all of our dreams, beliefs and behavior—is a complex of "needs" that we spend our lives attempting to meet. Actually, there are three levels of need from which we operate, and which we seek to fulfill when we seek "love."

The level of which we're most aware is that of our "physical needs." These are the preferences that have to do with lifestyle or physical attributes you're conscious of when you tick off the items on your checklist: tall, short, quiet, talkative, dark, blond, businesslike, artistic, etc. Beneath this level is a second category, of which we're usually far less conscious—our "emotional needs." These might be a need for protection, shelter, security or, conversely, freedom, room to grow, create and express ourselves. But there is a level even deeper than our "emotional needs" (here we really get to our bedrock)—the level we knew from the first moments of our lives and one that largely defines what we're after beyond all else: the need for "unconditional love." This is a state of complete acceptance—which you certainly experienced in the womb and very likely continued to experience as a newborn baby, dependent on and loved by your mother.

It's interesting that we *begin* with this innate knowledge of unconditional love and yet are so rarely conscious of it as adults. We have to work back *toward* a state that was completely natural to us when we were born! That unconditional love is a state worth aspiring to is abundantly clear to people who experience it, people who are *aware* of loving unconditionally in their relationships now. It's a transcendent state where you give and receive love without thought of gain or loss. This is truly the highest state of love—where love is most healing and nurturing. It enables you to rise above so much of the "warfare" you may now think is inevitable between the sexes. It is a state where you *accept* your lover and feel accepted by him. And it's a state where you experience loving without being concerned about whether, or how, the other person responds, where you feel spiritually connected, where you are not defined by what you do but by who you are at your core. For now, let's accept that we can only glimpse this as a goal—but remember it's where we're headed.

Your needs obviously comprise a basic determinant in your attraction script. But too often they can lead you astray. Say, for example, you feel the need to be creative—write poetry, or paint— but you're afraid to try your hand at it. To compensate, you may be attracted to a man who is himself creative, and attempt to live vicariously through him. The problem is, he's not really meeting your need—*you* still are not taking action to be creative yourself and so *his* creativity, attractive as it is, can never really fulfill you. In fact, you usually end up resenting him for not meeting your needs, which of course he can't! It's common to get short-circuited in this way: seeking from another person what we really need to provide ourselves.

Attractions like this can depend on emotional or practical bases. For example, in another script, it may be that you are missing some basic things—like a comfortable home or a reliable roof over your head—and so you're drawn to someone with an established home and money, someone who'll provide you with that roof.

The major problem with attractions like these—intended to compensate for what you need—is that they are at the mercy of your needs, and if your needs shift, the "love" may falter. For example, if you start to make enough money to provide for yourself, the man you've gone to for security may not be "necessary" anymore, and you may find yourself falling out of love or thinking of affairs. The man's "usefulness" will have disappeared—again, through no fault of *his* own, or yours, since you were responding to a basic need of which you may not have been fully conscious.

Ideally, relationships should be more than need-fulfillers. Unconditional love is what we're really aiming for, because in that state of complete acceptance, besides being able to fulfill yourself separately and together, your *capacity* to change and accept change in your partner grows immeasurably.

You'll get there. But first you have to recognize how the first two levels of need (physical and emotional) work in your relationships. Then you can start to change your checklist so you can grow and increase your chances of experiencing unconditional love. A man must be more than a means of fulfilling your needs: he's someone to share your life with. You can truly share your life with someone else only when you feel *complete* yourself. Or, as I said in the first chapter, to have a "whole" relationship, you have to be "whole" yourself. Then the relationship you have with a man will *enhance* your life, not merely fulfill certain narrow needs. (And, when that happens, you may discover that the right man for you may not be the person you once expected him to be. He doesn't have to be rich, handsome and conventionally successful to enhance your life. But you'll see that for yourself soon enough!)

Now that you have a sense of what drives you, here are the four factors that affect your needs and attraction.

## FACTOR 1: BRAIN CHEMISTRY

It's virtually impossible to be conscious of this factor—or have any control over it. The chemical reactions that occur in our brains regarding love and attraction will happen whether or not we want them to. One "chemical reaction" that occurs couldn't sound less romantic, either: the secretions of our bodies produce certain olfactory sensations that provoke sexual excitement in someone else. In other words, our bodily scents are a turn-on! In the human species, however, these scents are so subtle that you're generally not aware that they're what's causing you to notice the man you're next to—or him to notice you. These sexually provocative scents (called pheromones) trigger in your partner a chemical reaction in the brain's "pleasure" center, resulting in a host of emotional associations and appetites that can quite quickly lead to a very strong state of desire.

A number of cultures have clued into body scents' importance in attraction. In one Greek dance, for example, men wear handkerchiefs under their arms, then pass them to the lady of their choice. (You might consciously wince at the thought, but your brain chemistry—faced with one of those handkerchiefs—might make you feel very differently!) An experiment done in England in which the pheromone scent from women was applied to seats in a theater produced the predictable result: men tended to gravitate to the scented seats. Other research also indicates that the brain affects romance, because people with certain types of brain damage were found to be *unable* to experience "falling in love."

But perhaps the most interesting evidence that shows a correlation between chemicals in the brain and "falling in love" is this: studies by two researchers, Dr. Donald Klein and Dr. Michael Leibowitz of the New York State Psychiatric Institute, show that, in certain women, "falling in love" makes the brain's profile uncannily resemble an amphetamine high. The "brain in love" (as these researchers term it) pours out a chemical equivalent to an amphetamine, called phenylethlamine, which, because the woman can actually become addicted to the "high" it gives her, induces her to fall in love—to become, in effect, a "love junkie."

Clearly chemical reactions do have an effect on our attractions—but our desires and what we find erotic are dependent on so much more than that. Our minds direct our bodies as much as, if not more than, the reverse.

## FACTOR 2: CULTURAL STEREOTYPES

There are two major cultural stereotypes about love that especially affect attraction today. It's no wonder we've internalized them as if they were absolute truth: they've been around for centuries. The first is that there's a perfect other half, a Mr. Right out there waiting to find you. The second is a very unreal picture of love, promoted by everything from "Cinderella" to "Dynasty," but dating back (at least) to Tristan and Isolde. To appreciate the effect of these stereotypes on your love life—and why you may feel deprived (or guilty) because you somehow *aren't* living happily ever after with a perfect counterpart—let's start by looking at a little history.

First, the one-half-needs-another idea comes from the ancient Greeks—or, more specifically, from Aristophanes, in his account of the mythical Androgynes. According to this myth, the Androgynes were the original race on earth—extravagantly supplied with two heads, two arms, two legs and two sets of sexual organs. As mortals usually do in Greek myths, they misbehaved, and Zeus ran true to form by punishing them creatively. He split them in two: male and female. You can see where the idea of finding your missing half came from! This idea of man and woman as two halves comprising a whole underlies all of Western civilization's treatment of men and women, and our whole social evolution. All through the Middle Ages, up to the Renaissance—from Tristan and Isolde, to Heloise and Abelard, to Romeo and Juliet—the idea of two Fate-matched lovers (true passion against all odds) fueled men and women's dreams (and, worse, their expectations). By the eighteenth and nineteenth centuries, woman was hobbled and corseted and held down in an effort to keep her, in the Victorian phrase, "the angel of the house," whose duty was to her "keeper"—the "better half," or husband.

This centuries-old view of women is not, as we'd like to think, completely obsolete. Despite the struggles of women in the last one hundred years to attain an equal social footing with men, women's self-views have often still been grounded in the curious paradox developed through the centuries of what a woman *really* was—personally and privately idealized, but socially "inferior" and dependent on a man. Only "he" could validate her and make her "whole."

The message that a woman finds completion in a man is fostered—and made powerful—by being cloaked in some very powerful and appealing "love" packages. Look at the romantic myths that have fueled Broadway and the movies: *My Fair Lady, The Sound of Music, Casablanca, Gone With the Wind, West Side Story* . . . all celebrating two perfect lovers variously finding (or tragically parting from) each other. And—here we get to our second damaging stereotype—we find ourselves accepting without question an idea of love we think is just as possible to find in real life. Think of the encouragement we're given, even in the supposedly "sophisticated" entertainments of today! How many movies has heartthrob Tom Cruise made where he *hasn't* played a callous cad "transformed" in the end by love? (How many callous cads do *you* know of who've been transformed by love?) Why does it seem so "natural" for all the Colby men on "Dynasty" to be perfect, loyal husbands? Because they're rich, successful and handsome, of course! How could Blake Carrington (John Forsythe) be a villain? He's a mature Prince Charming—the man Cinderella (in the form of Linda Evans) comes happily home to after she's hit forty, who when he finds out she's dying of a brain tumor wants to marry her again to reaffirm their vows and ensure being together forever. He's a potent image of what we may realize is an "ideal," but nonetheless something we accept as possible—even inevitable if we ever have the luck of running into someone as rich, handsome and successful as a Colby male. It's no wonder we have some of the dreams and expectations we do.

Thankfully, we've recently gotten some healthier and more helpful images from the media. Witness a movie like *Bull Durham*, which showed that even a baseball "groupie" could be a strong, independent woman. Or *Crossing Delancey*, which features a literary woman who, miserable in her relationship with a famous writer (who's "supposed" to be her perfect mate), finds herself drawn to an intelligent, attractive pickle salesman—hardly in the script she could have imagined for herself. Or *The Nerd*, where the gorgeous cheerleader picks the studious student with white socks and too-short pants (who's an attentive, kind lover) over the narcissistic football captain. And Cher, in *Moonstruck*, chooses the brother with one hand over the brother with two —because the first has "soul."

Cher has been a role model in real life, too, taking a bagel maker for a lover. Likewise, Elizabeth Taylor, choosing a much younger construction worker over elder billionaire suitor Malcolm Forbes.

We can applaud these real-life and celluloid role models of love because they offer a fresh idea about new love choices, more than "Cinderella" ever could.

The grip of the old romantic myth is still, however, very strong—everything from the latest Danielle Steel novel to TV commercials for mouthwash reinforces it. Romantic stories that touch us the most may be decades old, but they continue to appeal because of our enduring desire to embrace their message. The media (whether in the form of a beloved old movie or a new torrid romance novel) give us, after all, what we *want*. Attempting to step back and be objective about the effect all these cultural stereotypes have on us isn't always easy; sometimes we're so attached to these myths we don't *want* to hear they aren't true. Still not convinced you're affected? Try the following exercise and see.

Imagine that you walk into a party where you are secretly hoping you will meet the One. You are prepared: you're decked out in your sexiest, slinkiest dress. You feel very "on": you've just gotten a raise, and in your new purple-silk trenchcoat you feel wonderful, in control, dazzling! As you approach the bar, you see four men ahead of you.

One is wearing an open-necked white shirt and tweed jacket. He's dark and athletic-looking and has curly hair. The second one next to him is good-looking, too, although in a different way. He's in a pinstripe suit, white shirt, red tie, his hair short and straight and light brown, and he's wearing horn-rimmed glasses. The third man is wearing washed-out jeans, a Swatch watch and an Italian sweatshirt. He's medium height with brown hair, clean-cut. The fourth man looks like a punk rocker, pouty and sullen, wearing black leather pants and an earring in one ear.

Which one would you be most attracted to? Take out a pen and paper and fill in the details of the one you like best. Be specific about how you imagine he'd speak, what he'd say to you, what he likes and dislikes, where he's from, what he does for a living—really flesh out the fantasy. If you want him to have a mustache, add that too. Add any other physical or sartorial details that appeal to you. Whom have you created?

You've just undergone the very complex and exacting process of selection. More than likely what you have in front of you is an amalgam of traits from ex-boyfriends, or traits *opposite* to those of ex-boyfriends who may have jilted you—as well as a hefty dose of media-inspired fantasy, a mix of Robert Redford, Paul Newman, Tom Selleck, Mel Gibson, Tom Cruise and (if he's your cup of tea) Woody Allen. . . . Any number of vivid media images may have entered your imagination. What you have your man talk about is also culled from any number of scripts, some of them literally movie scripts. We construct our fantasies from a rich mix of sources—not the least of which are the images and sounds of the media's love antennae. However, the important realization is that *you* construct them, even if you do so with blinding speed. So now, when you're tempted to say, "I don't know, the guy just turned me on," perhaps you'll begin to realize it's not that simple—*or* that mysterious!

## FACTOR 3: EARLY CONDITIONING

You may throw up your hands at the prospect of even trying to understand your early conditioning. Didn't it happen so long ago and in such complicated ways it defies analysis? No. I'm going to help you see clearly how what happened back then affects you now. In fact, there's a simple key to understanding how you were conditioned

from infancy on: *what is rewarded is repeated.* This comes from
B. F. Skinner's learning theory, which established that everything
we do is affected by reward and punishment. In fact, that's what
"conditioning" means: how we were rewarded and punished *conditions*
us to respond in certain ways now.

There are obvious examples of this in your own life. If mommy
yelled every time your room was messy when you were a little girl
—but gave you cookies every time you kept it clean—it's likely that
you have grown up having a clean room. Or, of course, you may
rebel, and do the opposite!

But often our conditioning operates on us far more subtly—and
sometimes response to punishment and reward isn't what you might
expect it to be. While we usually move toward what is pleasurable
and away from what is unpleasant, sometimes we'll repeat what was
unpleasurable in an attempt to *undo* the early punishment we received. In psychological theory this is called repetition compulsion.
A woman who as a little girl was treated badly by an ill-tempered
father—regularly yelled at and severely punished for even minor slip-
ups—may find herself compelled to seek out equally abusive men
now, out of the hidden need to repeat the former painful experience,
in the hope that *this* time it will turn out differently and she'll be
treated more kindly. Have you ever noticed how you throw yourself
into the fire even when you should *know* you'll get burned?

But, for the most part, people are drawn to repeating what makes
them feel good. And not all of what we repeat goes back to infancy
and childhood. Our first dating experiences can exert a powerful pull
many years afterward. You're probably aware of this to some degree
already: if, when you were in junior high school, you fell madly in
love with the captain of the football team who had broad shoulders
and blond hair, is it any secret why you look for broad shoulders and
blond hair now?

The pull of your early conditioning with boys can, however, be
a good deal more subtle. Suppose the first time you ever felt really
"turned on" was when you were "making out" with a boy who told
you you were beautiful—as he tentatively touched the "forbidden
territory" of your breasts while kissing you deeply (you were only
half-conscious of the tuft of chest hair visible at his open collar and
the feel of his dark, curly hair against your cheek). You came unconsciously to associate your first pleasurable sexual stirrings with
this particular young man—the way he spoke, acted or looked became

locked in your memory. You may find, today, that you're *really* turned on only by moderately hirsute, dark-curly-haired men—even though you may have completely forgotten *why*. Your fantasies are fueled by so much that you may not have been aware of even while the associations were being formed—or that you've simply forgotten. But, whatever your fantasies are, you can be sure they're based on very specific "data" that will tend to act as triggers every time you meet with them—even if you have no conscious idea why.

Circumstances that lead to romantic conditioning can be surprising. One study showed that people often found partners at their mailbox or in the supermarket. The theory is that in familiar surroundings (doing something as "normal" and nonthreatening as mailing a letter or buying a quart of milk) you feel less anxiety and are simply more open to people. You are at your most relaxed and receptive—you feel comfortable enough in these situations to risk approaching someone, or responding to someone else's approach.

The opposite circumstance may make you more receptive also. People can be attracted to others they meet in high-energy places (like football games or on mountain trips) since their physiological systems are already activated.

## FACTOR 4: THE FAMILY ATTRACTION SCRIPT

The role your early family experiences play in making you find certain men more attractive than others is so important that I'll be devoting an entire chapter (see Step 5) to it. Attraction commonly involves a reenactment of relationship dramas from your early childhood years. You may choose particular men because, unconsciously, they appear to allow you the chance to reenact those early relationships in order to experience them again. Why would you want to? The familiar may make you comfortable, or you *enjoyed* those early relationships. Or, as I suggested was the case in repetition compulsion, you may feel a need to change those early relationships to make them go right this time around. We're usually not aware of these early attraction scripts, but they are there, waiting to be acted out, filed away in our unconscious. We're like producers and directors scanning the population for the right cast!

Why make the effort to get in touch with these scripts and become conscious of them? Because whenever you're in the grip of a compulsion or a strong tendency you're not aware of, you're not fully exercising choice—you're simply responding to an old pattern that usually has nothing to do with the reality you're facing right *now*. I want you to have as much of a sense of choice as you can have—and that's what Step 5 will help you achieve. But I'll give you a hint of the effects your family can have.

Your family scripts start, of course, with your relationship with your parents: your emotional history starts at the moment you're touched by your mother. These early experiences with our mothers, and later our fathers—the way we were held and touched (or *not* touched), the way our mothers and fathers related to one another, and what might be called styles of affection in the household—played, and continue to play, a major role in our lives. These initial interactions "set" the patterns we have of relating to others today, the way we see people as giving or withholding, what they reinforce, and what they disapprove of. The groundwork for later attractions is set here, as you're taken out of or put back into your crib, as you're fed and held and played with and scolded, as you experience your first fears and joys and frustrations. You experience your first *response* to and from the World Out There—in the context of your family. You also experience—prenatally and, if you're fortunate, for a good amount of time after you're born—that state of unconditional love we identified as the source of such a deep need, that state of complete acceptance, of deep communion between you and your mother which really makes love *possible* later in life. That unconditional love is, in a sense, the simple happy ending our family dramas are always striving for—although the plots leading up to that ending often may be more convoluted! So, early in your life, the foundation is laid for your attraction scripts—the plays or dramas of your love life.

One common attraction script is the Oedipal script. As you may already know, Freud defined the Oedipus complex, which is a critical stage of childhood sexual development, as the unconscious tendency of the child to be attracted to the parent of the opposite sex. It will thus sometimes happen that, as an adult, a woman will choose a love object who is a father figure—and a man will seek a mother figure.

However, it's not always the case that people make Oedipal reenactments of their relationships with their parents. While some people do learn to find satisfying partners who are just like their parents—which usually indicates they had very satisfactory relationships with their parents, and are trying to repeat them—others may have had totally unsatisfying relationships with their parents and are looking to do anything but repeat them. In this case, your "model" for a partner might be a member of the extended family—or an early teacher or clergyman. Basically, you're attracted to the kind of person you're familiar with. It may be a person who made you feel safe, so you'll feel secure with a similar type of person now. The person you seek reflects an image you have learned to see as warm, accepting, nurturing. Or it might be someone you *wish* was that way, so all through life you try to change that person, or someone *like* that person—which is why, again, it's not surprising that so many people grow up in search of partners who remind them of someone in their original family or early childhood experience.

Invariably, when I lecture to large groups about finding Mr./Ms. Right, someone says, "Look, I *like* my father, but I don't want to marry him!" But look again. My first point is that this is a figurative, not a literal, statement. And, secondly, some people do hold back from loving a partner because, symbolically, they feel married to a parent. In other cases, the Oedipal script isn't always so neat—it's not always a case of your seeking a clear repetition of your relationship with your father, as father and daughter. The "daddy" dynamic can work in another, very surprising way: instead of acting the daughter, you might become the mother! You then act out your mother's role in the relationship—how you perceived your mother treated your father. Sometimes the roles are switched even more. You might take on the father's role and marry a man who reminds you of your mother. Or here's a very fascinating scenario: you pick a partner who acts like *you* did, and you "become" like your father. This is one of the most interesting dynamics, because here you get to identify with your parent and to "treat" the image of you (projected now in your partner) the way you wish you were treated.

Other family exchanges are possible, too. If sibling relationships have been intense, it may be that you find yourself attracted to someone like your older brother. In this case, you may have been disappointed in your real older brother, so your partner becomes the "ideal" brother you wished you had. You'll learn much more about these permutations, and why you follow them, in Step 5.

But it's important to say something additional here: when I describe these various family dynamics, you should not think there's anything wrong with them. We are marvelously adaptive, and we have the power to transform what may appear to be difficult or even disastrous beginnings into something we can learn from. Remember, *every* relationship can teach us a lesson. The point is to recognize your own family script so that you can see what role it plays in your own life, and take steps to avoid replaying it if it's causing problems.

Understanding your family scripts does take work. There are so many intricate ways they play themselves out in relationships that you can't expect to be able to uncover them all, right now, simply by lifting a psychological "lid" and looking in. But I will help you get that clear picture. Suffice it to say, there are *reasons* why you are the way you are, and when certain of your tendencies get in the way of your fulfillment, they bear looking into. However baffling and unconnected self-destructive tendencies appear to be—and they can sometimes seem to come from nowhere—there *is* always a connection if you take the quiet time to look for it and allow it to reveal itself.

Here's an important caveat to keep in mind. Remember that you choose certain men just as you choose other aspects of your life— *not* because you want to sabotage yourself (even if that's how it looks to other people, and even sometimes to yourself), but because you're convinced on some deep, unconscious level that you're *protecting* yourself. This is an extremely important idea, because it allows you to look at yourself with compassion and acceptance. You've been repeating old patterns not because you're masochistic or stupid, but because they provide you with the only courses of action you've ever learned to take, the only routes to *safety* you've ever known, the only hope of getting what you want.

You are not condemned to repeat the past. People can change. People do change. With some insight and hard work, you can vastly increase your own chances of happiness. The first step is to take a clear inventory of what dreams, assumptions and motivations you're starting with. That's what you'll do as we explore your own checklist, that fascinating collection of traits and beliefs and preferences that holds the key to why you live and love the way you do.

Our checklists are very important indicators of what our early family was like, what our parents wanted (and want) for us, what the culture tells us is "sexy," what our earliest sexual stirrings were, and what our experiences have been—in short, a roundup of all the four factors this chapter has dealt with. Our checklists, with their conscious and unconscious items, are a neat reflection of how we have assimilated all of those influences. But the checklist is especially important because it can be *changed.* In fact, you have the power to change your checklist, so that you can *choose* not to repeat what's painful and unworkable from your past.

The journey you've embarked on is an exciting one—even if you feel a little timid just now. Get ready to discover that the ideal man you've been assiduously seeking all these years may *not* be the goal you're truly after. The real goal has, in fact, nothing to do with "him"—it has to do with finding out about *yourself. You* are the one who matters—love yourself first. Then, you'll end up finding love in some unexpected—and wonderful—places!

## Step 2

# Determine Your Checklist

Congratulations! Simply by becoming more aware of the multitude of factors that go into making you attracted to a man, you've begun to question your motives a little, and dig a little deeper into areas you probably once accepted as "givens." No longer can you say *quite* so easily, "I don't know why I'm attracted to these kinds of men—I just am." You've stirred the pot a little now, and you can see many things surface that make your motivations grow clearer.

The next step is to refine that process, get down in black and white exactly what's going on in your own personal checklist—the inner "eligibility" test to which you put every man you encounter.

Here's what goes on every time you spy him across a crowded room. Your love antennae start to whir, and the console of your checklist computer lights up and buzzes. In your brain, thousands of bits of data are being entered, rated and evaluated. It will help a great deal to see what some of your own items are.

"Love antennae" is my favorite metaphor for the sensors through which you receive and send out love messages—a useful metaphor for the whole complex of attraction-reactions. The messages your love antennae receive are quickly spirited down to the data-receiving base of your checklist, and if the items "compute," those love antennae start to vibrate. You're *receptive*. That data bank of your checklist is consequently *very* important. It's the storehouse of information you depend on to separate the "right" guys from the "wrong" guys.

The problem, as we've already begun to see, is that sometimes your checklist is misguided: it tells you "right" or "wrong," based on outdated or untrue information—and it can steer you to a *wrong* man or away from a *right* man as a result. Or it can build up your expectations to such an unreasonable pitch that you don't have much hope of finding any man at all!

The first step to gaining control of your checklist is to take a good look at what's on it. Your checklist is sometimes conscious, sometimes unconscious—and usually a varying mixture of the two. That is, you may be very aware of exactly what you're looking for ("tall," "handsome," "articulate," "wealthy," "funny") and dismiss potential suitors who don't live up to your expectations or desires. Or your checklist might be a good deal less conscious; that is, you are drawn or not drawn to certain men "instinctively," without being able to clearly express why.

The exercises I'm about to give you are designed to bring up not only the conscious items on your checklist, but preferences of which you may not be so aware. But how can I get you to write down something you're not conscious of?

The secret is this: as you answer the following questions, don't *think*. Get a pen or pencil and write down the *first* responses that occur to you. It's important to write them down, too—don't just answer them in your mind. Committing them to paper will make them more real, ensure that you remember what your responses are and enable you to see them all in a series after you're done, so we can work with them. Be as free as you can be in your answers. Don't worry that there's a "right" or "wrong" answer or "best" way to be—there isn't. It does you no good to be anything less than truthful. The more honest you are, the more you'll be able to change what you need to change. Only after you've told the "truth" about what *is*, can you move to another way of being.

By telling the "truth" in the following exercises, you'll be able to see something more—a *pattern* of response that should give you a clear understanding of your love life and, ultimately, where it's gone wrong and where a new, happier, path can lead. Once you've determined what needs work, I'll show you in upcoming chapters how to accomplish that "work." But, first, let's see what we're working *with*.

We'll start with the type of man you continually find yourself attracted to—the question we explored in the last chapter and which can provoke as much resistance as it can clear answers. What comes to you if I ask, "What's your type?" One woman I worked with, Myra, thought she was being glib when she said, "Sure, I can tell you my type—easy. He's rich, powerful, gorgeous, fabulous in bed and treats me like a queen." Myra thought she was joking (or exaggerating) about this list of "perfect" qualities, but in fact she really *was* looking for a man who embodied all that. She didn't even realize it herself until she did a little more careful digging and saw that, even in her "real life," she was turning down men because they weren't the gods in her fantasies. She'd never really faced the fact that no man *could* live up to those standards until she took a hard look at her own hidden requirements.

What I guarantee *you* will see is the difference between what you *think* you should have and what you actually *need* to be happy. Here goes. Be spontaneous! Trust your responses. Don't dismiss any.

## LOOKING AT YOUR TYPE

What's your "type"? Write it down. Right now. Tell me whatever occurs to you. Include physical characteristics, traits, behaviors, or how he makes you feel or what he does for a living. Take as little or as much space as you feel comfortable with. If it makes it easier, imagine filling in the following: you meet a guy you're telling your best friend about the day after—he's your perfect type. He's:

Okay: now read it back to yourself. How did you *feel* describing your type? What are the thoughts that came up for you? Did you feel satisfied, like, "Oh yes, how perfect—that's what I want!" Did you feel a sense of peace that you'd found your perfect match? (When your expectations about something are fulfilled, stress dissipates— the fantasy is fulfilled, and you may catch yourself smiling.) Or did your mind bring up hesitations—were you skeptical? "I'll never find anybody like that," or "Even if I did meet him, something would go wrong," or "The things I'm looking for don't really count, they're not important."

Paying attention to the ancillary thoughts and feelings that come up when you express your ideal of a man gives you a sense of two things. One, you get to see what your ideal *is*. Two, you get to see whether you really believe you can ever achieve your ideal, or if you know it's an impossible dream.

Now, here are two more questions:

How easy was it to describe your ideal man? (Check one:)
☐ *Difficult*     ☐ *Easy*

Did your description "flow out" (come spontaneously)?
☐ *Yes*     ☐ *No*

If your answers were "easy" and "yes" (it flowed out), you probably have had lots of exeprience verbalizing to yourself what you like. In that case, you may have to look over the exercises in this chapter very carefully to make sure you're really answering honestly—if you have a fixed idea of what you like, sometimes you'll answer from the "surface" and fool yourself. Again, I'm not asking you to "think," only to listen to your own deepest responses—even if they surprise you by being very different from what you think you "ought" to be feeling.

If you answered "difficult" (it was hard to describe your type) and "no" (it didn't "flow out"), that may be an indication that you are willing to be flexible—the fact that you don't have a readily recognizable type may mean you're open to a number of alternatives. Of course, *saying* you don't have a "type" may be a coverup. It's possible you have a very strong type, but you've been reluctant to acknowledge it, even to yourself. Again, that will come out here, too—just be honest and answer from the gut. Whatever's going on will come out!

Before we leave our first question about "type," however, take note of how many characteristics you came up with to describe it. (Check one:)

☐ *One or two     ☐ Three or       ☐ Five to ten     ☐ An endless*
   *characteristics    four                              list*
               *characteristics*

Did you mention one or two things, or endless details? If you had a lot of details, that might indicate you are *very* particular—and, the longer the list, the harder it's probably been for you to find exactly the right eligible candidate. This might mean you need to learn to be more flexible (you'll find out about this when we get to our chapter about getting *over* your checklist, but take note of whatever you see right now, too). Having a long list of characteristics doesn't, however, have to mean rigidity—you can be giving yourself a very informative list of traits that vary in importance.

This is a good time to point out something crucial about checklists, and about the characteristics you've just listed about your perfect type. They *change*. They're not constant, or etched in granite. And thank heavens they're not—that's what gives us hope! As you'll see even more clearly later on, your checklist sometimes changes spontaneously—in response to your own growth. Here's an example.

Susie had a string of unhappy romances: she would always fall for the guy who stood out in the room—a room, that is, full of investment bankers. He'd be the guy with the perfectly tailored Brooks Brothers suit who'd likely gone to Wharton, played squash three times a week and had the lithe body to prove it, the guy who was making six figures when his classmates were still in the mid-five-figure range—the raging, number-one-in-his-class *success*. Susie, a very attractive woman, was fairly successful in hooking several of these impeccable specimens, but what she never realized was that they hooked up to her because she was one more conquest they could flaunt for a while (before they became tired and moved on to the next "status" symbol). Susie had an unerring eye for the guy with a huge ego, an ego that demanded *many* women to conquer. As a result, she was regularly dumped: when they were through with their conquering, they quite naturally moved on to other conquests.

Finally, Susie met a man who actually loved *her*—and kept wanting to be with her, even after the first days of infatuation. Susie was so unused to male persistence that she decided to test it. She refused him for a couple of weekends just to see if he'd call afterward (as none of her previous glamorous suitors would have). He *did* call—and offered to make dinner for her at his apartment, which thought had *never* occurred to any of the Brooks Brothers men in her past! Susie was taken aback, not only because of this man's extraordinary persistence and attention, but because he didn't have quite the pedigree his predecessors did. He wasn't rich (although he made what seemed to be an adequate living), and he was thin and drawn, with a kind of "mobster" look, which threw Susie a little at first but, to her amazement, intrigued her. When her father became ill, Susie was more than intrigued—she was touched that her new boyfriend cared so much and was there for her during the whole ordeal. Throughout the stress, he even helped her study for her extension course exams.

Quite without realizing it, Susie's checklist began to change. Had she been asked to write down the characteristics of her "type" during her days of pursuing what she came to see as "empty suits," she'd have come up with a far different list than she's come up with now. Before, the emphasis was on "success, power, good looks." Now the man she wants in her life has to: "Make me feel good about myself, be trustworthy—so I know he will do what he says he'll do, be faithful in his caring, treat me with kindness and consideration."

Take a look at your list of type characteristics once again, in light of the story I've just told you about Susie. How important are certain items as compared to others? Is "chiseled Greek features" right up there with "warm and responsive"? How might you reorder the list, so that the items on it appear in their real order of importance to you? Your checklist may begin to change a little even now, as you weigh what's really important against what may not be so important after all.

## HOW YOU PRIORITIZE

The order of the characteristics you've listed can reveal your thought process. And since we're looking for your *patterns* of thought as much as for the specific items that make up your thoughts, let's do a little formal reordering so we can see what emerges. I'd like you to decide how much weight you give to different aspects of a person. You might find out you're like the woman who met a wonderful man her *friends* adored, a woman named Lynn who, her friends told her, was unbelievably lucky in finding a man like Bill—warm, sensitive, very well off and crazy about Lynn. In fact, he put her on a pedestal. What Lynn didn't have the nerve to admit to her friends—because even *she* could tell it would sound ridiculously minor, even though it bothered her enormously—was that there was *one* trait of Bill's she couldn't abide. She felt guilty about it, and suspected she was being irrational. But Bill had a pot belly, and it drove Lynn up the wall. This may sound superficial, but for Lynn it wasn't. It was one "condition" she felt she could absolutely never accommodate. "Look," she said to me, "I realized that there were a lot of other things in a man that I could put up with. I'd rather have a cheapskate or a guy with a terrible temper than this. I don't understand it—in fact, I feel awful about it—but it's true."

Lynn knows the criteria on her checklist, and that's important. What she needs to do is take a look at what a "pot belly" symbolizes to her. She has begun to see that she interpreted Bill's being out of shape with not caring about himself, about what he looked like and, by extension, about *her*. ("If a man really cared about me, he wouldn't look like a slob!") Her aversion to this one trait is something she just hasn't been able to shake.

For Lynn, physical attributes are not something she can "negotiate." But it's possible that over time she may undergo a transformation, and perhaps this item on her checklist may seem less important as she grows to value other traits more. The better she understands that it's her own interpretation of that pot belly "symbol" that's bothering her, not the man Bill himself (who in every other way is *not* a "slob"), the more likely it is that she'll give less weight to it on her checklist, even though right now it's nonnegotiable.

I've told this story to emphasize that you'll discover items that may rationally seem unimportant but, for any number of reasons, really *are* important to you. Nothing is automatically superficial on your checklist. In fact, if it's *on* your checklist, it deserves close attention. Don't edit yourself. If you can't abide pot bellies or overly hairy chests or thinning hair, say so. We'll see what, if anything, we need to "do" about it later!

Let's start to prioritize. In the exercise below, write down the two characteristics that are the most important to you in a mate, both positive and negative:

## Love Priorities

*What I Absolutely Cannot Live Without*
*The man must have (be) (do) (say)* 1 _____
                                    2 _____
*What I Absolutely Cannot Live With*
*The man cannot have (be) (do) (say)* 1 _____
                                    2 _____

Now, write down what you don't like but you think you could live with or accept:

*He could have (be) (do) (say) 1)* _____
                                 *2)* _____

This will begin to give you an idea of how you weigh or prioritize attributes. It's very important: it shows what you're *deciding* when you "weigh" one attribute against another. It reminds you that you're the one calling the shots. What it's also implying is that, in calling the shots, you've got *choices*—you're selecting various traits over others. Later on, when you go over your checklist to *get* over it, you will recognize that *you are not settling, you are choosing.*

There are generally two parts to making a choice: what you look for, and how you prioritize its importance. You'll learn more about this process of choice in the next chapter on dream lovers. But for now, think about the key: your priority list reflects *choice*—and that gives you power. You can direct yourself—you don't have to settle for something you don't want.

## LOOKING FOR YOUR PATTERN

Now that you've given some "spontaneous" answers, I want you to thoughtfully go down the following list of questions in order to determine what forces were operating on your *very first serious* involvement with a man.

### MY FIRST CHECKLIST

*Who was the first person you were ever involved with?*
*Describe here:*

                       *age* _____
                       *sex* _____
*Appearance:*   *height* _____
                       *body type (thin, muscular, etc.)* _____
                       *coloring* _____
                       *he looked like (an Adonis, earthy, dignified)* ____

*Where were you in your life when you met?*
            *(graduating from school, wanting to move out of*
            *your house, etc.)* _____
*How did you meet?* _____
*What attracted you?* _____
*What did he find attractive in you?* _____
*How did he treat you? (e.g., always accepting, sometimes*
    *rejecting* _____
*What did you do together?* _____
*What was the best part of the relationship?* _____
*What was the worst part of the relationship?* _____
*What was your sexual relationship like?* _____
*What did you get from the relationship (what did you learn)?* \_\_

_____
*What didn't you get from it?* _____
*Other memories you have:* _____
*What happened to the relationship?*
    *How did it end?* _____
    *Was there any further contact?* _____
*How do you feel about the resolution?*
    _____ *good, because:* _____
    _____ *more bad than good, because:* _____
    _____ *mixed, because:* _____
*What did you want to happen?* _____

Very often you are drawn to a relationship because of the way *you* are allowed to feel or act with that person—what he brings out in you. And you are turned off when parts of you that you value are stifled. Three very important questions to include when you review your checklist are:

*How were you able to act or feel with this person?* _____
*What did he bring out in you that you liked?* _____
*What did he bring out in you that you didn't like?*

_____
*What was stifled in you in the relationship?* _____

Often we are influenced by what others think. Or we make choices to please others, like our parents. On occasion we rebel against them to prove it's *our* choice. Consider how much you were influenced or affected by others' view of this relationship.

*What did others think?*
_____ *approved, because:* _____
_____ *disapproved, because:* _____
_____ *indifferent*
*My reaction to their opinion:* _____

## OTHER RELATIONSHIPS

Now that you've thought about this first relationship, go back and fill out the same questions on this checklist for every important relationship you have had.

## PATTERNS

Next, let's put down a few key points about relationships at various key stages in your life.
**Your twenties:**
*What were your partners in these years like?* _____
*What did you want out of a relationship? (Companionship, marriage, just fun, etc.)* _____
*How did the other person treat you?* _____
*How did you treat your partner?* _____
*How close or distant were you with these partners?* _____
*How were you able to feel or act in the relationship?* _____
*How did the relationship end?* _____
**Your thirties:**
*Answer the same questions as for your twenties, then add the following:*
*Were these relationships different from what you experienced in your twenties?* _____
*Answer the same questions for relationships in your forties and fifties.*
**In addition (useful for all ages):**
*What are the advantages/disadvantages of being alone now?* \_\_\_\_
*Whom/what are your friends choosing as partners/lifestyles?* \_\_\_\_\_
*How do you feel about commitment and exclusivity?* _____

*What kind of relationship do you think you want now?* _____
*What kind of person do you think you want now?* _____

Perhaps some things have come up on these lists that surprise you. Perhaps you're not surprised yet. But I want to make you aware of what has been going on in your relationships. And the best way is for you and me (by my asking you the right questions) to map out a pattern of your relationships. In the following questionnaire, write down on the left-hand side the names of the men in the last four relationships you have had. Just list the names, as I have indicated on the questionnaire, and then proceed to place a dot on the scale on one to ten where that person falls. By the time you "connect the dots," you may be able to see a pattern in your relationships that will have eluded you up until now. For example, you may find out that you always had relationships with rich men who were all non-communicative, or your best sexual relationshps were with men who had no formal education. Now what does this mean? It means that you have a unique, individual pattern to your behavior. Through the exercises in this book, I am going to help you open up and discover the part of your behavior that is getting in your way. It does not mean that everything on your checklist is "bad" or a "problem." Not at all. But somewhere, something in that checklist is getting you into trouble. I am going to help you find out what it is and *help you change it*.

## LOOKING FOR A PATTERN: YOU AND YOUR CHECKLIST

*PHYSICAL PROFILE*

*Facial Characteristics*

| Unattractive | Handsome |
|---|---|
| 0 | 10 |

(Mark)
(Ken)
(Paul)
(Leo)

*Body Type: Height*

Short                                                          Tall

0                                                                10

_____

_____

_____

_____

*Body Condition*

Too Thin or Fat           Average           Great Shape

0                                                                10

_____

_____

_____

_____

*EMOTIONAL PROFILE*

*Awareness*

Insensitive                                               Sensitive

0                                                                10

_____

_____

_____

_____

*Expression*

Withdrawn                                          Shares Feelings

0                                                                10

_____

_____

_____

_____

*Temperament*

Calm                                                          Angry

0                                                              10

——————
——————
——————
——————

*Confidence*

Insecure                                              Very Confident

0                                                              10

——————
——————
——————
——————

## COMMUNICATION PROFILE

*Talking Style*

Withdrawn                                                     Open

0                                                              10

——————
——————
——————
——————

*Intimacy*

Afraid of Intimacy                                 Likes Intimacy

0                                                              10

——————
——————
——————
——————

*Talking Content*

| Talks Only About Ideas and Business | | Talks About Feelings |
|---|---|---|
| 0 | | 10 |

## INTELLIGENCE

| Average | Very Bright | Brilliant |
|---|---|---|
| 0 | | 10 |

## EDUCATION

| No Formal | | Extensive and Impressive |
|---|---|---|
| 0 | | 10 |

## BACKGROUND

| Unprestigious | | Very Prestigious |
|---|---|---|
| 0 | | 10 |

Poor _____ Wealthy

0                                          10

———————
———————
———————
———————

*LIFESTYLE*

Not Interested in                    Very Interested in
Family _____ Family

0                                          10

———————
———————
———————
———————

Likes to Stay Home
a Lot _____ Goes Out a Lot

0                                          10

———————
———————
———————
———————

Shy _____ Gregarious

0                                          10

———————
———————
———————
———————

|  | Lots of Activities |
| No Real Interests | and Interests |
| 0 | 10 |

———
———
———
———

*MONEY*

*Spending on Self*

| Tight | Generous |
| 0 | 10 |

———
———
———

*Spending on Others*

| Tight | Generous |
| 0 | 10 |

———
———
———
———

*Present Income*

| Poor | Moderate | Moderately Rich | Rich |
| 0 |  |  | 10 |

———
———
———
———

| *Potential Income* | | Moderately | |
| Poor | Moderate | Rich | Rich |
| --- | --- | --- | --- |
| 0 | | | 10 |

———
———
———
———

### LIFE CIRCUMSTANCES

| | Uncomplicated (no problems with |
| Complicated/Problematic | ex-wives, etc.) |
| --- | --- |
| 0 | 10 |

———
———
———
———

### PERSONALITY

| Self-Centered | Cares About Others |
| --- | --- |
| 0 | 10 |

———
———
———
———

| Withholds Emotion | Expresses Emotion |
| --- | --- |
| 0 | 10 |

———
———
———
———

Untrustworthy/Unpredictable    Trustworthy/Reliable

0                10

Difficulty Being Loving        Loving

0                10

## SEXUALITY

*Attitude Toward*
*Monogamy*
Not Interested       Committed to Fidelity

0                10

*Sex Appeal*
Not a Big Turn-On      A Big Turn-On
for Me           for Me

0                10

*Sexual Desire*
Not Very Interested
in Sex                                              Very Interested
_____
0                                                             10

——————
——————
——————
——————


*Connection Between Love and Sex*
Separates Sex and Love          Connects Sex with Love
_____
0                                                             10

——————
——————
——————
——————


*Sexual Activity*
Very Traditional                              Wild in Bed
_____
0                                                             10

——————
——————
——————
——————


*ATTITUDE TOWARD WOMEN*
Macho                    Mixed                  Feminist
_____
0                                                             10

——————
——————
——————
——————

*Attitude Toward Women in Marriage* "Modern"
"Traditional" (e.g. Equal Share)

0                                                                    10

———
———
———
———

## ATTITUDE TOWARD COMMITMENT
Not Interested                    Ambivalent                    Eager

0                                                                    10

———
———
———
———

## ATTITUDE TOWARD MARRIAGE
Not Interested                                                  Eager

0                                                                    10

———
———
———
———

## ATTITUDE TOWARD LOVE
Not Interested                                         Very Interested

0                                                                    10

———
———
———
———

## ATTITUDE TOWARD CHILDREN

| Not Interested | Ambivalent | Eager |
|---|---|---|
| 0 | | 10 |

———
———
———
———

## APPROACH TO LIFE

| Fearful/ Very Conservative/ Very Rigid | | Willing to Risk/ Open to My Ideas |
|---|---|---|
| 0 | | 10 |

———
———
———
———

## SOCIAL BEHAVIOR

| Isolated | Some Friends or Activities | Lots of Friends/ Enjoys Socializing |
|---|---|---|
| 0 | | 10 |

———
———
———
———

## MORALITY

| Dishonest | Very Honest |
|---|---|
| 0 | 10 |

———
———
———
———

*RELIGION*

| Declared<br>Atheist | Undeclared<br>Atheist | Traditional<br>Religious<br>Affiliation |
|---|---|---|
| 0 | | 10 |

_____

_____

_____

_____

*SPIRITUALITY*

| Not Spiritual | Very Spiritual |
|---|---|
| 0 | 10 |

_____

_____

_____

_____

## CHECKING OUT THE CHECKLIST

Look at your checklist "history." People often repeat themselves picking partners. You may notice that you are attracted to similar types of people and that the relationships begin and end in similar ways. Pick any one question and look at your answers for the different relationships you listed to see if the answers are the same. Think about it. What are the characteristics of those men? Compare them down the line. Are they the same type? Were those characteristics essential to your attraction to them? Notice where your cluster of tastes lies. Are they always physical, for instance?

In Eastern philosophy there are three "planes" you evolve through as you return to earth in each "new" life. They are the physical (the lowest), the emotional, and the spiritual (the highest). Were your patterns mostly in the physical, the emotional, or the spiritual plane? If you noticed you're more attracted to physical qualities, think about what will happen to those qualities. People do get older; they do change. You will inevitably be disappointed if that is the major characteristic that attracts you. Although physical attraction *is* important in our society—and research shows that attractive people do get better jobs and are more successful socially—that doesn't mean this should be the most important thing to *you* in a relationship. Or maybe it is. Maybe the determining input in your love computer is the "pot belly"—the one thing that you can't "give up."

Follow the lines. Look at the other characteristics of your type. You are likely sticking to that type for a *reason*, because essentially there are no rules when we are born that we have to fall for a certain type of person. You develop those tastes, just as you decide you like mashed potatoes or hate peas.

So, ask yourself where might these "tastes" be coming from? As we began to explore in the last chapter on attraction, are the patterns you notice similar to early relationships with your parents or a sibling? People are often attracted to family figures because they are familiar and comfortable, like marrying dear old dad. Or you may, at the other extreme, seek the *unfamiliar* because you are trying to avoid the patterns of your parents, either the relationship you saw between your mother and father, or between you and one of them. (For example, if your father was domineering, you may seek a milder-mannered man.)

By the time you arrive at the chapter called "Step 6: Change Your Checklist," your "reasons"—I promise—will be a lot clearer to you.


## YOUR FEELING PATTERN

It's very important to realize how you felt about yourself during each of these relationships. Remember that one of the most fascinating aspects of attraction is not just the characteristics of the other person but what they trigger in you—how you feel and act as a result of the interaction between you. Review how you answered the questions about what each relationship brought out—or stifled—in you. Are *you* very different with each person, or the same? Go to the next exercise and rate *yourself*. Make a new column for each partner.

Rate on a scale of 1 (not at all) to 10 (very much). Make sure to add any characteristics that come to your mind.

| **How I Felt With:** | **Barry** | **Larry** | **John** | **Ernie** |
|---|---|---|---|---|
| *I felt sexy* | | | | |
| *I felt intelligent* | | | | |
| *I felt capable* | | | | |
| *I felt creative* | | | | |
| *I felt happy* | | | | |
| *My feelings varied (extremely happy one minute and absolutely miserable the next)* | | | | |
| *I felt in control* | | | | |
| *I felt secure* | | | | |
| *I felt attractive* | | | | |
| *I felt* _____ *(add whatever was important to you)* | | | | |
| *I didn't feel* _____ *(add whatever was important to you)* | | | | |

Do you look for different people to bring out different parts of yourself—that is, can you feel charming with Larry, but not with Barry? Are there differences because you are not secure or stable in who you are? It's important to realize how *you* felt, or wanted to feel but didn't.

This is one of my favorite observations about love: we pick partners to treat us the way we *need* to be treated. (There's that element of *choice* again!) It is not a mystery. You may be attracted to a person who is rejecting or inaccessible. This could mean that you're not really ready for someone who is "good for you" or ready to be there for you. Therefore, by choosing someone who you sense will reject you, you fulfill your own expectations: you're choosing *not to be good to yourself.* Maybe, when the man *is* "good" for you, you find you're not very interested. Again, you may have chosen a man who will "prove" to you something of which you're already unconsciously convinced: that even when you're with a "good" man it won't work, because you don't feel worthy of a good man. The point is, again, *you*'re the one who's choosing to be where you are.

## CHANGES IN YOUR CHECKLIST

Sometimes your checklist will change spontaneously when you grow to feel more secure about yourself and what you want. (Remember Susie, who discovered her checklist had changed to include traits that had to do with emotional warmth and faithfulness—traits not high on her list when she'd limited herself to all those glamorous but empty-suited men.) In fact, it's virtually axiomatic that when you find yourself in a relationship with someone who truly is "good" for you, it's because you've put yourself in that relationship, because your checklist has changed and made you responsive to different traits in people. At twenty, you may have nothing but "Brat Pack"–movie and Jordache jeans–commercial fantasies of sullen, tightly muscled young men. By the time you're thirty-five, your fantasies may have mellowed, softened, broadened—you may find that simply as a natural function of *maturing*, your checklist of traits will have changed to accommodate the person you feel yourself to be *now*.

Sometimes your checklist will change simply because you've *awakened* to a reality you'd managed to ignore or previously deny. I'm reminded of another client of mine, Gail, who had started seeing Mark—a lovely, responsive, exciting man who fit her fantasy in so many ways, except in one that she couldn't quite bring herself to fully acknowledge: Mark was married. But Gail fitted Mark's scenario perfectly: he loved his wife and kids, but wanted a sensuous "mistress" on the side.

Gail had gotten into these situations a few times before. There was something about married she found symbolically "stable," even if they were married men to someone else; and, like so many women in extramarital affairs, she nurtured the illusion that they'd leave their wives to marry her. Of course they never did. Finally, with Mark, Gail had matured to the point where she could no longer ignore the reality—the fact that Mark had no intention of leaving his wife for her. And that the pursuit of him would never make her feel wanted, which was what she was really after. Her checklist changed—because *she* changed—when she discovered what she really needed for herself. No longer would she risk the kinds of disasters she'd gone through before, because, at a deep level, she no longer wanted to put herself in that kind of danger or state of deprivation. Even her sexual fantasies have changed. She says, "I know that my thrill, when I really get turned on, is when I feel 'He's the one—this could be the fulfillment of being together forever. Now I know I'm loved.' "

Gail's attraction to unavailable men was also based on the interesting twist that it was *she* who was really afraid of commitment, not they. Realizing this helped her face *her* fears and get over them. Her requirements have changed—married men are now out of the picture, and off her checklist.

I'll take you through changing your checklist in an upcoming chapter.


## HITTING BOTTOM SOONER

In addition to finding that your checklist will change organically, as you change, you'll also discover that you don't *have* to go to hell and back to learn every lesson in your life. Sometimes we're fed this myth—"If you go out with enough rotten men, you'll finally get so sick of them that you'll stop"—which may make you unwittingly think you've got to *continue* self-destructive behavior until that magical point when you're so "sick" of it you'll stop. This is tantamount to telling alcoholics that the only hope is to drink themselves into the gutter so that they'll finally want to change. In fact, you *can* hit bottom sooner—and *want* to change before you've done the worst to yourself you can do.

What I suggest is that you let your "bottom" be *now*—let your "bottom" be the place where *you decide you want to be happier.* Start to expand your horizons now, before the misery that can overtake you—about your life, your "marriageability," your prospects and your men—wields its power. You don't have to wait until you're feeling rejected and miserable and alone, crying yourself to sleep every night, to make important changes that will enhance your life and not bring it down.

Can that really happen? *Yes.* You can save yourself a lot of grief and wasted emotion if you start thinking about your checklist *now.*

## THE DESERT ISLAND TEST

I'll leave you with one last quiz before we go deeper into types of men you may harbor in your most secret fantasies (that's the dream lovers chapter, coming up next). This is one of the best ways I know of zeroing in on what you're really after in a man: it should leave you with a clear idea of who you really want in your life, and it couldn't be simpler.

Think of the man you're going out with, or want to go out with, or have just broken off with. Imagine the two of you on a desert island. There are no cars, no banks, no clothing stores, no jewelry shops, no limousines, no operas, no jeans stores. Just the two of you and the swaying palms against the blue sky.

What do you talk about? How would you be together? How do you rely on each other? Does he listen to you? Does he care about you? As you talk, do you speak about how you feel inside and what your dreams are? What do you like about being on the island? What feels good to you? What do you think about getting off the island— do you want to get off? Where do you want to go? Where does he want to go? Do you like being alone together? Does he? Do you feel good together?

This exercise is a good test of your relationship because it eliminates all the "trappings" we too often get stuck in—external, superficial values and experiences of the both of you.

If you didn't like being on the island together, you've got a pretty good indication that you have a relationship built on things that die, get lost or end. You may find yourself in a relationship that offers convenience, some pleasure or status from the "outside." There's nothing wrong with any of that. But if you discovered it's not enough (and you probably did, or you wouldn't have come this far with me!), then take another look at the desert island and imagine the man you *would* feel comfortable there with. Who is he and how does he make you feel?

You're getting closer to the picture of the man you're *really* looking for. But we can't bring him into precise focus until we do some more cleanup. It may take you into some surprising areas— the most secret areas in your mind, in fact. The place where you keep some of your most cherished fantasies. The next chapter—and the next step in our journey—will take you there.

He's the ultimate prize—the seemingly "perfect," though perhaps also unattainable, man: your *dream lover*. Sexy, accomplished, powerful, wealthy—the man you think can fix it all, take away your pain, give you exactly what you need. But can he really?

I promised to take you into your most intimate fantasies—and I will. But they won't just be the ones you dream about. They will also be the men you may actually have encountered in your love life, whom you *thought* were perfect for you. Owing to the nature of dream lovers—one or more of whom you'll probably recognize very clearly if you've ever had a real relationship with one—these "sensational" men do at least *appear* to exist. And they're not always inaccessible. (In fact, it's part of the very nature of some "dream men" that, if you fit at least part of *their* extensive checklists, they'll be attracted to you if you're wildly attracted to them: it feeds their own agendas and egos quite nicely.)

So what's the problem? If you're able to land a dream lover, haven't you "won" the love game? Your fantasy comes true—what could be better?

The problem is, something doesn't feel right. You should be happy, but you're not. After a date you may even feel "empty." You may question what you're doing wrong. That's a bad sign right away. Worse yet, you start to feel you're not

# Confront Your Dream Lovers

"enough," that the fact you're not feeling the "magic" you know ought to be happening is somehow your fault. And when it's really all over, you cry yourself to sleep, or endlessly engage your friends in analyzing what you did wrong and why you lost what you're convinced was the best thing that ever happened to you.

Actually, I don't want to throw a wet blanket on anyone's heated passions. Dream lovers are always instructive, sometimes even as wonderful as you hope they'll be. And not all checklist items that fit dream lovers turn out badly. The exceptionally handsome hunk may not be so wrapped up in his looks that he cannot genuinely appreciate and attend to you. And the rich man may not be so stingy or money-obsessed that he cannot be generous—with either his money or his emotions. The super-powerful guy may not just be overcompensating for some insecurity, but so mature in himself that he is able to support your growth and nurture your independence. I just want you not to be dazzled by the checklist items your dream lover embodies for you. I want you to truly see the man inside, how he really makes you feel, and if he's able to share real love with you.

I want you to go beyond the surface status symbols and get to the soul—the spirit and inner self—of a man, and of yourself. But even if you make a mistake, even if you find yourself hopelessly dazzled for a while by those surface attractions, don't despair. Remember that any relationship can teach you a lesson. Your relations with sensational men, whether they happen in your mind or in actuality, are no exception. When you confront the embodiment of what really turns you on, you have an extraordinary opportunity to see, first of all, if you're *right*—if your dreams really *are* what you want.

Sometimes, however, you'll find that your dreams are subtle cover-ups, vicarious attempts to get from Mr. Sensational what you really, unconsciously, need to provide yourself. We've met with that deferral motivation already, but it's especially clear when you conjure up (or actually meet and have a relationship with) the man of your dreams. Again, I don't want to take any magic away—but, as with every other inner motivation we've begun to reveal in the first three chapters, it can help enormously to see what's really going on when you're starstruck by the One.

In fact, before we introduce you to the first of our five contenders for Number One Dream Lover, let me give you a rundown of some of the unconscious reasons women have zeroed in on them. There are five strong reasons you sometimes fall head over heels for a dream lover that are important to look at, because they signal that you're not really facing reality, that you're not truly answering your *own* needs, even if your urgent fantasies temporarily convince you that you are. These are five motivations to be wary of when you fall for your dream. You seek "him," sometimes,

1. *To enhance some characteristic* you have yourself, but would love more of. For example, you may play tennis very well, but you want to be great. You think *he* plays "great," so you'll be able to reflect his glory.

2. *To replace some sense of inadequacy* you experience in yourself —you may want to know the stock market, but you realize you don't have a "head" for money matters at all, and he's a brilliant stockbroker perfect for teaching you *everything*.

3. *To be "where it's at."* He's so obviously trendy, so knowledgeable, so with it. A gallery owner whose art is the talk of the town, a rock musician who's the fantasy of millions of women, a body-builder whose muscles makes men jealous and women weak— there are any number of "fabulous" men who have an aura you want to bask in.

4. *To repair some hurt*. If you've always wanted to attract a certain type of guy, and never could—and that has become a sign of how unattractive or undesirable you are—then you may keep trying to get that type of guy to make yourself feel better (on the deepest level you are probably reenacting being a child, seeking Daddy's attention and love).

5. *To be accepted* into a lifestyle or group—to feel that he's the key to a whole world you feel you could never enter on your own (country house, yacht, commuting on the SST to Paris . . .).

You'll see in our next chapter, on emotional traps, how these motivations can wreak havoc in some very insidious and subtle ways. But, for now, be aware that there's more going on than may meet the eye (or the imagination) when your dream lover looms into view!

Take a look at the following categories of dream lovers—and what's going on in the women whom they attract. See what fits, and learn that the stuff dreams are made of is sometimes not what you're really looking for. Perhaps you've blamed yourself for the failure of a dream lover affair. Why couldn't you make it perfect, when you *had* someone so perfect? Or why, sometimes, does the guy you thought was Superman turn out to be one of the Three Stooges? Was it your fault? What happens when the dream goes bad—even turns into a nightmare?

Now that you've got a better idea of what's on your checklist, compare the checklist items you'll see after each category of dream lover. Do you fall for the same things? Again, don't feel it's bad to want the "best": if you're after a gorgeous, accomplished, wealthy, sexy man, by all means, go right ahead and find him! But, in your search, be wary of some traits that may only glitter. Sometimes what you *think* you're looking for turns out to be not enough. Be alert, too, to the five motivations I've just listed. They can mislead you: is your dream lover a symbol of who *you* really want to be, with traits you're really looking for in *yourself*? Try on the following dreams for size, and see.

## DREAM LOVER 1: THE MYSTERY MAN

Checklist items. He's:
- ♥ experienced
- ♥ challenging
- ♥ charming
- ♥ unpredictable
- ♥ daring
- ♥ sexy in unconventional ways
- ♥ suave
- ♥ dramatic
- ♥ unwilling to be pinned down
- ♥ like no man you've ever met

*Henri.* Just the sound of his name made Linda tingle—that rich, French rolled "r," the deep swallowed first syllable: *Ahn*-ree. Even now, now that it's all over, Linda can't help emitting a deep sigh. Something just *happened* with that man, she thinks. "From the first moment he looked into my eyes, it was like losing my center of gravity," Linda says.

"I was at a party," Linda continues, telling me about the first time she'd met Henri, "and it was ironic, because friends had invited me to meet someone else—a guy named Sam whom everyone thought

I'd be crazy about. Sam was okay—a nice guy, really—but no sparks. When I was in the middle of talking to him, this dark, compelling face materialized from nowhere right behind Sam—deep, brown eyes, strong lean jaw, arched and slightly bemused black eyebrows—that *face*! Whoever it was was gazing directly into my eyes, and I lost control of my lower jaw. Heaven knows what Sam thought was happening to me—actually he did ask me if I was all right!" Linda smiles. "I'm still not sure if I *was*."

Henri swept in with such grace and savoir faire that Don Giovanni could have taken lessons. "He was terribly polite to *Sam*, first of all, saying something like 'Didn't I see you at Aspen last winter?' in this faintly French-tinged voice, and when Sam, who'd never skied a day in his life, said no, Henri just laughed and quickly turned to me. 'Surely *you* ski!' he said, and I said, yes, sometimes, and Henri was off and running, flattering, witty, intuitive—and leaving Sam in the dust."

Henri was like a gust of wind from the Alps—quick-silver, flashing bright eyes, Swiss-French, with an unerring sense of how to get through to Linda. Before the night was over, Linda agreed to go with him to Vermont for the weekend. "Not the Alps," Henri said, apologetically, "but perhaps we can make up for that at some *future* time." The way Henri said "future" stuck with Linda: "He seemed to have made some, I don't know, *decision* about me—as if he could look deep inside me and knew exactly who I was, what I wanted, and knew he was the one to provide me with it. He seemed so *knowing*—like there was no question we'd have a future together. It was meant to be: Fate, Kismet, the stars." Linda was quick to relate that she wasn't in the habit of planning weekends with men after a half-hour of talk, but something just didn't seem under her control with Henri.

"I think if he'd said, 'OK, *chérie*, now we will go to the moon,' and escorted me to the nearest window, I would have jumped out." Linda pauses and looks a bit rueful. "As it turns out, maybe that's exactly what I *did* do."

Vermont was exciting—and *almost* everything she hoped it would be—but even in this first heady, days-long encounter, laughing on the slopes, looking deeply into his eyes, swept away in his experienced arms, something nagged at Linda. "It was like the longer we were with one another, moment by moment, his attention seemed to dim, imperceptibly at first, but by the end of the weekend I felt as if—I don't know, I guess he seemed slightly *distracted*, as if he had to consciously return to *us*, to what *we* were doing, to *me*. It's like there was something secret going on inside him, which he couldn't share —and which had nothing to do with me—but was sort of magnetizing his attention away from me. It was all very mysterious, but I felt a definite pulling-away."

Linda was still so taken by Henri at this early point that she managed to see his "pulling away" simply as part of his enigma— the mystery of who he was. "I began to have fantasies about what might have been nagging him—everything from some romantic existential despair to the fact that, maybe, he was hiding a Swiss hausfrau and two kids back in the Alps and was feeling guilty! But mostly I imagined the 'romantic' part—that made him seem more mysterious, and it romanticized his growing moodiness."

Henri *was*, in fact, getting moody. Their third or fourth dates, after they'd come back from Vermont, were romantic in setting. "We had dinner in a little bistro he knew and then walked around the park, late at night, bundling up and into each other, his arm tight around me," Linda recounts. But Henri didn't talk as much, and his "distractedness" was more pronounced than ever. Linda's fantasies grew more complex—and fantastic—since she had nothing "real" from Henri to counter them with. "I began to think maybe he was some sort of foreign spy, or into some sort of smuggling, espionage! He'd make cryptic remarks, sometimes, about his past—mostly boiling down to 'I can't talk about it' And I fell right into it, continuing the fantasy, imagining I was in some movie, playing the woman who's 'always there,' waiting for her mysterious lover, offering him a little peace, a little respite from whatever it was that took him away from me . . ." Linda smiles at the thought.

"And, boy, he was starting to stay *away*, too," Linda recalls. Their dates became less and less frequent. Finally, after a few weeks' silence, Linda called Henri to find out what was going on. She dialed his number and was met with a recording that informed her the number she'd dialed had been disconnected! "I couldn't believe it—I tried it again, but got the same recording, so I knew I hadn't dialed wrong. Henri had simply disappeared!"

## WHAT WENT WRONG

Remember what I said toward the end of Chapter 1: Pay *attention to what is actually there—what you actually let in*, as opposed to what you're striving to see in a man out of your own needs. Linda, in fact, was getting clues all along that Henri might prove to be somewhat less than reliable. She herself says that she tried to "romanticize" Henri's distancing tactics to hold on to the enigmatic fantasy that so attracted her in the first place. Not all "mystery men" disappear as suddenly and completely as Henri did—sometimes you can get them to hang on for a longer haul, and sometimes (usually unfortunately) you can actually get one to marry you. But, in the classic case (and admittedly we're talking about stereotypes), Mr. Mystery generally turns out to be far less "deep" than his carefully cultivated aura would lead the untutored woman to believe.

Most men who make an art of gliding in and out of women's lives—men who have "enigma" written all over them, and seem to be endlessly fascinating, endlessly complex, and unbelievably charming (and sexy) as a result—are in actuality running away from themselves. They're "mysterious" not because they're unfathomably "deep," but because they haven't taken a hard look at who they themselves *are*. So, quite naturally, they send confusing messages out about themselves. Henri (Linda later learned) traveled around, abruptly, as a habit, picking up the odd "yearning" woman here and there, enjoying the quick process of becoming a "fantasy come true" and then, true to form, making sure he became just as quickly unattainable.

Mr. Mysterious can get away with his hit-and-run tactics because he's got an unerring eye for a certain type of woman he knows will fall for him. Which brings us to:

## WHY WOMEN FALL FOR MYSTERY MEN

Why did Linda's love antennae go mad when she met Henri? What was she "reading" that drew her to him in an instant? It's not only that Henri represented some sort of slightly dangerous, enigmatic romance that made her feel as if she were in a *film noir* of the 1940s. It's also, as Linda eventually came to realize, that some women see their own "mystery" reflected in a mystery man. Intuitively, they sense they won't get complete satisfaction from an enigma because, often, they deeply don't believe they *deserve* commitment, an up-front assertion of love, a clear, cards-on-the-table understanding of what each partner can expect from the other.

There's also the sheer challenge (which is common to many women who pursue dream lovers) of attempting to land a man who's obviously difficult to land. "If I can get *him*," many women think, "it must mean I'm pretty terrific!" Specifically, women seek Mr. Mystery as their Number One Dream Lover because they're fleeing something in themselves; immersing themselves in shifting, uncertain, "excitingly unpredictable" romances allows them to *stay* in the uncertainty with which they've grown comfortable—out of the fear of what it might be like to show their true, far less mysterious selves.

It's a risk to show vulnerability: sometimes we resort to mystery as a camouflage for our *own* fear of opening up and getting involved. Our relationships almost always mirror, very directly, what we think about ourselves. Linda was at first surprised at the notion that it was *she* who picked Henri, not so much the reverse. When she began to see some of the reasons why she was so attracted to Henri—that it had to do with her own fears of exposure—suddenly Mr. Mysterious wasn't so mysterious after all.

## DREAM LOVER 2: THE INTELLECTUAL

Checklist item. He's:
- ♥ dazzlingly articulate
- ♥ intense
- ♥ insightful
- ♥ impatient with "stupidity"
- ♥ interested in many things
- ♥ knowledgeable
- ♥ witty
- ♥ wise
- ♥ passionate about the "Life of the Mind"
- ♥ uncomfortable with feelings

"He was every woman's dream of who to wake up with on a Sunday morning with the paper!" says Elly about Ross, a college professor with whom she'd had a lengthy affair. "That is," she continues, "if the woman's dream is that she have a live crossword-puzzle dictionary, a walking encyclopedia on the volatile situation in the Mideast and Central America, a breathing *New York Review of Books.*" But Elly is quick to point out that Ross wasn't simply a computer—some automaton who simply spouted arcane details because he had a photographic memory. To her, he was—or appeared to be—unbelievably perceptive, too, scoping out situations and getting to the bottom of things. "His judgment is so good," she thought at the time, "and that's so good for *me.*" But let's not get ahead of ourselves. Let's see how Elly and Ross hooked up in the first place.

Elly, an artist, was doing the graphic design on a book for which Ross was brought in as a consultant. It was a particularly knotty but important literary biography, and Ross was an expert in comparative literature and on this particular writer.

"When I read Ross's report on the book," Elly remembers, "which I did because it was attached to other correspondence that fell on my desk one day, I was amazed. I literally had to put it down on my desk and be quiet for about three minutes, just staring out the window. I couldn't believe how brilliant it was! Not just in what he knew about the literature and the life of the writer, but in the astonishingly sensitive critical view he brought to both. It was like he was reading something inside *me,* like he could read *souls,* almost. I'd never seen critical writing that made me ache to meet the author. But I couldn't let this opportunity pass me by. I had to meet the man who'd written this."

Elly made careful notes on Ross's report and called him up to set up a time to meet with him to talk about it. "I felt like I was calling up, I don't know, *Shakespeare,*" she laughs. "But he agreed to meet me." She dressed especially carefully on the day of their lunch date. Meeting men like Ross wasn't something that happened every day. "And the meeting," Elly recalls, "went like a dream. He had a rumpled, slightly skewed academic sexiness—like Harrison Ford playing Edmund Wilson. I was a goner." Ross's much-praised intuition did not fail him. He could tell he had Elly in thrall.

"We pretty much fell into our relationship; I've never gotten into an affair so quickly. And the trappings were so right—it really almost sounds like a cliché to tell you about them. He had this little country house he went to on the weekends all year round, even during winter, which was maybe the nicest time. It had a big fireplace, a library of much-read and much-loved first editions of just about everything and everybody, some nice beaten-up furniture and faded Oriental rugs on rough oak floors—and a big brass bed.

"I was thrilled I'd finally met a man who complemented me, a man who appreciated my artistic, impulsive, romantic nature, but who could also make up for the part of me I wasn't and he was— careful, analytical, controlled. But"—Elly's face falls a little—"it started to get really frustrating. Ross had all the intellectual moves down perfectly. His surface—the words and ideas and images he used as easily as you and I take a breath—was so dazzling that it took some time before I realized how really ignored I was beginning to feel. It's hard to describe. But we'd wake up in the morning and he'd open his eyes and it would be like 'Who are *you*?' I didn't feel he really took me *in*, somehow—there was always this distance. And then, when he started working on what he called his 'magnum opus,' Ross *never* came up for air. It was a big tome on the philosophy of literature in Restoration England, something that grew out of his doctorate and that he was teaching in college. And it wasn't just that he was passionate about it—it's that it turned everything else in his life into nothing. I didn't exist anymore. When I'd rush in to tell him about a beautiful leaf I'd discovered, I was abruptly cut off."

Elly says it was about this time that she realized she wasn't enjoying sex with Ross anymore. "It's not that Ross had ever been very 'free'—not like I was. But now he wasn't even *interested*. On the rare occasions we did make love, it was cold, mechanical and quick. He spoke to me less and less, too. He'd go for hours brooding in a rocking chair when he wasn't researching or writing. Soon he stopped acknowledging my existence at all. When I tried to broach anything about how hurt I was starting to feel, he'd firmly scold me. He said I should get control of my neurotic needs for constant attention and approval—and so it went. Finally I looked at him and looked at me and realized that those 'blank' times before he got so involved in his book were really a clue—he'd *never* really let me in. Not even during the 'good' times. He'd woven his intricate web of words so tightly that no one could have gotten through. All his words and brilliant thoughts didn't amount to a pile of beans when it came to communicating, or appreciating, feelings."

Elly was hurt—but she got out before she got more hurt.

## What Went Wrong

Again, to appreciate "what went wrong" between Elly and Ross, we have to see, objectively, what Elly was letting *in* about Ross and what she was ignoring. The traits she so admired—his intellectual brilliance, his verbal fluency, his wit, his wide-ranging mind—are all admirable traits, and it's no wonder Elly was attracted. There's certainly nothing wrong with being an intellectual. But her *need*—that is, her perceived need—for a man who excelled in these ways blinded her to something much more basic: could the man and woman beneath all the verbiage and intellectual posturing truly meet, open up to each other, learn to love each other?

Intellectual gifts can pose tricky problems: the very ability to verbalize and construct imaginative arguments for or against any stand allows an almost impenetrable defense, frequently covering (again, this is the classic case—we're talking about extremes in each of our descriptions of dream lovers) an obsessive-compulsive character who is really terrified of his feelings. It's as if Elly imagined an intricately meshed foliage of a gorgeous tree, and then discovered the tree had no trunk, no roots. Certainly, for her, the relationship ultimately bore no fruit—in the area (her feelings) that most mattered to her.

## Why Women Fall for the Intellectual

In therapy, Elly began to explore her own checklist, and realized that a woman is often attracted to an intellectual man because he represents the opposite of what she perceives herself to be. Elly felt herself to be deeply "emotional," and she was often afraid her emotions would cause her to capsize—that they would become too much to bear. She developed a desperate need for an anchor—someone who seemed to have it all together. Someone unbelievably, undeniably "smart." Someone who would have all the answers. Someone she could depend on to complete her own woefully inadequate overemotional self. Though she ultimately objected that he wasn't more like her, more emotional, Elly unconsciously chose Ross precisely because he *wasn't* like her—so he could "complete" her.

It's common that passionate, impulsive women who are afraid their feelings are "too much" will be attracted to controlled men. Something in Elly always knew that Ross was inaccessible emotionally; that's why she flew to him. Unconsciously he represented safety. But of course—as you've heard before and you'll hear again—a relationship can't prosper if it's one-half seeking its other half, one inadequacy looking to undo itself!

When Elly learned to trust that she wouldn't capsize from her own emotions—that it was perfectly all right to *have* her feelings—she began to surface from the "need" for men like Ross. (You'll learn more about this process in our next chapter, on emotional traps.)

While all women like Elly who are obsessively attracted to one particular dream man out of a feeling of inadequacy do have certain unconscious "negative" motivations, they may also quite *healthily* seek intellectual or other traits in men, too. Intellectual ability *is* attractive. You don't have to be "neurotic" to want the special stimulation of an intellectual man! It's just that when it becomes the *sole* trait you're looking for (or turned on by), it's usually worth looking at *why* you're limiting yourself to it, and how you may be blinding yourself to what else is going on.

## DREAM LOVER 3: THE POWER MONGER

Checklist items. He's:
- ♥ decisive
- ♥ effective
- ♥ well-connected
- ♥ self-confident
- ♥ strong
- ♥ reliable
- ♥ in control
- ♥ better at getting things done than anyone you've ever known
- ♥ used to getting his way
- ♥ the ultimate problem-solver

"If power is an aphrodisiac," says Helen about her relationship with wealthy and extremely powerful Ken, "then I suppose I can be forgiven for falling head over heels for him. The instant I saw him, I felt something in me surrender—totally. *He* would—and could, and was actually promising to—take care of *everything*."

Helen met Ken at a particularly vulnerable time for her. ("I don't know if Ken knows what the word 'vulnerable' *means*, at least from first-hand experience," Helen says.) She'd just lost her job. She was panicked about where the rent would come from now, what she'd do with her career, whom she could possibly turn to. She broke down, sobbing on the phone to a friend one night at about 3 A.M. Her friend knew someone who she thought could help. Ken.

"Call him," the friend said. "He's got a lot of influence, and he knows your field. He might know just the right position for you. I'll tell him you'll be calling."

Helen was immediately put at ease when she got Ken on the phone. Her friend had evidently done a good job preparing him for her call. "He was direct and take-charge," Helen recalls. " 'Of course, I can help you!' he said, as if I were foolish to think otherwise. 'Come in and see me today.' He made an appointment for three-thirty. Something in his voice really made me believe my problems were over. I can't tell you the feeling of relief—and the rush of pleasure I got about the prospect of meeting this amazing man!"

Helen continued to be amazed by Ken. "He had three job openings to tell me about—all of them were, he said, 'shoo-ins.' All I needed to say was which one, and he'd made the necessary call. 'But maybe,' he said, 'we should give you time to think about it. Like over dinner tonight. Is eight o'clock all right?' I was too baffled to do more than nod yes. 'Okay,' he said, 'see you then.' He buzzed his intercom and gave his secretary a cryptic command—the name of the most luxurious restaurant in town. Then he looked up at me. 'You look great in blue. Wear blue tonight!' I felt like saluting or something! But there was a genuine twinkle in his eye. I think I was already hooked—right then and there. He just took over. I loved that he told me what to do, even what to wear. He knew what I *needed*."

And seem to fill her "needs" he did, even though Ken wasn't anybody's idea of physical perfection: he was balding a bit, with a rounded face and belly. But he *exuded* strength. "I thought of him as a walking *oak*," Helen says. "I was convinced there was simply nothing this man couldn't do. It was an impression that was bolstered by the Rolls that appeared in front of my building, promptly at eight."

The splendid car whisked them away. During the ride, Ken told Helen of the deals he was making—how he was investing in films and buying property, even without a lot of disposable cash. Helen didn't feel Ken was trying to "impress" her: he was just so absorbed and enthusiastic about his work that he couldn't help talking about it. The phone in the car kept ringing, and as Helen eavesdropped on Ken's half of the conversations, she thought how exciting it all seemed. "He's so strong, capable, making so much happen!" she thought to herself. "I need a man like this."

When they got to the restaurant, Ken was greeted like royalty by a maître d' who Helen knew (from her own experience) treated anyone he *didn't* know as if they'd been dragged in by a cat. Helen smiled at the thought that she could just relax, lean back and be taken care of. At dinner, Ken deftly made perfect suggestions from the menu and went on to map out in the most concise terms imaginable the pros and cons of the jobs he'd made available to Helen, also managing to slip in a few equally concise compliments about how attractive she looked in her blue dress. Helen was overcome, hungry for what she knew she could learn from Ken. He knew so much about business and people, and Helen was eager for his guidance. He talked disparagingly about the powerful people he wined and dined while making business deals. "I hate every minute I spend with these guys, but they'd never know," he said. To Helen (whose every emotion showed on her face—she was almost constitutionally incapable of deception), this seemed the height of sophistication, the only way to get to the top.

Helen felt, in short, that she'd landed on Cloud 9—and she found herself hoping for a very long stay. She felt totally guided by Ken, and comfortable being led. Ken had yet another plan for the evening. After the perfect meal and a perfect ride in the purring Rolls, he shepherded her out of the car into the lobby, into the elevator, and into her apartment with the same quiet and deft expertise that marked everything else he'd done that evening. Helen felt a little woozy, although when he drew close to her—reaching out his bear-arms to hold her, his steel-gray determined eyes intent and purposeful—she began to come to.

"Ken—" was all she managed before he covered her lips with a practiced kiss. She tried to push him away, gently. "Really, Ken, I'm flattered . . . but . . ." But something melted. This oak of a man wanted her. She flashed on how often in the past she'd felt vulnerable—and here was a man who was ready and willing to take over, to take care of her, to control it all so she wouldn't have to think or worry. "Ken!" she half-whispered in one last weak protest. Then, as she realized she'd done from the first moment she'd heard his voice on the phone, she surrendered.

The sex was unlike any Helen had ever had. There were times when Ken would give her strict directions, but at other times he'd insist that she order him around. Such extremes are common with an overcontrolling man, who in sex will seek to dominate or be dominated, but all Helen knew was that she found it oddly thrilling. She came alive in bed as never before, alternately submitting and dominating, a dance of give-and-take that took her breath away.

And so began a series of weekly dinners and nights at her apartment: Helen felt she was in a trance, from the moment Ken picked her up to the moment he left, silently, the next morning. How she wished, sometimes, that he'd kiss her softly and whisper, "I love you and can't wait to see you again!" But Helen supposed Ken was too "powerful" a man to say anything so soft and expected. She began to realize, however, that Ken never said anything warm or affectionate to her. At first, this was something she accepted. Simply being in Ken's presence was a relief—she basked in his calling the shots. It was when things started to go badly at the job she'd chosen—when she really needed to talk to someone about the petty office politics—that she had to admit the dimensions of her affair with Ken were a little narrow. Every time she tried to bring up her own problems, to talk about something in her own life, Ken cut her off.

Finally it hit her. Ken believed he'd kept up his part of the bargain—getting her a job—and he did *not* feel that his responsibility included listening to her problems or engaging in mushy "love talk." Meeting her the way they met suited his plans perfectly. He wanted nothing more or less than what they had. "Get on with it" seemed to be his motto not only in business but in his personal life as well. Helen began to chafe against the limits Ken set. She realized he never wanted her to contribute an opinion, even about where they met and what they did. She suggested going away together for a weekend—Ken said it was out of the question. Perhaps a different restaurant—she knew a great little Mexican place—but, again, no. He liked the restaurants he chose—why should they change?

Then Helen discovered another reason for Ken's resistance to changing day, night or restaurant. She called Ken's office one day and a temp, instead of Ken's usually efficient secretary, answered. "Oh, you must be his wife calling again. I'll put you right through. Sorry I couldn't put you through earlier when you called!" Helen swallowed hard. Wife?

Looking back on her affair with Ken today, Helen is still in awe at what she now considers to be the man's colossal gall. "When I confronted him about his wife the next time we had dinner, he said, 'So what? What's that got to do with you?' Then I saw it all in a flash. Ken had organized his love life with the same efficiency he'd organized everything else. I was a well-oiled part of his 'machinery.' It was no wonder that sex—now that I had this new view of him—really *had* become mechanical, even if I'd never admitted that to myself before. Everything fell into the same rut—his way. I wasn't a *person*; I was simply a part of the master plan of his life. Taking care of *me*? What a laugh. He was taking care of himself. He'd never had any real feelings for me at all. How could I have been so blind?"

## What Went Wrong

Well, here's a classic case of the woman searching for the dream lover who plays a father/protector role for her. Drawn to a man who can take over her life, the woman ultimately feels empty or used, as she discovers that she's just another means of his exerting domination and control.

Not that men like Ken aren't admirable in their way, or able to "give" what they say they'll give. They may even meet certain of your needs. When Ken "solved" Helen's occupational problem and when he initially took charge of their affair, he was acting on some very accurate intuitions. He knew what Helen needed and he knew that he was the man to provide much of it. The problem is that the power-monger dream lover rarely goes beyond this level of need-fulfilling to see the woman, the person beneath. To *accept* Helen's vulnerability meant more than coming up with quick, effective "solutions" to it. It meant listening to her. Caring about her. Opening up to her. That was something Ken *didn't* know how to do. He operated solely on the levels he knew he could control—and he did that very well. But there was an entirely deeper level he couldn't touch at all.

Ken is the kind of man who is usually terrified to go beneath the surface, to accept his *own* unorderable feelings. And so he builds what he believes is a fortress of "absolutes"—virtually mathematical certainties that Helen + new job + regular affair with Ken will make everyone equally happy, will balance everything out as neatly as he balances his best business deals.

What Ken didn't anticipate was that Helen would end up feeling angry and frustrated at being manipulated. And indeed Helen felt like finding out who his wife was and calling her up to ask her how she put up with him! Instead, she did a little soul-searching of her own. And discovered what you'll learn about next.

## WHY WOMEN FALL FOR THE POWER MONGER

Sometimes it does seem that power is an "aphrodisiac." Helen surrendered to a very common fantasy—a seductive fantasy of a father figure taking care of a little girl, making it all "all right," protecting her, formulating decisions for her that are "in her best interests." What's curious about many women who are attracted to "powerful" men, however, is that they may be quite powerful *themselves*—but as soon as they get near men who assert enough control, they'll *give up* that power, shrinking into "helplessness," letting the man decide everything. Such a woman may have residues of anger at herself and at him for allowing this to happen, but she'll let him take over anyway. Why? Sometimes women give up power because they felt forced to be in control in the first place—out of survival, they learned to exert power to feel good or to make life tolerable without a man. But when a man comes back, they willingly give up the reins.

Other women don't really believe they are powerful, even if they're perceived that way by the world, even if they've learned to act "powerful" in their professional lives. But it never connects to their gut that they do have power—they feel like secret imposters. Again, when a powerful man comes into view, they're only too ready to cede power they never really believed they had in the first place.

But Helen also got seduced by another aspect of Ken's power: his confidence in barreling ahead and getting what he wanted. She envied it. She wanted this for *herself*, but it never occurred to her she could actually *do* it herself. Remember one of our five motivations at the beginning of this chapter—"to replace some sense of inadequacy you experience in yourself." Frustrated in expressing her own need for power and autonomy, Helen found Ken an irresistible beacon of that power—and she hoped, perhaps, she'd get some of it through osmosis. On a positive note, however, she was *learning* from him. By reacting to his control, she was learning that she wanted to, and could, make her *own* decisions! She was learning, too, to become more independent and to make up her own mind.

## DREAM LOVER 4: THE OPERATOR

Checklist items. He's:
- ♥ charming
- ♥ magically intuitive
- ♥ incredibly good in bed
- ♥ manipulative
- ♥ seductive
- ♥ physically graceful
- ♥ self-centered
- ♥ imaginative
- ♥ flattering
- ♥ impulsive

"It was his dreamboat *eyes*," says Pat about Luke. "He could look at me and say more than any other man I've ever met. It's like he inoculated me with some drug, simply by *looking* at me!"

Luke was the sailing instructor at the country club Pat belonged to. One day after a lesson, he sent her a small decorative box with a note inside, "The genie inside this box told me we were meant to be together. Tonight, Palm Court Bar. Be ready, because I am."

Their first night together, they ended up in bed. "Let's just hold and touch for hours," he told her, "or until you want to stop." It was music to Pat's ears. Luke massaged her feet and whispered to her what she had longed for but never heard before—how beautiful she was.

The next weeks were heaven for Pat, filled with long erotic nights. Some days Pat played "hooky" from work, which she'd never done. They shopped for Luke at Armani's. Pat loved looking at him. He was so gorgeous. She booked him tennis-court time. And a personal trainer.

"A gigolo," her friends called him, "out for a free ride."

"That's not all true," Pat insists. "Luke was a man who truly loved women. He was born to be a lover—every move he made, every word he said, every breath out of him was designed to attract women—and he was incredibly good at it." Even now she gets a rush down her spine remembering what it was like with him in bed. Or on the beach. Or in the bathtub. Or any one of the numerous imaginative places Luke would suddenly decide they "had" to make love.

There wasn't an inch of Pat's body Luke didn't know how to "play." She felt like a Stradivarius in the hands of a master. And on top of it all—on top of his incredible physical *expertise*—he had those dreamy eyes that made her feel so wanted, so adored.

Pat never cared to question whether Luke was taking advantage of her. She knew, as only a woman knows who's been made love to the way someone like Luke makes love, that she had something *very* special with him. He *appreciated* her more than any other man she's ever known. She wishes she could bottle his essence to remind herself of what mad, passionate, exquisite physical and soulful love was all about. If only . . . if only . . .

If only he hadn't turned out to be such a cad.

Luke is an example of one of the most maddening dream lovers. He is every woman's fantasy: he *does* seem to have a supernatural sense of how to please women. He *does* seem to simply love women more than most men do. He *does* have an intuition about what women need to hear and need to feel about themselves. He is the one dream lover who seems so convincingly to love you. How could someone who looks at you and touches you the way he does not love you? He *is* his love—his very body is the instrument of it. And he makes you the instrument of it too.

I've already summed up Pat and Luke's relationship in that somewhat purple rhapsody—the parts I've left out are the parts Luke would leave out if he were to tell you the story. The part about how, after making love to her the first night in her impressive neo-Georgian home (which she'd just bought out of the proceeds of the last investment banking coup she'd made at the brokerage firm where she was a vice-president), he decided Pat was the woman he'd always wanted to live with. And be clothed and fed and coddled by. Given a BMW by. And squired around to all the best places by.

And yet, Pat's experience was also valid: she *was* loved by Luke. He wasn't just in it for the material dividends. It was "in his blood" to be the lover he was. She feels lucky to have had him. His words ring in her ears: "I want to make you happy." "Tell me what pleases you." She yearns for him still, even after the lies, even after Luke's staying out that Friday night and coming home, too late, smelling of another woman's perfume. And then when she caught him, in her *own* home. There was so much that was galling, yet so much that was wonderful.

## WHAT WENT WRONG?

Pat was vulnerable to men like Luke. Like many women insecure and desperate about being loved, she was looking for the dream lover who would reassure her she was *wanted,* at any cost.

Also like many women, never thinking of herself as desirable, consigning herself to what she thought was an inevitable "spinsterhood" (that's what her mother called it) because she wasn't beautiful, Pat poured all of her energies and intelligence into her career. And she was a considerably wealthy woman because of it.

Then along came Luke. And Pat felt "turned on," "hot," for the first time in her life. She felt what it was like to be undressed by a man's eyes. And richly approved of. "You fascinate me," he'd tell her, "you do so many things so well. You're amazing." The words were like a tonic she couldn't get enough of.

When asked what he did, Luke would say he was "between sales jobs"—selling what exactly, Pat was never able to determine, until now. When it was obvious what he was selling!

It's important to note here, though, that while one might think Pat was being taken advantage of, she also *gained* from the experience with her dream lover—in many ways. She felt an electricity from him that taught her so much about her own desires. And she experienced a love with him that taught her she *could* be desirable. And she learned to appreciate her life and her abilities, through his pointing out to her everything she did, and appreciating it. And she got to play out being the "father-protector" role herself.

Luke is now out of town, plying his "wares" somewhere else, Pat imagines. She hates him and loves him, but is moving toward the realization that she no longer needs him. Because he has, after all, left her something very precious—the knowledge that she *is* a sexual woman.

Yet, of course, something *did* go wrong. And that something does need to be looked at—what motivates women like Pat to be swept off their feet by Luke's brand of dream lover isn't, perhaps, quite as obvious as it may seem.

With her dim self-view, Pat consciously felt she was out of the "love game" and thought she'd pretty much adjusted to her manless state. She poured all she had into her career. But, in fact, Pat was desperate to be loved. So she couldn't have been more receptive to someone as sensuous and experienced as Luke was. It didn't matter who Luke the human being was; it only mattered that he was willing to play "Man" to her "Woman." Luke became a needed symbol of masculine love. When Pat said she felt "inoculated" by him, she meant it: he was like a drug she hadn't realized she craved until she got the first dose of it.

But Luke also appealed to Pat's sense of dependency—not so much that she could finally "depend on a man" the way Helen thought she could depend on her power monger Ken—but that she could hold Luke by his dependency on *her*. Which is what we'll explore next.

## WHY WOMEN FALL FOR THE OPERATOR

Sometimes, falling for a guy *you* can take care of is a way of vicariously taking care of yourself—as if *he* is you. We've seen all along how relationships mirror the woman who gets into them. And, in Pat's case, the dynamic she allowed to happen with Luke precisely mirrored her desire to feel her own power as a sexual woman. In addition, materially taking care of a man was to her an assertion of her own strength. She *enjoyed* being in control, treating him. It was like a role reversal. The problem was that her need to take care of Luke was in fact a deflected need to take care of *herself*. Because she did not truly believe in her own power, in her own competence and self-worth, she held Luke as a kind of "hostage"—by giving him everything he wanted, she could vicariously get all she wanted. Further, she could feel she "deserved" (literally "earned") his attention and, even more important, make sure he wouldn't leave her.

But a relationship based on "buying" someone to please you, or projecting yourself into the other person, is doomed. Luke's half of the equation could never have been enough to satisfy Pat's real need: to believe in and love *herself*. She would have to do that herself.

But, do keep in mind, choosing Luke was not a fiasco. Pat grew: she discovered sexual feelings and capacities in herself she now knows she must address. As she learns to feel stronger in her own ability to integrate sexuality into the rest of her life—as she starts to accept herself as a worthy and attractive woman and human being—the "love" Luke awakened can act as a kind of guide.

All this emphasis on the sexual attraction to the operator shouldn't mislead you, however: there are plenty of platonic Lukes to be had —often younger men who are adept at flattering older women who feel past their peak of being able to attract men. You don't have to end up in bed with an operator to be profoundly touched by one. All it takes is one unsure, needy woman in search of an all-encompassing fantasy of a dream lover.

But give that woman some self-esteem, give her the sense that *she* has the power to direct her own life, and she'll be too clear-eyed to be prey to "Luke." She may still *choose* such a relationship, but she'll do so knowing the trade-offs, what each is giving and getting, instead of being a victim. You don't need a romantic cure-all when you don't feel romantically inadequate. And you won't feel inadequate when you learn to love and trust yourself. And that's, of course, what we're going to get you to do!

## DREAM LOVER 5: THE CELEBRITY

Checklist items. He's:
- ♥ admired by many people
- ♥ at the center of "where it's at"
- ♥ narcissistic
- ♥ exhilarating to be around
- ♥ forceful
- ♥ sure of himself
- ♥ ambitious
- ♥ concerned with appearance
- ♥ fast lane all the way
- ♥ recognized in his field

In the blue light of the rock club, Max looked like someone from another planet—a weird mix of early Brando and David Bowie, his skin blindingly blue-white, sweat gleaming on his bare torso, slender hips, wiry legs sheathed in black leather. And his voice—that incredible rasping voice somehow made ballads out of the crashing, angry sounds his band poured out. Max was incredible. It was no wonder *Rolling Stone* started to take notice of where Max's band was playing. No wonder *The Village Voice* had just named him the decade's *new* Angry Young Rocker. Max's star was definitely in the ascendant. A record contract was clearly on the way—just a matter of time.

Amy couldn't believe her luck. She was responsible for booking Max into the club, and Max was the *one* musician she'd wanted to meet out of the many the club presented. Now, watching him perform, writhing to the band's insistent beat, Amy felt her heart pound.

"He was a *poet*," Amy recalls, "not just with his lyrics, but in the way he performed. I've never seen someone use his body to communicate a song the way Max did. Imagine men as well as women screaming every time he lunged out with his guitar—every time he moved at *all*. He had a little of Elvis, a little Springsteen, but something also entirely his own. He riveted me—I'd never seen anybody with such *power* onstage."

Amy was determined to meet him. Not, however, without having to wade her way through a much larger-than-usual crowd of groupies who flooded the dark corridor from stage to dressing room. Assuming as much authority as she could in the squirming mass of girls—and they *were* girls, Amy thought, little more than seventeen, eighteen, nineteen—Amy marched through to the sacred door, unlocked it with the club's key and slipped in out of the roar.

Max and his band were slumped onto a variety of folding chairs and an old sofa, like beaten gladiators. ("Even *exhausted*, Max stood out," Amy remembers.) He looked up at her wearily. "How do we get the hell out of here?" he mumbled, the sullen rasp of his voice as mesmerizing as it was when he sang. Amy felt like their guardian angel. "There's a *back* way," she confided, and Max's eyes lit up. "You mean we can get out of here *alive?*" he said, and jumped up and threw his arms around Amy. Amy thought she'd faint—he was strong and wiry and hot and pressed against *her!* "Is this really happening?" she nearly said aloud—then recovered enough to push Max reluctantly away and tell them how to get out of the club.

"You're coming with us," Max said. "I mean, that *is* part of the deal, isn't it?" Amy stammered that she "hadn't planned to," and Max cut her off. "Don't be ridiculous. You're saving my life!" And she found herself sneaking out the back way with the most incredible human being she ever thought she'd meet in her life. "The gods *had* to have been smiling," she now says. "There was no one on earth I wanted to meet more than Max. And here he was kidnapping me!"

Max had a sullen kind of male beauty—pouty, moody, intense—which made his smile, rare as it was, something that made you weak-kneed. He beamed that light on Amy this first night not two but *three* times—"A record," Amy says, "not equaled before or since!" He said she was his savior, he owed her everything, and whatever she wanted from him, she had only to ask. He also managed to get rid of the rest of the band using, Amy now suspects, some sort of silent code that clearly broadcast "Get lost, I'm with a chick"— a code, Amy discovered later, he used quite a bit. But Amy didn't know that then. All she realized was she was alone with Max. Charismatic superstar Max. The new voice of the decade was talking to *her*.

Thus began one of the most exhilarating and exasperating encounters Amy ever expected to experience. "Max latched on to me like I was a new toy—a toy he couldn't get enough of. He told me how lonely it was going from club to club, fighting off bimbos, turning on all that energy—and for what? Yeah, he knew he was good— brilliant, even—but who really appreciated what he was trying to do? Some glib tight-ass reviewer from a trendy tabloid? Certainly not the teen groupies he had to swat off like flies. Nobody—nobody, anyway, till he'd met me.

"I was the one 'chick' Max could tell might understand him. Understand what it was like to be the kind of tortured, brilliant, incredible human being he was. I was the one chick he decided he really needed to get to know better. By which he meant, take to bed. My head *swam*. I felt like some photograph of Max had suddenly come to life and made a beeline for *me*. Who was writing this script? I couldn't have come up with anything this good if I'd *tried*. It was better than any *fantasy* I'd ever had!"

That was, until, after holding him off for one, then two nights, she finally had sex with Max. ("I don't know how I got the nerve to refuse him," Amy says. "It was like saying no to a hurricane, but I couldn't let myself drown so soon—I just wasn't ready to go to bed *instantly*, in case it would be over.") Max was like a whirlwind—all that incredible energy quickly came to a peak and then disappeared. Completely.

"It was like he lost all his *air*," Amy recalls. "He went to sleep almost immediately, woke up a few hours later and started to grumble that he had to get out of here, what did he think he was doing— something about how making love to so many women on tour was *not* good for his karma. . . . When I heard that last part, something snapped. I asked him to repeat what he'd just said. He did, so there was no mistaking the 'making love/karma' part. I felt terrible, humiliated. This guy—who'd once been my *idol*—now was treating me like dirt. 'Who do you think you *are*?' I remember shouting. And I remember him drawing back, pathetically, puffing out his thin chest. 'You know damned well who I am. That's why you're in this damned bed.' I was crushed. I didn't know whether to throw *him* or myself out the window. Instead, thank god, I threw on my clothes and ran out the door of his hotel room, to the safety of my home."

## What Went Wrong

Fame (or excessive wealth or beauty), to too many women, including Amy, is often equated with "worth." Max had undeniable talent, but it was his public display of it that really awed Amy. Celebrities attract such enormous attention because of our need for icons—for symbols of what real beauty, talent, self-esteem should *look* like. And when one of these gods deigns not only to descend from Olympus but to notice *us*, who are we to say no? If this isn't a dream coming true, then nothing is! Amy wasn't given a blank canvas. She was given an already painted canvas—one she couldn't have improved on if she'd tried. She was, she thought, being given one of the perfect icons most of us only get to dream about. Consequently, she was blind to a lot of signals someone *not* turned on to Max's brand of celebrity would have seen and sensed in a moment: he was a selfish, self-absorbed, narcissistic egomaniac. The *gap* between the kind of deification Amy succumbed to and the reality of the disappointment she feels she ended up with couldn't have been more dizzying.

Amy might have realized she was with this dream lover for the wrong reasons if she'd been alert to the following tip-offs: (1) it's not the guy who matters, but what he does or represents; and (2) if, when you are rejected, you feel rejected by the world he represents. (For example, for months, Amy couldn't go to concerts because Max's not wanting her made her feel she didn't belong with any crowd she saw as "hip" or "cool"—despite the fact that she rationally knew Max had treated her badly, she still felt rejected by the world he represented.)

### Why Women Fall
### for the Celebrity

We've seen in other breakdowns of women's attractions to dream lovers—whether they represented power, intellectual genius, mystery, sex, or any other phenomenal promise of a "perfect partner"—ways in which women seek outside of themselves what they really need to provide themselves from within. As the magnet for all a woman's fantasies—from power to sex to talent—a celebrity can *really* blind a woman to what her real needs are. She's being given something prepackaged, somebody she already feels she knows intimately through fantasies she's nurtured, sometimes for years. Seeking the approval of someone this magnificent can become the focus of that woman's existence. She'll offer a torrent of whatever she is, whatever she can give in return for—what? A glance? A smile? A night? It doesn't matter, sometimes: any reciprocal gesture tells her that if "he" finds her attractive, she *must* be okay. But the dream is doomed. She inevitably wakes up to the fact that the icon she worships has all the faults and flaws of any other human being. Her own dream of perfection is dashed. It's not only the devastation of seeing an icon crumble—it's the abrupt realization that she's given herself to nothing.

There can be another dynamic going on, too. Sometimes the woman drawn to a celebrity is as narcissistic as he is—and she really wants not only to *have* him but to *be* him. His life seems so exciting and so full that her own pales by comparison. Living vicariously through him means that getting dumped by him can be unspeakably devastating: some women become suicidal. They deeply believe that the end of the relationship means something has died in themselves.

Clearly, developing a strong sense of your own self-worth can guard against this kind of dizzying rise and fall. So does becoming alert to the "pull" we've identified throughout this book—that, sometimes, what you're attracted to in *him* is what you long to have and be yourself.

## WAKING UP FROM THE DREAM

Dreams are wonderful: they offer, in capsule, a rich and enticing picture not only of what we want in someone else—but, unconsciously, of the person *we* want to be ourselves. When you start to look at your dream lovers in that light, they can become an extraordinary guide. They can show you traits you really want to develop in yourself. They can inspire you to increase your own sense of self-importance, to be creative in ways that will please you, to enjoy your sexuality, to appreciate all of the powers of mind and body to which you have access. When you turn a dream on its ear, it ends up helping you focus not on what's *out there*—not on some perfect counterpart who will erase your inadequacies in one magical sweep, or give you the life you dream of—but on the person *you* could become. As you slowly sweep away the dust from your eyes and allow yourself to awaken from your dreams and see what they are really telling you, you begin to see some of the obstacles that keep you away from adding *real* love to your life. You may think you want a knight in shining armor—that's what your dream may appear to tell you. But you will probably find that *you* long to be as strong, as wise, as loving, as purposeful as you imagine your perfect knight to be.

When you focus on increasing your own powers and delight in who *you* could be, something astonishing almost always happens. You look up to see that somebody else has noticed. You look up to see that you've attracted someone to you who cares about who *you* are—because you so fundamentally care about yourself.

There are more obstacles to become aware of; we'll delve into some even more subtle ones in the next chapter. But don't lose sight of where you're going. You're heading toward a new vision of *you*— so you can get a clearer vision of the man you'll be happy with.

One thing I can guarantee: you won't need that man to be a dream lover. Oh, he may have *traits* you admire—wonderful traits —but he won't be a phantom. He'll be as real as you're allowing *yourself* to be.

## Step 4

## Wake Up to Emotional Traps

It takes some courage to look at your fantasies dispassionately. They're *fantasies*, after all, and you've learned to cherish and protect them—not subject them to dissection. But now that you've made the effort to look at them a little more objectively, you've probably already begun to be rewarded. You know a little more about yourself. One of the things you've discovered is that you often create dream lovers to provide you with something you may really need to give yourself. Nowhere do we more urgently project our needs than on our fantasies of an ideal man. But often what you find when you take a look at those needs is that they can't be fulfilled by "him." You need to do something about them for yourself. You've been looking outside for answers that you can really only find within.

To get an even clearer idea of your needs, you need to dig to a level of "obstacles" *beneath* your fantasies. Dream lovers often signal the existence of what I call emotional traps —insidious, automatic assumptions we have about how we're *supposed* to behave that often end up blocking us from happiness. However self-protectively we created these traps, we've got to lessen their hold on us if we want to increase our chances of finding real, satisfying love. And, as with other blocks, we can start to get over them only by becoming aware they're *there*.

There are four main categories of emotional traps:

1.  Fear of Attachment
2.  Dependency
3.  The Power Trap
4.  Saving the Family

All have surprises—and the biggest one may be how often you fall into them! Before we break them down, let's talk a little more specifically about how all emotional traps work.

As you've seen in your checklist, it's neither a random "mistake" nor a mystery that you're attracted to certain traits over others. Every preference you have you've got for a *reason*. And I can't emphasize enough that you are perfectly entitled to your preferences—whatever they are! I only care that some of your expressed preferences keep getting you into trouble—making you unhappy. When you keep making choices that make you unhappy, your choices emerge from "emotional traps."

Emotional traps spring from deep needs and fears operating in your psyche that you're probably not aware of—and that lead to problems. For instance, if you think you want a deep relationship, but deep down you're afraid to "get involved" with a man—to truly open yourself up, share your feelings and make it clear the kind of relationship you're after—you likely have two warring basic urges: the need to be loved and the fear of being abandoned. When the need battles the fear, your psyche creates a protective rationale—an emotional trap. So you may act cozy and tell a man you're totally interested in him, but reflexively you send out a clear message to any prospective partner: "Keep your distance—I'm not really ready to get involved!" It comes out in the men you pick and in subtle ways you end up acting. You'll let a man in just so far—but when things threaten to get truly intimate, you'll find you've lost interest in him —that suddenly he "turns you off." What's actually happened is that the emotional trap *you*'ve set up acts as a safety valve. You conveniently "turn off" because he's getting too close. And your deep fear that if he gets close he might abandon you is too strong to resist. So you protect yourself by not risking what you fear you'd never be able to survive: being abandoned.

This points out a central truth about all emotional traps. We create them to protect ourselves from hurt—from what something in our psyche has taught us must *never* be allowed. Sometimes this taboo is the risky "love" of another person. Sometimes your psyche tells you you couldn't possibly make it on your own, so you'd better get someone more competent to take care of you or you won't survive. Sometimes you re-create early family dynamics because, again, those patterns are what you learned were essential for love and survival. Whatever the threat, we're not talking about minor preferences. We're talking about something that, to your psyche—your unconscious mind—is a matter of *life and death.*

You may not be *conscious* of being "terrified" of a relationship (even though that's exactly what you are inside)—you may think you merely "prefer" not to get into an intimate relationship because, vaguely, you're not "ready" for one. Or you're not conscious of being threatened senseless by the thought of being alone—you merely "discover" that you seem to bounce from relationship to relationship without stopping, and without really knowing why.

To understand your emotional traps, you must begin by respecting them. You haven't created these trap doors for nothing—they developed because something in you was convinced that you had a desperate need for them. The first step to waking up to the fact that you may *not* need them is to look at these defenses with love and compassion—for yourself. Don't get angry when you find a new emotional trap. Accept that you've only been trying to take care of yourself. Then you can accept that there may be a better way.

Here's the rundown of emotional traps. You may have more than one of them, and it may take some time to realize it. Just let these descriptions resonate a bit, and see if you identify. That will be the first step to lessening their hold on you.

## EMOTIONAL TRAP 1: FEAR OF ATTACHMENT

The fear-of-attachment emotional trap may be one you resort to if you answer yes to one or more of the following questions:

1. Does it seem that every guy you meet complains he has "cold feet" or he's "afraid of commitment"? Are you convinced the entire male population has this problem?
2. Do you never date anyone for longer than two months? Do either you or he lose interest quickly and become eager to get on to the "next one"?

3. Are the only men you ever get emotionally involved with married or in some other way "involved" or restricted?

4. Do you think a relationship is fine until he starts getting "serious—even in minor ways, like giving you an unexpected present, or suggesting a visit to his parents? Then, do you begin to notice his flaws and begin to cool toward him?

5. When he asks you to stop seeing other people, do you get nervous—and then become fairly certain he wasn't really right for you in the first place?

Let's start with the question about all those men who are "afraid of commitment." What warning bells does it ring?

I've just given you part of the answer. When a woman says "I only meet men who don't want a commitment," she's betraying her *own* fear of commitment.

I've seen this pattern over and over: you're in exactly the "right" relationship, in one sense, every time you get into one. Why? Because you've put yourself there. You may say you're after commitment, but if you keep being attracted to men who quite expressly are not interested in settling down, you're responding to something deeper in you that tacitly agrees with them: you're not really willing to settle down either. It's strange how something this obvious can be so elusive. Women can go for years consciously *thinking* that they're after a permanent relationship, and yet showing quite clearly by the kinds of men they habitually end up with that they're after no such thing. Again, it's not a conscious decision. The women are merely following the only safety route they've ever really constructed for themselves: making sure that they don't get too intimate, out of the deep fear that it might end and leave them hurt and abandoned.

Your attachment to this emotional trap can be astoundingly subtle. You may be able to quote chapter and verse about statistics that prove "there are no good men left." You may have airtight arguments about society and the role of men and women that virtually "guarantee" marriage simply doesn't work anymore. You may be heart-rendingly eloquent about the terrible things your last lover did to you—and you'll never let your guard down again. Your rationales can be wonderfully convincing. In fact, they've *got* to be persuasive for you to hang on to them! But what you're hanging on to isn't "logic."

It isn't "proof" that you're doomed never to get involved. You're hanging on to your own fear—the roots of which go terrifyingly deep—that it's just too risky to let love into your life.

There *are* ways to learn to take different risks, which it's the goal of this book to teach you. But, again, the first step is to realize and accept your own fear of taking those risks.

## EMOTIONAL TRAP 2: DEPENDENCY

You are caught in the dependency trap if you answer yes to one or more of the following questions:

1.  Do you imagine that all your problems will probably be solved as soon as you find the right man?
2.  Do you feel like half a person without the right guy?
3.  As competent and intelligent as you know you are, do you seem to lose your strength and abilities when you're with a man?
4.  Is one of the nicest feelings you have that you're with a man who'll "take care of you"?
5.  Do you have a vague sense of unease when he does for you what you could do for yourself—even though you asked him to?

Katharine, who comes to me for therapy, now laughs about what once had her totally baffled about David, a man with whom she's had a relationship for quite a few months now. "I can run an entire office at work without a hitch, but as soon as David's around, I forget my keys, can't add two and two, can't open an aspirin bottle, and even though I can press forty pounds at my health club, when he's there, I can't lift my end of a canoe."

Katharine still has what she calls "lapses" of competence when she sees David—although she's learning to shake her head briskly and "get out of it," to realize that David's presence doesn't have to drain her of the ability to do anything other than depend on him! But it's hard, because Katharine has a *very* well-oiled dependency trapdoor. We've gone over a good deal about this trap in the power monger section of the dream lovers chapter, where I pointed out that even women who are very powerful in their personal and professional lives are often willing to give up that power as soon as a man comes into view. Why is this such an alluring trap to so many women? And how can so many women be so blind to the split personalities they exhibit when "under the influence"?

Katharine helps illuminate, from her own experience: "I began to realize something was wrong when David kept pleading with me to *stop*. Stop what, I wondered? I mean, I had totally given my life over to him, did exactly what he wanted, even shopped for him when I went to the grocery store. I was always trying to figure out what would make him happy. Then, after weeks of what I was sure was completely selfless, loving attention, he said he just wanted to be left alone for a couple of hours while he read a book. I was amazed. Surely I hadn't kept him from reading a book? Was I that much in the way? I felt terrible. And terribly apologetic. I kept saying I was sorry—that I promised not to bother him—until, as he pointed out, my *apologies* were keeping him from reading his book! So I made myself be quiet."

Katharine pauses, her brow creasing in a frown. "I couldn't leave him alone! I felt a kind of terror about simply being with myself. And a growing resentment toward David. I mean, all I was trying to do was help him! How could he not appreciate me? Maybe, I thought, if I fixed him a bowl of popcorn, and we snuggled together while watching one of his favorite movies on the VCR . . ." Katharine laughs. "I'd really gone round the bend."

What Katharine has grown to see about her insistent dependence on David ("there was no question about who would drive the car, or choose a restaurant, or decide what movie we'd see—it was always David") and her insistent demands to know whether or not he "loved" her ("I drove him crazy asking him that," Katharine now says) is that they were founded *not*, as she'd thought, on her abundant capacity for selfless love, but on a huge need for reassurance. She had a nearly insatiable desire to be told she'd be taken care of, that she would be loved "forever," that she'd "never have to worry again."

The dependency emotional trap is, like the fear of attachment trap, predicated on a terrible fear of being abandoned. In fact, it's not uncommon for someone with a fear of attachment to *switch* to a dependency "mode" when she finally does risk the plunge. In a sense they're opposite sides of the same coin. But they're equally damaging to a relationship: while fear of attachment prevents a relationship from ever happening so it won't end in abandonment, dependency can virtually guarantee abandonment through one partner smothering—and driving away—the other.

"David had really almost had it with me," Katharine says now. "It was only when *I* could begin to see that I was acting paranoid about his leaving me that he could let me know he did love me— and I could believe it." Katharine was lucky—David was willing to grow with her as she recovered from her overdependence. And, as you'll see, the good news is *always* that you can recover from your dependency trap—once you accept that you'll survive without the constant presence and attention of someone else.

Demanding constant attention can become a real art to dependency "addicts." In fact, many women who use this emotional trap are very sweet and giving. Thus, they are all the more devastated when the man goes away. And the man himself is often baffled—he very likely can't put into words what it *was* that drove him away. He knows she had done everything for him, but somehow he can't accept it. He's not conscious of anything, usually, other than a vague sensation of being smothered, and he'll often think it's his fault that he can't accept such apparently pure, selfless love. What he's really responding to, however, is something quite different: a need for love and reassurance so vast that he senses (quite rightly) he could never fulfill it. And so he's driven away.

The dependency emotional trap as described above is by far the most common, but don't forget our story about the operator in the last chapter—the dependency Pat encouraged her dream lover Luke to have on her. One of the lessons Pat learned was that she was actually submerging her own dependency needs by picking a man to depend on her, so she could shift into feeling independent. It was an unconscious agenda. Sometimes we derive satisfaction in yet another way when another person—or creature (many people have pets for just this reason)—utterly depends on us. We get to give and, through our imagination, *receive* our own relentlessly "loving" ministrations. (Sometimes when you pet your cat, you may really be "petting" yourself!) If dependency were cake, we'd get to have it and eat it, too.

Again, it's important to point out that none of the impulses to give and receive attention (even vicariously) is "bad." In fact, it can be very therapeutic to take care of someone else—or allow yourself to be taken care of. It's only when your need to depend on or be depended on becomes a means of escaping reality—escaping taking responsibility for your own choices and for your own life—that it can be a problem. That's when we need to wake up to the fact that this emotional trap really *is* a trap, and not the safety valve we may have thought it was.

## EMOTIONAL TRAP 3: THE POWER TRAP

If you answer yes to one or more of the following questions, you probably fall into the power trap.

1. Do you gravitate to men who "take over"—who seem to control all situations *and* you?
2. Do you give in to a man in an argument—even if you still disagree?
3. Do you admire and envy men who intimidate or control others?
4. Do you feel like a nobody if a man you think of as powerful ignores you?
5. Do you think you need a powerful man to guide you in life, or to keep you from being too emotional or falling apart?

Notice how the power trap questions are similar to the dependency questions. These two emotional traps are indeed closely related. But the attraction to power—even if the man who embodies it abuses you and doesn't make any pretense of "taking care" of you—persists in its own peculiar way. The woman who typically falls for the power monger is not, as we've already seen a "doormat." She is often—in fact, usually—very competent on her own. But something about power in a man makes her melt, and lose any sense of her own power.

"I couldn't believe how strong my reaction was to Dick," a rising young advertising executive Angela said to me. "He was short, physically unimposing and unattractive, with—I guess—a real Napoleon complex. But he ran the company I worked in with an iron fist. He had his finger on every aspect of what everyone did. You never knew when he'd blast into your department, telling you how inefficient you were, catching you on the *one* coffee break you allowed yourself all day with some snide remark about how he wasn't running a Dunkin' Donuts. He was *awful*.

"But he was also one of the most powerful advertising bosses in the industry," Angela went on. "I would rail against him to everyone I could find who'd listen—about what a tyrant he was, what an unfeeling bastard—and yet my obsession with him struck all of my friends. 'Why don't you just ignore him?' they'd ask me. But I couldn't ignore him. He'd gotten under my skin."

One hectic day, Angela got one of Dick's dread "memos," which she assumed was a list of picky complaints, like the kind he sent periodically to everyone. Angela steeled herself for the onslaught she was sure she'd find when she opened the envelope. Inside, however, was an uncharacteristically terse one-liner: "Come see me now. D."

"My stomach went through the floor. It was as if every authority figure in my life had somehow coalesced into this little runt, and they were pointing their collective finger: my third grade teacher, my junior high principal, my father, the Pope and the President of the United States—they had all become Dick. I prepared myself for the absolute worst, that he was calling me in to fire me, and began preparing a speech that would tell him what an unfeeling monster he was and how no one in his company could stand him, and . . ."

Angela was bristling with fear and defensive rage when she walked into Dick's office. Dick, however, didn't seem to notice she was on the verge of exploding. He looked up from his desk and said—"*grunted*, really," Angela now recalls—"Good job on the Barclay account. You're due for a raise."

"I must have looked at him with such a blank, shocked expression, because he actually looked *concerned* about me for a moment. He asked me if I were all right, and I think I caught him with the faintest glimmer of the first smile I'd ever seen on his face. I stammered something resembling thanks and stumbled backward out of his office. I felt like such a *jerk*. But I couldn't believe what had happened! Suddenly, the world changed. Suddenly, this man I'd never been able to tolerate (or stop talking about) became this incredibly wise—omniscient, even—mentor, somebody who might have appeared arrogant and unfeeling to people who didn't understand him, but who I knew was really a genius. I had a whole new view of him. He became a heroic Napoleon to me, now—a fiercely driven man with a vision that, if I were lucky enough, I'd be able to help him achieve. . . ."

Angela's obsession with Dick hadn't changed intensity, merely direction. She was compelled by the aura the little man had, an aura of absolute tyranny. *Power:* the very idea of how much power Dick had made Angela breathless. He was at the top of a field known for its cutthroat competition. *He* outmanueuvered the best of the best. And now he actually thought well of *her* contribution to his empire. It was unbelievable. How could she have been so blind to have ever thought he was anything but wonderful? Then Angela noticed another change in her opinion of Dick: he was really very attractive. In fact, she found herself fantasizing about him—about what he'd be like. . . .

Poor Angela suffered from a severe case of poweritis, the power trap being a particularly strong emotional trap for her, as it is for many women. We've accepted "Power is an aphrodisiac" as a truism. It's so ingrained in us that a wildly successful man (whatever he's like as a human being, whatever his capacity for love is, whatever he *looks* like) *has* to be a turn-on. Certainly you'll find a lot of gorgeous, competent women on the arms of outwardly nondescript men, men whose sole recommendation is, to these women, the only important one: they wield enormous professional power. Why is this so addictive to so many women?

Remember what we learned in the dream lovers chapter about Helen and Ken's relationship, our "power monger" story, and from Amy and Max in the celebrity story. In each case, the woman needed to learn that what she was truly after in a "powerful" man wasn't really *his* power but rather a feeling of power in *herself.* In Angela's case, this is particularly vivid. *She* wanted to be powerful, too—and here was this man "lording" it over her! When he threw her the crumb of a quick compliment and a raise, she sprang at it like a hungry animal: here was some of that precious "power" she always craved. As she unconsciously shifted to see Dick as the source of power (rather than withholding it, which is how she'd seen him before), he became a magnet for her admiration, her devotion, even her sexual fantasies. But the real problem—the underlying condition that caused Angela to be obsessed with Dick from the start—really had nothing to do with Dick at all. It had to with Angela's own *fear of powerlessness.*

As in other traps, this is a life-and-death struggle to the psyche. Deep down, you imagine you won't survive if you don't make the right accommodation to the person who seems to have what you need, in this case, "powerful" people who, you're convinced, have what you need to *live.*

## EMOTIONAL TRAP 4: SAVING THE FAMILY

You are trapped by trying to "save your family" if you answer yes to the following questions:

1.  Do you always like what your mother and/or father likes?
2.  Do you worry about your parents' opinion even today when it can't keep you from doing what you want to do (and do you feel at ease with a prospective partner only when you know your parents approve)?
3.  Do you feel relationships work best if you both come from the same background?
4.  Do you feel responsible for your parents' (or other living relatives') happiness?
5.  Do you spend a lot of energy trying to get your parents to see something your way?

Here we get to one of the trickiest of all emotional traps. As with the other ones we've covered, however, we just have to look back a bit at what we've already seen to realize we've been dealing with the issue of saving the family all along. Remember back in the attraction chapter (the first step of our program) when I isolated the family attraction script as one of the strongest factors of attraction? Many of the women I've since talked about in this book have been operating from an unconscious checklist made up of items "given" them by their earliest family experiences. It is in fact inevitable that you'd be influenced in this way. We have to learn from *somebody* as infants—and whoever teaches us inevitably makes an indelible impression, laying down our first family scripts in the process.

We attempt to control our relationships on the basis of what we knew as children, what we saw or experienced in our parents' actions. Then the choice of a mate often revolves around some reenactment of a family relationship—either to repeat it or repair it. You could have been happy about your family relationships and now seek to repeat them, or been deeply unhappy about a family experience and seek to undo it or do it better this time around in a present relationship. Either way, what you're doing is saving the family.

This can be a trap for obvious reasons: the ancient scripts you're following are illusions and prevent you from really experiencing the person you're with now. But try to tell your unconscious mind this!

Until you can find a way to risk taking a route different from the one you followed as a child, or to make peace with the hurt or disappointment you felt as a child, you won't let go of your early patterns. You need to realize, deep down, that it's okay to let go, that you'll be all right, that you really *are* free to enjoy new relationships now. Relationships don't have to automatically end in the same way—starting, perhaps, with an initial comforting feeling but ending in pain, pain you've unconsciously been trying to "fix" all your life.

Samantha, a lovely woman, still bears strong traces of the very popular, upper-middle-class, private-school upbringing her parents strived to give her. Her straight mid-length blond hair is carefully combed back, like a schoolgirl's; she's soft-spoken and polite and carries herself with self-conscious care, as if she had a stack of books on her head. However, she says, she went through years of rebellion against the class to which she now bears witness and felt, for a while, she'd pretty well succeeded in breaking her ties to it.

Pushed to excel in school by a mother and father who pushed themselves to excel in the community (by living in an impressive white colonial house in their "respectable" Connecticut town, driving the right car, belonging to the right clubs), Samantha very early on resented all the pressure. She found herself attracted to the arty, "bohemian" set at school—not the collegiate, bound-for-six-figure-incomes set her parents wanted for her. At first she kept this rebellion under wraps. She kept up appearances at home, even if at school she sneaked cigarettes with her new "loose" friends and planned exciting trips to avant-garde plays in nearby New York. But when she got into college, a place "classy" enough to suit her parents but "arty" enough to suit the image Samantha was attracted to, she let loose.

Her parents couldn't believe it when she came home on her first vacation from school wearing a sweatshirt, jeans and no makeup, toting a pile of radical socialist literature. Thus began a tug of war between Samantha and her parents that lasted through college and later, as she eked out a living as a "radical" journalist in New York, living in vast overpopulated lofts, sharing the rent with a random migrant group of men and women who were variously actors, writers, artists—but mostly hangers-on with no clear mission except to "live the way they wanted to."

One of these men—Stan—Samantha found particularly attractive. Something about him seemed so "right" to her: his quiet purposeful approach to life (he was a poet who made his living teaching in a dangerous inner city school); his genuine desire to help make other people's lives better. And the way he *looked*: he had a lean, tall, Ichabod Crane physique, big hands, a boyish shock of hair. Samantha and Stan fell in love and, despite not especially believing in the "institution" as it existed in their "corrupt" society, got married. They figured, why not? At least it was a public announcement of the love they felt for each other.

Samantha's parents made it clear they did not approve at first, but they gave in to her choice. They felt perhaps marriage would mellow Samantha and her radical ideals and would make their son-in-law "accept responsibility" and get a high-paying job. Samantha's mother even grew to like Stan after a while—there was something she felt was curiously familiar about him. "I feel like I know that boy," she'd announce, and then plunge into the "usual": "Now if I can only get you to save a little money, get good jobs, plan for kids, move to the suburbs, maybe you really *will* have a chance. . . ." This sparked what seemed to Samantha their eternal argument— capitalist materialism versus equable distribution of wealth.

Stan began to notice some unpleasant changes in Samantha about six months into their marriage—changes for which he was completely unprepared. She began to carp about little things, the very "materialistic" things they had spent so much time telling Samantha's parents they didn't want or need. Suddenly, according to Samantha, they didn't have enough furniture. They should be buying better quality paper napkins, paper towels, shampoo, soap. And why wasn't Stan paid more for the hard work he did? Samantha seemed to be getting worried, all of a sudden, that their little apartment wasn't big enough for them. She thought they'd be happier in something larger and in a better part of town. When Stan pointed out this growing "materialism," Samantha became defensive: she just didn't want to live like an animal, that was all! But her carping got worse, and Stan was really beginning to feel their perfect marriage wasn't so perfect after all.

Tensions between them increased, and Samantha suddenly felt the urge to go back to her childhood home for a weekend—just to let things "cool off," and spend some time with her parents. Stan was baffled: how was she going to relax there, of all places? She always got into such rip-roaring arguments with them! But Samantha was curiously adamant. She hadn't seen them in a long time, she said, and she knew that, as much as they disapproved of her, they'd welcome her back for a couple days. Privately, she found herself dreaming of the clean, white, expensive linen sheets she'd known as a little girl—and then abruptly "came to" as she remembered her and Stan's futon mattress on the floor. She missed a bed, a real bed.

During that weekend with her parents, looking through an old family photo album, Samantha was hit by a revelation. Looking at a picture of her father taken a good twenty-five years previously, noticing his long, lean, lanky body—that shock of hair over the forehead, that sort of goofy smile: she was looking at Stan! "Oh, my god," Samantha thought. "No wonder Mom always felt she 'knew' Stan. My father looked just like him!"

Now that Samantha's been in therapy for a while, she's come to see that she's re-created—or tried to re-create—a good deal more than she ever knew. She wasn't only attracted to Stan because he unconsciously reminded her *physically* of her father (a similarity her own mother took in when she said "I feel like I know that boy!"). There was a whole host of other similarities she'd responded to and was attempting to play out so that *this* time around she could make them come out "right." From the very start of their relationship, Samantha sensed Stan had potential for great success as a writer and teacher. She had picked the *one* man in the crowd she'd been hanging out with who had real purpose and proven ability, an approach to life that—albeit in more conventional garb—mirrored her father's. When she started to carp about her life with Stan not including enough material things, she was both trying to re-create the comforts of the home she'd grown up in and responding to the need she'd strongly sensed (as a little girl) her mother express for the family. More than she realized, Samantha had identified with her mother and her mother's desires, including "keeping up with the Joneses."

Samantha had also sensed a "poetic" streak in her father, buried as it was over the years in his career as a successful corporate attorney. Unconsciously, she picked Stan because he was actually giving voice to that poetic nature: he was actually doing what Samantha sensed her father longed to do.

Now you can begin to see how many family dynamics were at play—and how many secret demands were being placed on the relationship and the partner. To fit these scenes, Stan had to succeed monetarily *and* be "poetic" for the catharsis Samantha unconsciously sought.

Stan, having no idea what was going on in Samantha's unconscious mind, simply felt irrationally pushed. It was only when Samantha awakened to her real motivations that she could begin to ease up and see who Stan, her husband (not a "stand-in" for her father), really was. He was not clay to mold into a better image of her father; he was his own man, with his own dreams, abilities, flaws, potential. Samantha could begin to escape her family emotional trap when she realized she wasn't responsible for "saving her family." It was not, as she thought it was when she was a little girl, her fault that Daddy felt inhibited from doing what he really wanted to do and that Mommy felt as if they weren't prospering fast enough. She did not have to replay this script now, to "fix" things, to make everything better.

Taking on responsibility for everything that goes on around you when you're a small child is very common. You try to understand why Mommy and Daddy are angry or depressed or withdrawn, or why they become warm and loving and playful. And, if they're not completely consistent, it's easy to think it's your fault when they seem to turn against you. The scripts that have to do with loving approval, as well as those based on unpredictable withdrawals of love, get etched very deeply into our psyches—it's no wonder that we're so attached to them long after they first bewildered us. We want the good ones again. And we don't want the bad ones to happen ever again. So we can fall into the trap of attempting to restage the bad ones. Now you can begin to see what problems you set up for yourself when you attempt to replay a family drama.

You can also begin to realize that some items on the checklists you carry around often aren't yours at all. They've been bequeathed to you by a complicated mix of what your parents have instilled, what you've observed of your parents' behavior and all the other factors we've been talking about in this book—everything from brain chemistry to how you responded to your first date, first kiss, first rejection on a date.

But the part that was instilled in you during your earliest childhood has to be looked at carefully. Every time you voice a strong opinion about "how a man ought to behave" or "what love should feel like"—every time you observe yourself about to react reflexively to a man—stop and examine what's going on. Where did this response come from? Do you really want to hold that opinion or act in this way? Is it, in fact, really *your* opinion or action, or just something you vaguely think is "right"? Where did it come from?

When you start to ask yourself those kinds of questions, you allow the power of those gripping "assumptions" to lessen. That's the point of looking at them: to see if they're really yours—if you really want them.

## UNHINGING YOUR TRAPDOORS

The emotional traps we've looked at in this chapter are only examples of ways you can appear to sabotage yourself. No doubt your own fears of attachment, your dependency issues, your problems with power and your family scripts take many different contours, some very different from the ones I've outlined here. But I want, again, to stress something very important about the process of coming to peace with your emotional traps. First of all, there is no easy way to identify something on which you've depended all your life—and then, with a flick of the wrist, get rid of it!

Awakening to the power of your emotional traps is a gentle process—it happens by degrees. The most any of us can hope for is *progress* as we go along. *Expect* that you'll resist giving up your favorite defense mechanisms, which is what emotional traps really are. Resistance is natural. The traps are what you've been unconsciously convinced are really saving you!

But they're *not* saving you. They're holding you back. The more conscious and more *aware* you become that your emotional traps are preventing you from living a full and joyous life, the clearer your eyes will be to real possibilities open to you. We've already illuminated a good deal of the undergrowth that holds you back: the false checklists you use to keep you from meeting men with whom you might really find lasting love; the dream lovers who can't really exist because they're perfect projections of your *own* desires and fears; and now some of the deep-seated attitudes—the emotional traps—that you use in the mistaken assumption that they're saving you. Can you see that all of these elements mesh together? In fact, "undergrowth" is a good word for how your various fears and assumptions and desires get mixed up together to keep you from growing.

This undergrowth has some very peculiar properties, chief among them that it tends to disappear in the strong, clear light of understanding. We'll get you into the clearing yet!

But first, get ready to meet your family again—in a way you've never seen them before.

## Step 5

## Recognize Family Dramas and Scripts: How to Stop Reenacting the Ones That Don't Work

Let's repeat the premise: you didn't come from a blank slate! And neither did your preferences in men and your view of the world. We've already seen some pretty clear ways in which you're bound to your past and had some glimmers of how, through awareness, you can begin to free yourself. But to get to the *real* source of why you behave the way you do, you've got to go home. With apologies to Thomas Wolfe, you not only *can* go "home" again, but have *got* to go "home," to see what you can do about cutting the tethers that keep you uncomfortably trapped.

That's what I'll help you do in this chapter on the family dramas you've learned to reenact. We've already explored this a little—at the outset when we identified family scripts as a major attraction factor and, just now, in our discussion of the emotional traps I call saving the family. A family script is like a play where the characters are members of your original family (including yourself). The plot is any one of numerous vivid scenes from your childhood that are critical to your feelings and actions today. They might have to do with whether you were allowed to stay out late at night, whether you were inconsiderate of someone (and how you were punished, if you were), whether you were a "good" or a "bad" child. These scenes are "frozen" in your memory—and later get reenacted in adulthood.

Here's an interesting aspect of

family reenactments I know will surprise you. You don't always replay yourself; you may just as easily play the role of your mother, father, one or another sibling, or any other family member who had an impact on you. And as them, you may relate to either yourself or any other important person in your life.

Just to help stimulate you to see whether your relationships reenact family scripts, think about your partner and answer these questions:

- ♥ What characteristics does he have that resemble your mother's?
- ♥ How does he resemble your father?
- ♥ How does he resemble other important people in your life?

Now think about how *you* act in relation to your partner.

- ♥ In what ways does he stimulate you to act so that you behave (think or feel) like your mother, like your father, like other significant people in your life?

As I've been careful to stress as we go along, don't automatically think replaying a family script is bad or wrong: sometimes it's the healthiest thing you can do! If you learned to be open, caring, warm and supportive from watching your parents—and you replay that script today—consider yourself blessed! You're repeating a useful script, one it's good you learned.

The problems come from the scripts that aren't so healthy— ones you're obsessively attached to (to the point where you're out of touch with the present) and ones you resort to because you want either to repair or to redo whatever you perceived went wrong in the first place.

Another tricky problem arises. Because you're using real live people in your *current* life as if they were pawns on a chessboard, you're bound to run into some unwilling players. People don't like to feel they're playing out somebody *else*'s "drama," especially when they have no idea that's what you're trying to get them to do!

Sometimes several of these problems arise in the same situation, as with Stan and Samantha. When Stan began to sense Samantha's criticism of him (which is really what Samantha was doing, even if it was unconscious), he resented it. From *his* point of view, Samantha had simply changed with no warning. What Samantha was doing, however, was playing out a family script where she was taking on various family members' roles, unconsciously seeking a "retake" on her childhood.

As you'll soon see, Samantha was playing a "mother script"—attempting, as she sensed her mother once did with her father, to push Stan in the same ways. She was also, however, playing out a father script. In being attracted to Stan's poetic nature, she was unconsciously encouraging her own father to express his buried talents—talents she sensed her mother undervalued. In being attracted physically to Stan—who closely resembled her father—she was also playing herself as a little girl, in a classic Oedipal script (which you'll remember from Step 1), by trying to win Daddy for herself. There were obviously a lot of family scripts playing on Samantha's "stage" with Stan—none of which she was conscious of! At least not until she went into therapy and began to see the puppet strings she was trying to pull.

You may have a stronger mother script than father script, or perhaps you're following a sibling script. Whatever, it helps to become conscious of these childhood mini-dramas when they trip you up today. Until you've examined them and understood them, you're like an actor in some avant-garde movie where no one knows who's playing the other parts, who the director is, how the whole story will work out, or even what the story *is*. That's not a particularly clear way to put on a show!

Let's start by examining some of the most common scripts women follow so you can see the larger picture: who's behind the camera, who's in the starring roles, why you can't stop running this movie—and why, maybe, you should!

## THE MOTHER SCRIPTS

It can take volumes—and it *has* taken volumes—to explore your relationship to your mother! But I can help you see the essence of what's going on in this relationship, at least in how it affects some of the patterns you reenact romantically today. Let's get to the first one right away.

## Mother Script 1: Marrying Mom

Carolyn was twenty and in her last year of college when she met Roger. He was a bright, sensitive man, ten years older than she and established very successfully in a law firm. He was devoted to Carolyn—and Carolyn loved to talk to him. He listened patiently and was genuinely interested in her dreams and ideas. He was also wonderfully attentive in surprising ways: he regularly made breakfast for her, brought her flowers, expressed his love for her in a thousand spontaneous gestures. He was everything in a husband that Carolyn knew her mother would boast about, and she was right. They married, and at first Carolyn was extremely happy to feel so extravagantly loved. Carolyn's mother was as happy about the marriage as she'd expected, saying she never dreamed her daughter would make such a "perfect" match. Not only was Roger a "great catch," but he would "take care of her."

But something nagged at Carolyn. Certainly she was "happy" with Roger—who wouldn't be with all that attention and love?—but she had a secret dream: she wanted to be an actress. When she finally admitted this to Roger, she was amazed at how quickly he supported the idea. He encouraged her to quit the "dull" job as a translator she'd gotten right after college ("Learning a new language opens up a whole new world," said Carolyn's mom on frequent occasions; Carolyn wondered why her mother had never taken up a language herself) and take whatever lessons she needed to start her new life.

Carolyn, delighted, took dance classes for movement and a beginning acting class. Every night she'd come home to find Roger had cooked dinner, or was ready to take her out to dinner. He was, as always, more than willing to hear about her new life—he was as enthusiastic a listener as always. And when the classes got tough, he gave her needed moral support. "Whenever I sobbed I'd never make it, he was there," Carolyn told me, "insisting that I *could*, that he believed in me."

But within months, Carolyn's cocoon life with an adoring and indulgent husband was crushed. She found herself very attracted to a man in her dance class and could feel the attraction reciprocated. She allowed herself to say yes to "coffee at his place," and they began an affair. As soon as she became involved with this new man, Carolyn found she could not have sex with Roger. She was tormented with guilt: how could she do this to such a wonderful man? But she felt driven to be "bad," and she was too irresistibly drawn to the other man to stop herself.

One day, when Carolyn was leaving the "other man's" apartment, she glimpsed Roger rushing away. "He *knew*," Carolyn said. "The worst that possibly could happen finally did." Carolyn was terrified —she didn't think she could bear the look of hurt and anger on Roger's face. She went home with a decision. She'd "go into therapy" to find out why she'd gotten into all this mess. Roger *was* hurt and angry—but, again, he supported her decision. He'd wait to see if they could work out their relationship.

Carolyn discovered in therapy that she'd been following a classic mother script. She'd married a man with many of the characteristics of her own mother. And she responded—or rather rebelled—in the same way as she'd rebelled against her mother, frequently, as a child by being a "bad girl" from time to time. These rebellions caused both mother and daughter a lot of pain, because Carolyn's mother had been as warm and supportive as Roger was with her. When little Carolyn came home from school, "Mommy" would always have cookies and milk on the table and would be ready to talk for hours about what little Carolyn had done in school, what she was feeling, what she was angry about—everything. Her every minute reaction was discussed, considered and discussed again.

On one level it was extremely gratifying to Carolyn to share this experience. But Carolyn began to sense that her mother was beginning to live, vicariously, through her own life. Carolyn began to deeply resent the attachment and thus, periodically, would "misbehave." She'd stay out later than she was supposed to, not do her homework, forget to do what her mother asked. Today Carolyn continued to feel the same conflict: she needed to be adored and cared for, and yet she was in a rage at the very person who *was* taking care of her—it harked back to the attentions of her mother that pleased her so, but also stifled her independence and made her feel suffocated.

Why this rage? Because Carolyn wanted on some level to take care of herself, but she lacked the confidence to do so. So she was locked in a relationship of *angry dependency*.

It has taken some time for Carolyn to see Roger *as* Roger, to accept that his interest in her life is *not*, as it was in her mother's case, an attempt to live vicariously through her. And to see that she could accept his attention without feeling smothered by it. But Carolyn had to wake up to the mother script she was following before she could enjoy Roger's attention and not be victimized by her own conflict over it. She needed to accept that indeed her attraction to him may have been partly based on his similarity to the way her mother treated her, but that ultimately she had *not* married her mother.

## MOTHER SCRIPT 2: NOW I GET TO BE MOTHER!

Essie put it succinctly: "Mother was always trying to *fix* me." Whenever Essie was about to go out on a date, her mother would fuss over her dress and her hair, and check her nail polish and stocking seams. "She was relentless," Essie said, and while she never protested, inside she was furious.

Now watch how these scenes played out when Essie fell madly in love with Jed. "I felt like he was perfect for me," Essie told me. "Though he was often messy, I actually enjoyed thinking of him like rough clay. I thought, 'Think what I could make of this man!' "

What Essie didn't at first realize is that she set about turning Jed into a revived "little Essie," someone she could treat as her mother had treated her. It was a classic case of the guy who gets lambasted by his boss at work and goes home to kick the dog, a deferred reaction where he treats the dog as he was treated.

Jed, while attracted to Essie's "take charge" approach, did *not*, however, feel he was quite in need of the urgent, scolding attention he got from morning to night. He was not, he felt, a slob. He merely liked things "comfortable and lived-in." But he liked Essie: she was strong and really "loved" him. So he put up with her constant do-this and do-that assault, until it finally became too much and he exploded.

"If I'm so terrible," he asked with what seemed to be impeccable logic, "why did you marry me?" Essie was furious: didn't he see she was only trying to make him, and their life together, better? A terrible tension grew between them, not helped by the fact that for a long while now Essie was refusing to have sex with Jed. Finally things got to such a stalemate that they decided to come in for therapy.

They looked like two angry fighters at opposite corners of the ring. Each was convinced he or she was being "reasonable." "*He's* the one acting crazy!" "*She's* the one who's causing all the trouble!"

I decided to ask a crucial—if intimate—question. "What's it like for you in bed?"

"I'm not interested," Essie replied, turning away.

"How is a man supposed to take that?" Jed said in anger, but softly.

"I'm sure that it's painful for both of you," I said, "but maybe it will ease the pain to know that neither of you is at fault. The problem is *between* the two of you. It's related to your being locked into patterns you saw long ago—when you were very little and couldn't change those patterns on your own—and now you're repeating those patterns without awareness, without really choosing them. Let me be specific." I turned to Essie. "Is anything about the way Jed behaves with you reminiscent of your childhood, maybe of your mother?"

I'd obviously hit a nerve.

"Oh, my God," she said. "I'm ordering him around like *she* always told me what to do."

"And if you feel like mother and you make Jed the child, how will that affect your sexual feelings for him?" I asked.

"I won't have any," she answered.

"Right," I said. "When the relationship smacks of the underlying parent/child relationship you once knew, you stop feeling sexual. This could happen if you treat each other like brother and sister, too. You might say incest fears and fantasies get in the way."

This new understanding helped Essie to separate her unpleasant "stuck" way of treating Jed from her real desire to love him and feel erotic with him. Now, every time she's about to nag Jed, Essie tries to tell herself, "Mother was like this. I don't have to be!" And Jed says to himself, "I don't have to withdraw and sulk and punish her by being obstinate." They *choose* to react differently, she in a less controlling way, and he in a more assertive one.

## MOTHER SCRIPT 3: MARRYING THE RIGHT MAN—FOR MOM

This isn't just a mother script—it's often a parent script, too, where you respond to your parents' collective wishes. It's a very common script: see if you identify with Karen's story.

Karen's story starts in much the same way as Carolyn and Roger's—her mother was thrilled that she'd found someone like Bob. Bob had gone to an Ivy League school and had also just gotten an MBA. He was obviously headed for great success as a businessman. He was a real "gentleman," from a family Karen's mother approved of—a family much like their own but richer. If there were ever a storybook tale of perfect girl meets perfect boy and lives happily ever after in a perfect marriage, *this* seemed to be it.

Bob and Karen did get married, Bob did enjoy success as a much-promoted and well-recompensed corporate executive. They did get the house they might be expected to, a lovely suburban spread in a beautiful section of town. "I think back to those years," Karen says, "and it's funny—in a way, I really was happy. It was an elated kind of feeling that I'd really gotten the life I was supposed to get. Sometimes when I watch that television show 'Kate and Allie,' I feel a lot like Allie—that perfect husband, perfect kids, perfect home and world she thought would never end. But the difference between Allie and me is *she* would have gone on in that world if her husband hadn't dumped her. When it all started to break apart for me, it wasn't because *Bob* had done anything different—it was because *I* needed to. I was starting to feel like a Stepford wife. I was beginning to feel if I saw one more bed of petunias, one more perfect patio barbecue, one more invitation to join the Junior League, I was going to *kill* somebody. Why did this change when it did? I don't know. I only know I felt terribly guilty—here I had *everything*, and everything started going sour. Was I just a spoiled brat?"

Karen's first strong impulse was to blame herself. But now that she's in therapy, she's beginning to see things differently. I've been able to reassure her that while Bob—and her life with him—may have seemed perfect on paper, there was something heartfelt that she felt was missing and that she had every right to want to explore. What Karen was beginning to realize was that Bob had never really been *her* choice. He was the logical choice in the script she was following, the script she'd been handed by her parents about the man she *should* want for a husband. This might have been all right if Karen had discovered, after marrying Bob, that he had reserves of the kind of love and attention she truly craved—but that wasn't the case.

"I'm still not sure what Bob's own agenda was," Karen says. "Maybe I was the girl *his* parents wanted him to marry. I only know I never felt connected to him—never. We went through the motions—we've even got a child whom we both do genuinely love—but nothing in our lives *together* seemed quite real. It's no coincidence that I think of sitcoms as a basis for comparison to my life. That's what it seemed we were playing. Something on television. Something for *other* people. The problem with doing that in real life is that everything isn't resolved in a half hour. Life just goes on—and on. The shallow stuff never changes. There's always one more petunia bed to ooh and aah over at your neighbor's. Always one more bridge party with people you don't especially like. Bob seemed to have adjusted okay to all of this, but finally it was too much for me."

Karen didn't truly acknowledge to herself that "it was too much" until, when Bob decided they needed a family room built onto the house, she met Tony, the carpenter responsible for most of the work. He had long curly blond hair and bright blue eyes. He was rough-edged—he'd barely finished high school—but he liked to read and would surprise Karen, between hammering nails, with the odd literate quote, from Shakespeare, Keats, Shelley. He seemed, Karen remembers, "to know exactly how trapped I felt inside. It was just something in his eyes that said 'I know.' One day he walked into the kitchen while I was fixing lunch and said, simply, 'What do you want to be when you grow up?' I looked at him and—burst into tears! He held me. He understood. He also sensed that, in the short time I'd seen him, I was so much more in love with *him* than I'd ever been in the years I'd lived with Bob. Who would have thought—a *carpenter*! How could this be—this wasn't supposed to happen! But it did. When Tony talked to me, it felt real. Not like I was in somebody else's script."

During the weeks it took to build the family room, Karen allowed herself to get closer to Tony—not yet to have a physical affair, but to *talk*. She realized what a wonderful man he was, how right her first instinct was to be so madly attracted to him. Something deep inside her sensed Tony was the man she could be happy with. The feeling was so strong that she got the courage to tell Bob she wanted to separate.

Karen's mother, when she got wind of this, was horrified. "You're giving up a successful businessman for a carpenter?" She couldn't understand how Karen could so willfully, selfishly, idiotically throw her life away. "My mother knew exactly what buttons to push," says Karen. "What about our little son—did I know what hell I was consigning him to—growing up in a broken home! Why was I always thinking of *myself* when so much more was at stake? What kind of daughter *was* I anyway? Mother spared me nothing. And it was very hard. Sometimes I thought, maybe she *is* right. Maybe I am throwing everything away. But then I thought—*no*. I knew my life was empty with Bob. I knew I had a right to a full life with Tony. And as for my son, he'd be much happier seeing his *parents* happy even if it took some adjustment getting used to two homes. There is nothing worse than growing up in a home where you sense mommy and daddy don't love each other. I knew I was doing the right thing."

Karen is still, over a year into her marriage to Tony, convinced she's done the right thing. Not that there haven't been adjustments: "We're constantly reeducating ourselves," Karen says. "Tony and I don't come from the same backgrounds, and lots of times we've got to take great care in listening to each other, instead of just assuming we know what the other is feeling deep inside. Sure, there are problems. But our love for one another is so real and so important to each of us that we always seem to work it out smoothly."

Karen realizes that her first marriage didn't really take place between Karen and Bob at all—it was really between Bob and Karen's mother! At one point in therapy I asked Karen to tell me how her mother reacts to Bob when she sees him, even today, more than a year after Karen's divorce.

"She lights up when he comes in the room," Karen said. "She clips all the newspaper articles on him—because he's such a successful businessman, our small town paper *loves* to run articles about him—and has made a scrapbook. Sometimes when she's telling me what she and dad did, she'll say 'Bob and I' by mistake. My father's name is Chet."

"How do you feel about that?"

"Infuriated!"

"So who was married to Bob—you or your mother?" I asked.

"My mother," she said. "She picked him."

It may be some time—maybe never—before Karen's mother accepts Tony, Karen's carpenter husband. This causes Karen a fair amount of pain, but nothing compared to the barren state she'd experienced trying to make her marriage to Bob work. She's shifted her need for love from her mother—whom she was really trying to please by marrying Bob—to her husband, Tony, who has become a much more satisfying source of the love she's always been seeking. She's rewritten her script: now it's *hers*, not her mother's.

## Do You Follow Mother Scripts?

If any of the above descriptions strike a bell—and if your answers to the following questions lean decidedly toward "yes" rather than "no"—you may have to take a close look at whose dialogue, entrances and exits you're really following in your life. If it's your mother's script, don't hate her or yourself: just get comfortable with the idea that you do have other alternatives.

But first, find out if this is your dynamic (there are others coming up). If you answer yes to one or more of the following, there's a good chance it is!

1. Does your partner remind you of your mother in the way he behaves, reacts or treats you?
2. Do you behave, react or treat your partner the way your mother treated you?
3. Are any dynamics between you and your partner like the ones you witnessed between your father and mother? Do you play your mother's role or your father's? (Either could indicate you're playing your mother's script.)
4. Do you always seem to pick a man you *know* your mother will like, or disapprove of?
5. Do you get upset if you don't have your mother's approval—or argue with her to make sure she sees it your way?

## THE FATHER SCRIPTS

You might have already said something like "I know what I repeat with men definitely has more to do with my father than my mother." You may even be a bit pleased with this: some women are pleased to think of themselves as "Daddy's little girl." But unfortunately, playing "Daddy's little girl" sometimes does not lead to the emotional structure you need to have a truly fulfilling life, such as autonomy and independence. What could be better than feeling that you were the most special person in your father's life? Yes, feeling loved by a man, and feeling special, can help you. But you'll see how it can also get in the way.

Many women with whom I've worked wake up to some surprising

truths about this. One of them, Judy, couldn't understand why she kept getting into relationships with abusive men, when she'd been so highly praised by her parents—especially her father—when she was a little girl. Shouldn't she have had more self-esteem now after all that praise? But, when Judy looked a little deeper, she realized that she'd actually felt more pressured than praised by "Daddy." She was responding to an underlying message that said, "I'll love you as long as you *perform*." Judy thus had no real sense of being loved for herself—only for her accomplishments. It was therefore no surprise that she gravitated to men who supported her secret view of herself as inadequate and "not enough."

This is only one of the awakenings about being "Daddy's little girl" that we'll explore here. Let's look at how, in these family scripts, there's usually much more than meets the eye.

## Father Script 1: Pleasing Him at All Costs

"Mick is nothing like my first husband, Grant," Arlene said. She'd come for therapy because she thought she'd need help making this transition in her life. "Grant was always mushy, always letting me have my own way, always the guy who gave in. He was a little like my mother."

Arlene was already conscious that her relationships with men mirrored some dynamics she'd had with her parents. So she was very aware of why she consciously chose Mick. "I love that he's so much more like my dad," she told me. "He's my idea of a real man—a guy who isn't a pushover." Arlene decided she had to become as "tough" as she saw Mick was, to make this relationship work. She thought it would be good for her, a good change from the indulgence she thinks she had too much of in her first marriage. "I needed to grow up," she said. "Mick wouldn't stand for the crap Grant took from me—my moods, my demands, my insecurities. That made him wonderfully attractive."

What Arlene did not realize is that she'd really traded one script, a man like her mother, for another, a man like her father. But neither would be fulfilling. Arlene's first thrills about Mick's "toughness" eventually faded as she grew to see she had picked him to make herself work as hard for his approval as she had for her father's. But it ended in frustration.

"Nothing I did was right," she said. "Well, that's not strictly true—sometimes, like when I managed to get his eggs exactly the way he liked them, Mick would beam at me as if I were the perfect woman he'd always dreamed of. That was terrific, and I fed on that for days sometimes, since it seemed to happen so rarely—his approval of me." She paused. "Sex was that way, too. He'd criticize me for moving around too much, or making too much noise. Then at another time he'd say I was the sexiest woman alive. And I swooned.

"The same thing happened when I'd want to talk about my feelings. My ex-husband, Grant, would always listen. I never knew if Mick was in the *mood* to listen. I began to feel like a starving dog, waiting for any scrap to be thrown to me. It was a dynamic, now that I look back on it, I can't believe I put up with for so long—but somehow it seemed so good for me. I kept telling myself I'd found a real man at last, who was making a 'real woman' out of me. He was forcing me to handle my feelings on my own instead of allowing me to spill them out. He was making me grow up."

(Arlene now laughs. "What kind of masochist was I?")

As I've said, Arlene was following a different script from that of her first marriage, but it was just as unhealthy. It was, instead of a mother script, a father script. However, when I suggested that there might be a similarity between Mick and her father, at first she resisted the idea. Mick wasn't a successful executive like her father; he was a building contractor. "They couldn't have been more different!" she insisted. But then she started to compare how she *felt* with Mick with how she'd felt as a little girl. She would, she said, bend over backward to get her father to notice her. It was hard, because he had such high standards. But every once in a while she'd manage to strike "gold." She'd bring home a perfect report card or do well at field hockey, and her father would grace her with one of his huge smiles and rare hugs. "*That*'s my girl!" he'd say. "I lived for those moments," Arlene said. "I thought my father was the most wonderful person in the whole world then—there was nothing I wouldn't do for him!"

Arlene began to see that her attraction to Mick was an attempt not only to relive her relationship with her father, but to make it *better* this time around. Remember our concept of "repetition compulsion": we sometimes seek to repeat something painful in the hope that, this time, we'll make it turn out all right. Unconsciously bound by the belief (forged by the dynamics with her father) that "men" rarely tell you they love you—but sometimes, if you were lucky, they'd come through—Arlene had made Mick a "test" of how much love she could get from a man. It was eventually exhausting, and Mick soon grew in resentment against her as he sensed her trying to *extract* approval from him as if it were a tooth!

Arlene's story is interesting because it shows a switch from mother script to father script. What she was doing in an even broader sense was *depending* on any childhood pattern to get her through—not accepting, in any deep sense, that *she* might have the power to make decisions about men *herself*. She had to work out both mother and father scripts to learn this. She now sees—from the clear evidence that the scripts she grew up with didn't work in later life—the necessity of coming up with some of her very own. This is frightening: it can mean, for the first time, really looking at "reality," really seeing yourself for who *you* are, not for what you once knew or even who your parents told you you had to be.

We'll see more of this struggle in the following two father scripts.

## FATHER SCRIPT 2: LOOKING FOR YOUR PERFECT FATHER

Briefly, this script works as follows: you're convinced Daddy was perfect, and thus no man, whatever his traits, however much he "proves" he loves you, however "right" anyone tells you he is for you, can possibly measure up.

The problem is simple. You're really trying to *marry* Daddy—as shocked as you may be to realize it. To release yourself to love a less-than-perfect man, you have to mentally divorce him—a painful process, but a necessary, and freeing, one. We'll go into this "divorcing Daddy" problem in much more detail in later chapters, but you should be alert that this is a common father script.

## FATHER SCRIPT 3: BECOMING THE DADDY YOU NEVER HAD

Remember Pat and Luke in the dream lovers chapter, how Pat, the accomplished and wealthy businesswoman who thought herself too "plain" to attract a man, fell for the operator—Luke? In taking care of Luke, Pat was enacting the family script of becoming the father she wished she'd had. Let me tell you a little about how Pat grew to become the woman she was. Pat grew up, quite simply, disappointed in her father. They lived in a small house at the wrong end of town. Pat always dreamed of having the mansion on top of the hill at the end of the road. She worked at washing the cars of wealthy families, dreaming one day of *owning* one of those cars. Her dad, a paper cutter, earned a meager wage. And he was meek, completely without ambition. Pat remembered that when her mother yelled at him for putting his feet on the coffee table, he'd sulk and go off to the basement and restack old paint cans. Pat always wanted him to yell back at her—to show he had guts. But he never did.

Pat vowed she would never be like that. And she cried herself to sleep many nights wishing and hoping that her dad would change. Frustrated at his ineffectual nature, at their poverty, Pat did everything she could to learn about managing money. She became, as you learned in the dream lovers chapter, a very wealthy woman—with three cars—counting the BMW you'll remember she bought Luke. She lived in that beautiful neo-Georgian mansion that had so attracted her operator, Luke. She had made it, just as she wished her father had.

In choosing Luke, however, Pat showed she was still in the grip of an old script. She *became* the ideal father she wanted, since the real one had never been adequate. She took on, cared for and loved Luke just as she'd always wanted to be cared for herself (plus the fantastic sex, which was Luke's special contribution to this mix).

Granted it was not as successful an adaptation as we might wish, since Pat was blind to the fact that the "child" she'd chosen, Luke, was really out for himself—to use her, not to give her the equal and deep love she craved. Again, I won't diminish the lesson Pat did learn from being with Luke—that she *was* a sexual woman, and that she was a capable, strong person who had created a fun, successful life—but the father script at work here put her at a huge disadvantage. Being driven to be the perfect "father" blinded her from seeing fully the "child" she chose to take care of.

There's also a gnawing sense of worthlessness still at work in Pat that all her money and success and ability to father other people can't quite erase. And that feeling comes from identifying with her real father, much as she tried to become the "ideal" father.

Pat came to see in therapy that she can become *herself*. She can trust in her own ability to take care of herself; she doesn't need to continue to *react* to her father's inadequacy, as if that were still happening in her life—as if she were still back in her small house, listening to her mother berate "Daddy" and watching Daddy disappear down into the basement. And she needed to see that she doesn't have to pick a man she can "father" as a way of vicariously getting better fathering herself.

Some women in Pat's situation seek a man to replace their inadequate father. In Pat's case, she symbolically *became* that replacement. Again, there's nothing wrong *per se* with these adaptations—sometimes "becoming" supportive, loving and caring because you need to feel supported, loved and cared for is exactly what you need to do. But there's a difference between taking on these traits and attempting to reenact scenarios with your father for the rest of your life. You have to let him go—forgive or forget him—and learn to cherish your own ability to take care of yourself. That's when your eyes start to open and you see it's okay to be who you are. You've survived, and you *can* survive, despite the fact that "Daddy" might not have been the father you needed or wanted.

## Do You Follow Father Scripts?

If you think you're trying to work out feelings you may have about your father, it's important to look at the following questions:

1. How are the men you date like your father?
2. In what ways are the men you date *unlike* your father?
3. How are the men you date like your *ideal* father—the father you wish you had?
4. Do you always seem to pick a man you *know* your father will like or that he will dislike?
5. Do you get upset if you don't have your father's approval—or argue with him to make sure he sees it your way?

## OTHER FAMILY SCRIPTS

Certainly any member of your family who had an impact on you when you were growing up can be the source of a family script. While mother and father scripts are probably the most common, you can also be playing out a sibling script.

You already know, if you've got a brother or sister (or brothers *and* sisters), that kids in a family usually scramble competitively for their share of the family pie. When there's more than you seeking parental love, you can have very ambivalent feelings about your rivals. Sometimes this ambivalence is so acute that it creates scenarios you play out long into adulthood—sibling scripts. Perhaps you competed so fiercely with an older brother that you find yourself, today, picking men with whom to compete, men who are in the same professional field as you or in the same general money-earning bracket, men who—once you've hooked up with them—you make sure you're "doing better than."

Such sibling rivalries can come in many different packages. If you grew up hearing Mommy and Daddy praise an older sibling, which is very likely (older brothers and sisters can appear to get head starts on younger children—they get to ride bikes first, go to school first, play sports first), you may feel a tremendous need, later in life, to "catch up" and even overtake your romantic partner. You're playing a sibling script, and it's probably exhausting both of you—you and the lover to whom you're laying siege!

You may also be following any of the permutations we've already discussed about fathers and mothers. Perhaps you were "embarrassed" by a chubby brother, whom none of your friends wanted to date. Maybe then you'll choose a partner who is either a better version of the brother you were ashamed of, or someone similarly "inadequate" whom you'll now try to change.

Relationships with sisters can be even more ambivalent. Competition tends to increase when you share the gender of a sibling, and any of the scripts we've been talking about can be adapted to relate to your older or younger sisters. Whatever the sibling script, you tend to follow it if it's been, in some way, reinforced by your parents. (Perhaps you really *did* sense that "mom liked you better," as one Smothers brother perpetually tells the other.) It may take some time to identify where you got your script. But, wherever it comes from, if it's causing you trouble in your romantic life today, you don't have to keep replaying it!

And don't think that family scripts include only family. Any "significant other" in your past or childhood can be the source—only you will know who it was who initiated the pattern.

## The Perfect Family Fantasy

There is one final family script I'd like to talk about because it's so prevalent among women—and especially difficult to identify given many women's fierce attachment to it. In this script—the perfect family fantasy—no one ever fights. Everyone expresses love all day long, in wonderful and surprising ways: Mommy bakes cookies just when you want them; brother good-naturedly teases you, but you can tell he loves you; Daddy thinks you're a princess; the house is bright and spotless; you've got plenty of friends. But most important—everyone loves each other. You're all caught up in an unending flow of unconditional love.

This fantasy seems especially prevalent today. Just look at the return we've seen in recent years to home and hearth—all those gorgeous Ralph Lauren interiors that say "perfect home," all the cookbooks offering us "comfort food" like oatmeal and macaroni and cheese and beef stew. There seems to be a huge tug back to the family. But whose family?

This is such a tender, vulnerable area for all of us—it's why Christmas and other family holidays can be such a trying time. Often, we are *so* bound to the idea of perfect family love, we blind ourselves to the fact that our own childhoods were *not* perfect. ("Of course I had a happy childhood!" you may say defensively, even if you know, deep down, you didn't.) Or, perhaps more depressingly, we're simply convinced that we never *knew* true family love, and never *will* know it.

The perfect family fantasy script is, however, really sugar-coating. Desiring either to see your own original family as perfect, or to create a perfect family today, is almost always full of your own denial of what you *know* to be true: people aren't perfect. They're flawed. Sometimes you argue. Sometimes you're in a bad mood. Hank doesn't always look as handsome on Monday as he does on Tuesday. Sometimes you "hate" him. Sometimes you wonder why you *had* kids when they act up the way they're acting up today. Sometimes it's a gray day. And, sometimes, it's a sunny one.

Love, relationships and people don't always go according to plan. But life—and love, relationships and people—can be wonderfully rewarding, *too*, as long as you see them for what they are, not what you ache for them to be.

As I hope you've seen—by looking into yourself and comparing your own family scripts with the ones I'm offering as examples—the role of family dynamics is important. Clearly, it can have a very significant impact not only on who you are but on whom you like and get along with. And, of course, whom you say "yes" or "no" to on your checklist.

What I'm really helping you to do is widen and change your *perspective*—that's been my goal throughout this program. I want you to see new angles in the prism of love choices. Your chances of happiness increase when you can allow yourself to look through as many angles of the love prism as you can. And when your love antennae vibrate to more of these new choices. And that's what I'm going to ask you to do in these final exercises, which I know you'll find fun and rewarding.

Get out some paper and a pencil and get ready to draw!

## SEEING THE FAMILY PICTURE

*Here's another opportunity to see what you might be feeling about your family. When you do these exercises, different emotions may surface than when you simply "verbally" answer questions. We're going to rely on a different resource for these answers—by getting you to draw. You can draw on any piece of paper.*

**First Exercise**
*Draw a picture of you and your mother doing something— anything—whatever comes to your mind. Don't worry about how well you draw. It doesn't matter. Let it come out however it does.*
**Second Exercise**
*Draw a picture of you and your father doing something— anything—whatever comes to mind.*
**Third Exercise**
*Draw a picture of you and the first man you really loved.*
**Fourth Exercise**
*Draw a picture of you and your current lover, or your most recent one.*

Now answer the following questions about the exercises with your mother and father (the first and second exercises):

1. *How close were you on the page?*
2. *Is one of you much larger than the other? Which one? Is that unlike the way it is in real life?*
3. *Are hands missing, in pockets or hidden? Or are hands out or touching one another?*
4. *Are faces looking out or toward each other, or facing away?*
5. *What are their expressions? Happy or sad?*
6. *Was there something you wanted to draw but couldn't? What? Why didn't you draw it?*

You can see by the very nature of these questions what some of the answers will mean. Keep in mind that what you draw may be the way things *are* or the way you *wish* they were. What about your closeness? How close you drew yourself to your mother or father is an important indication of how close you *feel* to them, or *want* to feel.

Now, what about equality? If one of you is larger or smaller than the other (way out of proportion to real life), that indicates how much power you give to whom—who's "bigger" or "stronger." (If you're equal in size, then you may see yourself as a peer.)

Openness is also important. The degree to which your hands and expressions are *open* on the page also indicates how open you feel or want to feel.

Was there something you wanted to draw but "couldn't"? You may insist that it wasn't important or you just couldn't draw it. Let me gently but firmly tell you that an omission probably reflects an important need you may be afraid to face. Suppose you "wish" you had drawn the figures closer to one another than you did. What you're really expressing is the wish that you were closer to your parents— not that you made a mistake. Similarly, whatever you "left out" or "did wrong" in your drawings wasn't a mistake either. Your drawings are very clear indications of what your *first* feelings or wishes about your parents are, not the feelings you'd like to go back and "edit" in.

Look at those first two drawings again. What are you doing together? What's the significance of it, now that you accept that *you* chose to depict this activity? What about the expressions of your faces—blank, smiling, frowning? In what order did you draw the figures—you or him/her first? If you took a long time to draw a figure or had a hard time drawing the whole figure and could only draw part, that means you're very conflicted about the person or that part of their body and what it represents. (For example, trouble drawing your father's smile may mean you fear his disapproval.) If you decided to put someone *else* in the picture with you, that may mean you feel a need to diffuse the relationship you feel with the parent; or you feel that someone else comes between you.

Now take a look at the last two drawings—you and your first love, and you and your current (or most recent) lover. Ask the same questions of these drawings.

Quite a revelation!

These drawings are *speaking* to you. They are your heart and your mind and your dreams and your fears—all trying to get your attention. Look at them closely. Keep them for a while, and see what they bring up when you look at them next. You're projecting unspoken—and sometimes unconscious—feelings and needs in these drawings. Analyzing them can show you what you feel and need and want.

Learning to listen to those pleas from yourself is what will mark your growth. And what will enable you to take the next step in our journey: to get *rid* of the old voices, the old scripts, the wrongheaded items on your checklist that keep sabotaging you over and over. And to find the happiness and fulfillment you seek, by knowing yourself and being freed to make new love choices.

As enlightened as you now are about yourself, you may still feel resistance to changing your checklist. Having come this far in the book, you know more now about how your family scripts and emotional traps may constrain you. And you're more aware of what's really going on beneath your "attractions" —why you fantasize about certain men and don't about others. But the prospect of changing, so that your love antennae respond to *new* men, may still seem overwhelming.

You may even worry that I'm telling you to stop responding to those things which really turn you on. No. I'm not asking you to give up what really attracts you, or to settle for less than you dream about. As a psychologist, I'm into helping you fulfill your desires, not making you deny them. I assure you I want for you what *you* want: the fulfillment of your needs. That doesn't mean slapping your own wrist when you feel a craving for a certain type of man. But it *does* mean taking a closer look at that craving to see how you might *fulfill* it most satisfyingly and have the best chance of lasting happiness. And it *does* mean selecting more carefully—retraining and retuning your love antennae.

You'll be surprised, I think, to learn how much you *can* "have your cake and eat it, too." The fact that you're attracted to powerful or athletic or suave or brilliant men doesn't mean these traits are automatically dangerous or superficial. These are perfectly fine traits— and there's no reason you

# *Change Your Checklist*

shouldn't seek them. The goal is simply to make sure that the man these traits are *attached* to is good for you, too. As we saw perhaps most clearly in the chapter about dream lovers, you can get into trouble when you allow a man's "attractive" traits to overshadow everything else. It's when you mythologize the reality out of love that you get trapped—and unhappy.

So blaming what goes wrong between you and the men in your life on the fact that powerful or handsome or brainy men are always "bad" for you isn't the answer. Let's say you get weak in the knees over the take-charge, successful, no-nonsense CEO type. There's no reason not to admire this kind of man's approach to life—but there is good reason to beware that he doesn't throw *you* around the way he throws his weight around at work. You may want to see whether his business contacts are more important than *you* are. You may, in short, want to see how much his power intrudes on your own happiness. Allowing yourself to pull in the reins a little bit and take a calmer view of a man's real effect on your emotions and your life can reveal some surprises. The power trait may still be a turn-on, but you may want to weigh it against other traits that, on calm reflection, turn out to be just as important. The good news is that CEOs *can* be nice, sensitive, decent guys—not all of them will treat you like a doormat. But your chances of finding the decent variety only increase when you open your eyes to more than the power trait that may have triggered your fantasy first.

That's why I want you to change your checklist.

One goal of changing your checklist is to see the range of what you're *really* after in a relationship with a man, as opposed to the knee-jerk attractions that prod you to jump in without thinking.

Another goal is one we've already explored in this book: to see if the trait you think you're after in a man is one you really want for *yourself.* It's common, as we've seen from a number of stories in this book, for women to get involved with artistic or sexy or intellectual men out of a buried desire to have these traits themselves. What you create when you do this is a no-win situation: you can't help (however much you're conscious of it) *resenting* the very men you're attracted to if they've got something *you* want for yourself—and if you really want to *be* them more than be *with* them.

Taking a new look at your checklist and attempting to change it will, I promise, provide you with an extraordinarily effective "love map." For one thing, you'll have expanded the choices in your life enormously. I know from years of experience as a psychologist that the more choices and options you give yourself, the better you'll feel, especially when those choices and options are based on reality. That's the overall goal of changing your checklist—to wake up to *achievable* ways of bringing love into your life.

This said, you may still be digging in your heels. It's a sad truth that we sometimes cling to the known even when it makes us miserable, rather than make a move toward the far more hopeful unknown. All I can do is urge you to do it anyway. Take the leap to seeing your love life differently than you've ever seen it before. Don't "try" to do it—there's no such thing as "trying." Right now, try to raise your right arm. Is it raised or not? See, you'll either do it or you won't. There's no such thing as "trying."

Respond with that same kind of decisive, positive, active spirit now in your life. Which, ironically, you'll best be able to do by looking at the reasons you may still be *resisting* changing your checklist. Let's take a look at the barriers that may still be holding you back—*and* at how to clear them away for good.

## BARRIERS TO CHANGING YOUR CHECKLIST—AND HOW TO GET THROUGH THEM

### 1. YOU CAN'T SEE ALTERNATIVES

Sometimes the inability to see alternatives is just a bad habit, one which you can start to break simply by *hearing* that you have alternatives you never realized. That's what I hope much of this book has already done for you—elicited the response "Oh my, I never thought of that before! Yes, I can do that." Just planting an idea in your mind can be a powerful tool for extending options and expanding choices.

For now, just adopt the attitude that there *are* alternatives, even if you don't yet have a clear idea what they are. Experiment with this a little more specifically. Next to your list of "tall, dark and handsome" on your first checklist, write another list—"kind, understanding and a good sense of humor." Add other emotional traits, and some new physical details (like "warm hands" or "great smile") that might not have occurred to you before. Your list of "possible" men will grow —as will your chances of meeting one of them.

## 2. You Don't Know What You Really Want

Some women are miserable that they don't have what they want, but they actually can't say what that is! The closest they can get to verbalizing their deepest desires may be too general to help much ("I want love, I want to be cared for, I want to be fulfilled"). Pressed to make more specific choices, they may end up choosing a man their friends, parents or professional colleagues think is appropriate. While I hope you have already begun to get a clearer idea of what *you* want, I know it may take some more courage to stand up for yourself and come out with it. For now, just accept the idea that you won't be happy until you meet your own needs. And I promise, as you go through the rest of this book, you'll develop more courage to elucidate them—and act on them.

## 3. You're Afraid to Change

Change, as you know, can be frightening. Even if it seems that it might eventually bring more satisfaction, you probably also worry that it will bring disappointment—and so you're afraid to go through with it. But being afraid of change to the point where you take no new actions in your life means only one thing: you're sacrificing any *probable* gains. Again, as you read on, you'll get even more inducement to face your fear of change, and do it anyway.

## 4. You're Lazy

This is a big one. Instead of taking the effort to investigate new types of men that might be more interesting or satisfying, you may find good reasons to rationalize why you are where you are—and why you're still stuck with the same unsatisfying love life. You may protest, "But I *like* this kind of guy," when in fact what you're saying is, "I've learned to *settle* for him." Few women are truly lazy—if you scratch the surface of "laziness," you usually find fear. So, take a look at the preceding barrier again and see if it fits.

## 5. You're a Perfectionist

You simply won't settle for less than your ideal: it's perfect or nothing. I don't have to tell you that this kind of thinking is bound to lead to disappointment. Hopefully, in some of the stories I've given you in this book, you've already begun to examine the reasons why your standards are keeping you from "real" love—and to see that you may be responding to old family scripts or emotional traps rather than to your own real desires. In any event, you, too, may be hiding a fear of change, which we'll address more fully as we go on.

## 6. You've Got an Investment in Keeping Love Away

Wait—don't leap to the next barrier because you're sure this doesn't apply to you. Unfortunately, women who have an "investment" in avoiding intimacy rarely realize they do; they may tell you in all earnestness that "love" is the only thing that matters to them. But look at their track records and you may see evidence of the opposite. Why did no man ever "work out"? Why has no one ever measured up? Why was real intimacy so impossible? Some women actually wallow in the misery of being alone—unconsciously "preferring" it to a real relationship with a man. Is this masochism? No—it's a "secondary gain," a kind of compensation. Perhaps you figure that if you stay alone, you won't have to face any compromises or disillusionment from being abandoned. When you examine your own investment in keeping love distant, you usually find some deep fears—which, again, the rest of this book will help you to face.

## 7. You've Got a Terrible Self-Image and Poor Self-Esteem

This may be the most important resistance we've talked about, obviously one I'm devoting a lot of time to in this journey of ours. Why? Because it underlies almost every problem with love and intimacy a woman has. Women who have low self-esteem and believe deep down that they don't deserve to have what they want (happiness) usually persist (unconsciously, of course) in looking for someone who will corroborate their own view of themseles as unlovable and unworthy.

Almost all women struggle with self-esteem issues, and when it's a big problem, there's no area of life it doesn't affect—love, work, all relationships in the world. If you suffer from feelings of unworthiness, you're always on shaky ground because you're never pretty, smart or good enough for the man, job, friends and family you have or would like to have.

It's so important to address this area that, in addition to the implicit emphasis I've already given it so far, I'm adding some special exercises in their own section following this chapter. If self-esteem is a recurring problem for you, pay special attention to them.

You've already begun to deal with these barriers to change by reading about them, which means you've begun to *face* them. If one or more fit (and it won't be uncommon if *all* apply), "own" the fact that you've been holding yourself back that way. Don't berate yourself. Merely take note that perhaps some of the biggest obstacles to change (and thus happiness) in your life are ones that can be *removed*—because *you* put them there to begin with! Your power in choosing is an attitude to nurture throughout your life. Ask yourself, "What's holding me back that I have power to change?" Once you've owned the resistance, you can go on to change. You'll be freer to make the next choice—or choices.

## TRUTH TRAINING—CHANGE FROM WITHIN YOU: THE FIVE-STEP PLAN

What we're basically trying to do is to see the *roles* you play—unconsciously as well as consciously—and realize what in those roles may be holding you back from intimacy and satisfaction in your relationships. As we've seen along the way in this book, whether blindness about yourself comes from emotional traps or family scripts or the dream lovers to whom you bond in fantasy, the good news is that it's possible to "train yourself for the truth."

How? First by *seeing* what's really happening, then *feeling* on a gut level what's really happening, and then by learning to *act* in new ways appropriate to the reality you've discovered. The following five-step plan is a good way of allowing you to undergo this process. Every time you need to surface from a dream lover fantasy that threatens to capsize you, you can make this five-point program work for you:

1.   Face the Fantasy
2.   Separate Fantasy from Reality
3.   Write the *Real* Screenplay
4.   Change Your Self-Talk
5.   Detach from the Past

That's the program in its bare form. But let's look at exactly what each of these steps means—and how it can be used—in a real-life example. Jane's story illustrates this nicely.

Jane went on a skiing trip with her friend Alice—and she had a mission. She was *not* going to allow a weekend romance to throw her. She was *not* going to fantasize wildly about "inappropriate" men. She'd had a history of getting involved with men who looked, sounded and, at least at the beginning, acted "perfect," but to whom she'd almost always blinded herself in some crucial ways. She'd excuse one man's narcissism, another man's selfishness, another's insensitivity in any number of ways ("That's just how men are" or "He doesn't really mean it" or "He's very good at taking care of himself") and end up getting badly hurt as a result. So she was watching out for herself a little better, and while she fully planned to have a great time on her ski trip, she promised herself she wouldn't fall head-over-heels at the first provocation. She'd also learned my five-point plan—and was determined to use it.

Unfortunately, she hadn't banked on meeting Peter. Their meeting was right out of a fantasy. She knew she looked good (she was wearing a very flattering brand-new, form-fitting, powder-blue and silver ski suit) when Peter swooshed in beside her, his skis spraying snow, in an impressive dead-end parallel stop. He was breathtaking: a Robert Redford jaw and straw-blond hair, sexy Vuarnet dark glasses and tight silver ski pants. His approach was thrillingly direct: "Who are *you*?" he asked with obvious interest. Introductions were exchanged, revealing that Peter was a Club Med ski instructor who happened to be working this season at this resort. A ski instructor! Peter couldn't have known how perfect this was for Jane. She had dreamed of being "saved" by the strong arms of a handsome expert on some dangerous run. And now here He was.

Jane ignored the distant warning bell that she was about to fall blindly in love again—she could only concentrate on turning this expert into an escort. She nurtured a romantic vision of an intimate dinner at the ski lodge, followed by a long night. Her revery was abruptly broken by Peter's invitation to join his ski class the following day. The warning bell momentarily got louder: was that all he was after? Trying to scare up students for his class? Then Peter saved the day by adding that he'd "love" to have dinner with Jane, too— that evening, if she thought she could make it. Jane beamed, and the warning bell receded. She did, indeed, think she could make it. (She also agreed to be in his ski class.)

Jane met Peter that night at the bar in the lodge. More accurately, Jane met Peter and roughly twenty other women he seemed to know (and get to know, right then and there). Jane began to wonder why Peter had singled *her* out when it seemed obvious that any of the other women would have done just as well. He smiled at and joked with this or that female passerby—they all seemed to be his ski students. Perhaps, Jane thought, they'd all gone this "dinner" route.

At first Jane was crushed—"Here goes another fantasy!" she thought—but then she was grateful she hadn't gotten more deeply involved and allowed herself to be hurt later, the way she used to engineer things. She was grateful she had a mental remedy she could start to make work right then and there: my five-point plan. It became more and more obvious through dinner that Peter was putting himself on "display," that he was an inveterate ladies' man, that he would inevitably end up telling her what she dreaded hearing—that she was rushing him, that he liked her but it didn't mean he wanted to be committed, that he was only after fun. Although Jane continued to be dazzled by his good looks and charm (even if that charm was a bit distant), she was able to check her reactions. She was able to stop herself from snowballing into what she had always done before —bend over backward to get his attention, laugh at his jokes, flirt outrageously, become pushy in her desire to win Peter. She was able instead to work on the first of the five steps:

## 1. FACE THE FANTASY

Jane allowed herself to *see* who Peter really was. She didn't automatically have to have him. In fact, by allowing herself to enjoy his good looks and charm and wit without falling desperately in love, she could actually appreciate him more. When you face the dream lover fantasy, you drain it of some of its obsessive power and free yourself to become receptive in other, more expansive ways. It would have been fine for Jane and Peter to have a brief exciting romance —as long as she *knew* she was playing out her fantasy. But Jane also knows that acting out a fantasy has its dangers: it rarely lives up to expectation, and it's hard to remain emotionally neutral when you give in to it. So she was ready, in the first step, to let go of the dream and complete another step in telling the truth to herself.

## 2. Separate Fantasy from Reality

Here's how Jane did this. She let her mind run freely and came up with all of the traits she fantasized Peter had. She "made him up" as a perfect lover, fantastically attentive to her, falling for her totally, pledging undying affection. Then she made a quick mental note of the *real* Peter. The real Peter was flirting with other women when he could, totally interested in his own "studliness," not in her. To correct her tendency to manufacture a dream lover, she mentally listed, as impartially as she could, the facts. Who *was* Peter, really? A good skier, but not, as in her fantasy, the "greatest skier in the world." A man who obviously liked women, but a *lot* of women at the same time. A good salesman who was trying to sell his ski instructor services to as many women as he could. A guy who was charming and handsome, but not really capable of developing a deep, long-lasting relationship.

Jane recalled this fantasy-versus-reality list a few hours later, when she was back in her room and the tendency to romanticize the evening began to overtake her. Her "facts" list kept her from floating away, but it also stopped her from doing something else destructive. Always before when she'd sensed coolness or rejection from a man, she blamed herself. She was never good enough, pretty enough, athletic enough, smart enough. With Peter, she could see it hadn't very much mattered who *she* was. He was so obviously following his *own* agenda, an agenda she knew wouldn't have changed for any woman.

By reminding herself of these facts, Jane could continually allow not only Peter to be who he was, but herself to be who she was—

and have that be okay. She didn't need to feel resentment against Peter or hate herself for some imagined inadequacy.

However, fantasies are persistent. Even after steeping herself in the "real truth" about Peter, the memory of his touch still threatened to wash all that truth away. Luckily, Jane had recourse to a third step.

### 3. WRITE THE *REAL* SCREENPLAY

Jane now imagined her dinner meeting with Peter as if it were a movie—and then became the movie's critic. "How does he treat the heroine here?" she asked herself. "Poorly" was the inescapable conclusion. She went through their conversation, taking the same critical stance, and something became very clear. She didn't enjoy talking to Peter! The "movie" in her mind came to a dead, disappointing halt whenever she replayed their dialogue. It was time, she realized, to change the movie—bring in a new writer, director and cast. There just wasn't enough chemistry between the "stars."

Jane was further able to detach from Peter by using another mental step.

### 4. CHANGE YOUR SELF-TALK

What this means is that every time Jane felt the impulse to berate herself for not being "good enough" for Peter—or to fall into an old rut of telling herself, "He's so great and I'm nothing"—she could replace that inner voice with something better. "I feel good about myself. I am excited by him and flattered by his interest, but I know the type of man he is and how that 'type' has treated me in the past. I've always been hurt and I don't want to be hurt like that again. I don't want to make myself vulnerable to someone as vain and self-absorbed as he, even while I accept that he's a great-looking man. I don't need to be anyone other than who I am. I'm fine *right now*." When you change what you say to yourself (your self-talk), you are more likely to change your beliefs *and* your behavior.

The result of these steps was to allow Jane to begin to detach from Peter and to open herself up to *other* men. In the clarity these steps afforded her, Jane was able to meet Arthur. Arthur, ironically, was in Peter's ski class too. He was, in fact, the best beginning skier in the class. He did not have Peter's flash—no color-coordinated outfit, no drop-dead shades—but he had a quiet humor and self-effacing charm that Jane allowed herself to see and enjoy, now that she'd separated herself a bit from Peter. When she fell on the course at one point, it was Arthur who flew to her side to help her up. (Peter, Jane noticed, made a dutiful turn in her direction, but Arthur didn't hesitate a moment—he was there instantly.) Arthur asked surprisingly competent medical questions. "Can you move your leg inwards, turn it out the other way?" And, when he finally pronounced her okay, she felt a surprising rush of warmth toward him. Heaven knows, Arthur was no knight in shining armor. He wore a beat-up parka, an old woolen cap pulled down low on his brow, and glasses. In the world of fantasy, from which she'd so carefully extracted herself with Peter, Arthur would never have measured up. But in the world of reality . . .

Jane was able to "accept" Arthur more completely by employing the fifth step in the plan:

## 5. Detach from the Past

You'll remember back in our attraction chapter how clear it was that much of what turns us on comes straight out of our pasts. Our fantasies, in fact, are usually based on "ancient" images and pleasures and fears—feelings that go back to infancy and get refined through all experiences up to the most recent ones. In Jane's case, she had to admit that Arthur reminded her of a smart kid in her high school who wasn't especially popular—and that was a half-conscious obstacle to her "letting him in" today.

Examine how you are similarly blocked by past experiences, beliefs and rules you made. You may have a romantic idea of what eyes are supposed to look like from someone who kissed you when you were sixteen; you may hate certain noses because they remind you of that awkward boy in seventh-period chemistry class, and so on.

What Jane has learned to do is be sensitive to old, inappropriate messages getting in the way of her happiness today—and focus on what's *positive* in men she likes but whose traits may activate an old prejudice that prevents her from seeing something good. She could do this with Arthur more easily because she really did like the way he "held" himself. He had a nice, relaxed aura about him that she found attractive, and she focused on that instead of his less glamorous aspects.

And so Jane allowed herself to respond to Arthur's attentions, even though certain initial physical "cues" about him might once have turned her off. She'd learned that those cues just held her back from enjoying a lot she *could* enjoy. In the lodge that night, Arthur and she sat and talked, she with her legs curled under her on a couch in front of the fire, he sitting cross-legged on the floor on a braided rug, leaning against the leg of the couch. Jane was amazed by how "natural" it felt—how unforced, how warm, how enjoyable it was just to *be* with somebody, without feeling she had to impress or dazzle. It was, she had to admit, a relief from the way she'd felt with Peter. "It wasn't that I was falling madly in love with Arthur," she says. "I just really liked him." Jane remembers glancing across the room toward the bar, where Peter was holding court, and breathing a slight sigh of regret—Peter *was* so physically gorgeous—followed by a much deeper sigh of relief. She genuinely *liked* Arthur better than Peter and was certainly having a better time with him.

What this five-step plan really accomplishes is something simple: it enables you to *use your own judgment.* Jane realized she had to do what was right for *her*, not what would have made her look impressive to someone else. Alice, with whom Jane had gone on this ski trip, was unbelievably envious of Jane when she hooked up with Peter. ("I can't believe you got the hottest man in the resort!") And Alice was much less impressed when Jane turned to Arthur. But it was a moment of real triumph for Jane. She allowed *herself* to choose some-one, not knuckle under to Alice's or her own old expectations of the man she "ought" to have pursued and caught.

## MAKING YOUR CHECKLIST YOUR OWN

This final lesson we've just learned—use your own judgment—brings up something very important. Just as Jane learned that she had the power to seek out what *she* wanted in a man (not merely what she'd been taught she was *supposed* to want in a man), you can learn to sensitize yourself to respond to what *you* really want from love. This doesn't mean you have to give up what turns you on. It's extremely difficult and unproductive to censor your desires. You have to begin by accepting them—and then, if you see that they keep getting you into trouble, take steps to reorder your priorities.

But the important point is to own your checklist—to make sure that whatever is on it is there because *you* want it there, not because you think mama or your ex-roommate in college would approve. A client of mine, Esther, helps me illustrate how important this is. When I asked Esther to come up with her checklist—to choose the three most important things she looked for in a man—she didn't hesitate. She scribbled down the following:

1. Great wealth
2. Great social standing
3. Fancy lifestyle

"At least I know what I want!" Esther said brightly. "I mean, okay, I know it sounds materialistic, but you asked me to be honest, didn't you?" Esther gave me some background about her desire for the "good things in life." Her mother had grown up in lower-middle-class circumstances and vowed she wouldn't marry until she'd found a man "of means." In fact, she did "land" a successful dentist, and her lifestyle did improve. But while she found herself living in a nicer house, wearing nicer clothes and going on the occasional vacation to nice places, she was never happy. She continued to feel socially and economically inferior to the people in her husband's circle, and she overcompensated by putting on airs—and a great deal of jewelry and clothes that strained her husband's income. The clear message Esther got was: "Marry rich. If possible, richer than *I* did." It was the only way a woman could be happy.

It was at this point Esther came to me. She'd been dating wealthy men of high social standing and she was miserable. She'd written down "great wealth, great social standing and fancy lifestyle" as goals—and yet, having found them in the men she met, she knew they obviously *weren't* what would make her happy. She was miserable, she said, because she'd met this schoolteacher who made about one-fifth of what most of the other men she'd met made—and she found herself falling in love! This was a disaster. "What would my mother say? She'd disown me!"

Through therapy, Esther slowly gained the courage to stick up for herself—and for the man she really loved. I asked her to write a new checklist months after she first came to see me, and already it had changed. Out of a vestigial deference to her mother, her first item was "able to provide for me," but the next two traits were "kind" and "intelligent"—traits that described her schoolteacher beau. Esther had already begun to make her checklist her own, but she was facing something even more difficult. By sticking to this man, a man her mother felt was completely wrong for her, she would have to learn to live without her mother's approval. Esther had never done this before! She'd always managed to merge her own wants with her mother's. She'd gotten immense security ever since she was a little girl from knowing that her mother approved of her. She desperately wanted her mother to approve of her choice of man, but her mother wouldn't. Esther found herself getting very angry, and a situation that had begun as tense now threatened to explode. Much of this anger came from Esther's deep-seated fear that "mother might be right." She'd aligned herself with her mother's will for so long that rebellion wasn't something she felt she could *survive*.

What Esther came to realize is something I've found very important: we get angry or are hurt by what others say only if we feel, deep down, the same way ourselves—and wish we could get rid of it. Esther was obsessed about her mother's disapproval of her beau's finances because she *herself* was worried about his schoolteacher's earning power. Once she realized this, it cleared the way for her to face other powerful feelings as well—feelings of love for him, feelings of wanting to make a commitment. Finally, she realized she had no choice but to form, and stick to, her *own* checklist, painful as it was to go against her mother's wishes.

I helped Esther separate from her mother (and from her mother's checklist) in ways that can be clearly outlined in steps. These steps can help you, too. Here's the three-step process we used. It took courage, but the rewards have been immeasurable for her—and will be for you, too.

## OVERCOMING THE NEED FOR APPROVAL: THE THREE-STEP PLAN

### 1. FACE YOUR NEED FOR APPROVAL

If your need for approval is getting in the way of your happiness, as it did with Esther, give yourself time to weigh how important it is to go ahead *without* approval. If you feel it's important enough, mentally stick up for yourself, tell yourself you're responding to what only *you* know will make you happy. Build your inner decision up so you feel good about yourself. Ask yourself, "Do I really need (his, her) approval?" Keep asking the question until you can say "no."

Recognize that your need for approval comes from a fear—that you'll lose the person's love whose approval you seek if you don't do it his or her way. Risk it. Real love is not based on others doing what *you* want them to.

Trust your own judgment. That way you'll never be a slave to someone else's.

### 2. STOP THE ESCALATION

You don't have to "take the bait." If someone whose approval you used to depend on suddenly has withdrawn support—and taunts you with "How could you do this to me?"—give yourself permission to withdraw. Say what it is your right to say: "I don't think this is the best time to discuss this." Then wait until both of you are calmer. If you know the situation will be explosive and it's likely you'll say hurtful things, step back, calm down, and wait until the "mental weather" is clearer.

### 3. FEEL GOOD ABOUT WORKING THROUGH YOUR NEED FOR APPROVAL

Bucking someone's approval—someone very important to you—takes a lot of courage. But when you do it in the service of what you know is right for *you*, you've triumphed. You deserve to build yourself up about it—not at someone else's expense, not to build up steam for "vengeance," but to bolster the inner sense of rightness that made you want to separate from someone else's checklist in the first place. You're a good person when you treat yourself well, not when you've lived up to somebody else's dream rather than your own.


## MAKING ALL THIS WORK: TEN-STEP GUERRILLA TACTICS FOR MEETING "THE NEW MAN"

"Enough! I understand more now," I hear you saying. "But I've got a party to go to tomorrow night, and there will be any number of men there I haven't met. What do I do?"

It's amazing the time women put into their makeup, hair and clothes and how little they put into mental preparation—when, as we've seen, it's the *mind* that ends up running us (rarely our makeup). So, let's condense a plan of attack. (I know this isn't exactly a war, but sometimes it's a good idea to get the adrenaline up a little so we face the pursuit of love courageously. So—to arms!) I guarantee that this will transform your evening, and increase your chances of meeting a man who's right for you. You'll end up using everything we've learned so far—and it'll be a lot easier than you think.


### 1. REWRITE YOUR CHECKLIST

I mean, literally write a new checklist—with pen and paper, not just in your head. In light of everything we've just discussed about making your checklist your own, take a hard look at your priorities. Go back to Step 2 of this book and review what you wrote down under your type—the spontaneous list of what you want in a man.

Put these items in a column you'll label "The Old Me," and that will be your old checklist. Go over these and alter any that would lead you to a dream lover. For example, in Jane's list about the ski instructor, Peter, she changed "charming" to "charming *but* only having eyes for me." Record the new checklist items in a column labeled "The New Me." Add to it ways you want a man to make you feel—like "he makes me feel beautiful" or "he lifts my spirits when I'm down" or "he's available to give me affection when I need or ask for it." See if you can eliminate items that can change (like looks) and choose characteristics that last (like loyalty).

## 2. Delay

Once you've gotten to the party and find yourself talking to a man, don't allow yourself to make snap judgments. One survey has shown that people form their first impressions in the first fifteen seconds of meeting someone. Hold back on the reins. Allow the man you're talking to *five minutes* of your time. And instead of plunging into a conversation, take a few deep breaths. Don't interrupt—let him finish his sentences. Take it slow—take it easy.

## 3. Don't Judge

Allow yourself to listen to what the man has to say. Don't automatically rate his opinions or his tone or his vocabulary. Give him a chance to be himself. Tell yourself to suspend all judgment for this first encounter. You'll be amazed at how fresh and clear your ideas of who people are will be as a result.

## 4. Be a (Discreet) Talk-Show Interviewer

Pretend your TV ratings depend on making the person you're with look and sound good—help him to feel comfortable, bring him out without being unnatural yourself. Show interest in what he has to say—let him blossom. (This doesn't mean you have to *like* him as a result, but at least you'll have given him—and yourself—a real chance!)

## 5. Change Your Inner Voice

We touched on this before, but it's especially important here—at the moment before you first talk to a man. If you find yourself standing alone at the party and playing yourself the old inner tape ("I'll never find the man I want. I'm just unlucky in love. It's impossible"), or anything else that drums in a negative message, you've got a pretty good chance of proving yourself right. It's a profound truth that we get what we expect to get. Change that tape the instant you hear it to something like: "I deserve exactly the right man for me. I'm going to find someone wonderful tonight. And, if I don't, I'll have a good time anyway." Of course there are no guarantees you'll find the man of your dreams, but feeling relaxed about the possibilities almost ensures that you're as *open* as you can be to meeting the right man. Positiveness always works better than negativeness. When you communicate "I'm having a good time," you attract; when you communicate "I'm miserable," you repel. It's as simple as that. So—attract! Make your inner voice positive.

## 6. "Translate" Physical Traits

There are alternative traits in men you can free yourself to enjoy—alternatives to the ones you *thought* you were after exclusively. Let's say your initial checklist for a man's physical attractiveness runs as follows:

1. Full, sexy lips
2. Broad shoulders
3. Dark, curly hair

These sound fairly definite, don't they? But what if you've just met a man who interests you but who doesn't live up to your checklist? Allow yourself to "meditate" for a moment, to transform each item into something that *does* appear in the man you're talking to. You may find that "full, sexy lips" transforms into "deep, searching eyes." That "broad shoulders" transforms into "strong, self-confident posture." Allow yourself to "see" the man you're with romantically, and you may spontaneously enjoy the thought of running your fingers through his hair—even if it's blond and straight rather than "dark and curly." It's not that every item on your checklist is negotiable, but you'll be amazed by how allowing your mind to "float" for a moment can open up new possibilities. You'll awaken to *alternatives* in the man to whom you're speaking—even if he doesn't check out on what you *thought* was your checklist.

## 7. Get to Bottom-Line Traits

By going one step beyond translating traits, you can get to their bottom line, to what they really mean to you. You can peel away the layers of emotional and other nonphysical traits by using a free-association technique. Let's say you've listed "wealth," "enjoys traveling," and "kind" on your list. Meditate on "wealth," and ask yourself what it really means to you. Are you attracted to the power it can confer on a man? Or the ability to acquire material things—the emotional security it may represent to you—the feeling that you wouldn't have to work if he were rich? Do any of these broader alternatives apply to the man you're talking to right now? What about "enjoys traveling"? Are you really after a sense of adventure—experience—fun? What does "kind" call up for you? Empathetic—understanding—willing to overlook your flaws—nonjudgmental? Suppose he has to be a doctor. Does that mean you feel you'll always be taken care of? Every item on your checklist has synonyms and associations and underlying meanings that make what you're looking for a lot broader than you once thought. Get to the deeper layers of what you want as if you were peeling an onion. Different and more people may "fit" than you realized.

## 8. Value-Load

Just before competition, some athletes do what they call carbohydrate-load. They fuel up on what they know will bolster performance and help them maintain stamina. Do the same emotionally by "value loading." Look at the following list of checklist items—and if they don't already appear on your list, add them. Repeat them to yourself until you own them, until you can *feel*, not just think, how right they are and how much you deserve them in a man. Scan this list before you go to the party—and make it your inner guide, a part of your positive inner voice. "The man I'm looking for":

- ♥ Treats me well.
- ♥ Makes me feel good about myself.
- ♥ Cares about my happiness and well-being.
- ♥ Is thoughtful and generous.
- ♥ Is willing to commit to the right relationship.
- ♥ Is honest and trustworthy.
- ♥ Is willing to cooperate, compromise and communicate.
- ♥ Is able to express and receive affection.
- ♥ Respects my independence—and my vulnerability.
- ♥ Supports rather than competes.
- ♥ Others you come up with: _____

## 9. Personalize

Often what we're really attracted to in people is not just who *they* are but how we allow ourselves to feel around them. Go over each of the items on your checklist and rephrase it into "how it makes me feel" or "how he allows me to be." For example, must he be "exciting" so you can allow yourself to act uninhibited? Some partners, of course, will stimulate you in different ways or bring out certain parts of you, but the key is to allow yourself as much as possible to think, feel and act freely regardless of how *he* is.

## 10. Learn to Balance Your Brain

"If only I could change my brain," I can hear some of you say. In fact, the brain you've got is perfectly fine! What I'd like you to do is to balance what may be your slightly lopsided use of it! People generally fall into one of two categories—either they're analyzers or reactors. You've undoubtedly heard about the right and left sides of the brain, and the roles they appear to play in the way we feel and think. The right side is spontaneous, emotional, reactive—this is the reactor's dominant side. The left side is analytical, focusing on facts and records—this is the analyzer's dominant side.

Take a look at your checklist and see if feelings or facts predominate. You can usually get a clear idea which type of "brain" you tend to use, but what *we're* after is balance.

If you're predominantly a reactor, your list is likely full of things like "sweeps me away with romance," "attends to my every thought and feeling," "is empathetic and kind." This may lead to wonderful romances. But you may also find yourself getting involved with a lot of irresponsible, childlike men who are incapable of managing their own lives. If so, what you need to do is make a new list that will help open the left side of your brain—your analytical self. What does the analyzer self want from a man? Let *it* have its say. It may be difficult to coax it to respond, especially if you've spent most of your life denying this part of yourself. But coax it anyway—give yourself time to come up with this new list. "Responsible" may pop up. "Able to pay bills" may be the next item. "Organized" or "competent in daily affairs" may be others.

Similarly, if you tend to be an analyzer, ask the feeling side of your brain—the reactor—to have *its* say. Let the "feeling you" express itself. Perhaps, because the analyzer in you always held sway, you've found yourself in a series of frustrating relationships, with men who are cold and unresponsive. Let the reactor part of you guide a bit more, and your love antennae will be more sensitive to emotional capacity in the men you next meet.

One part of the brain is just as important as the other—in fact, that's the point. We're only happy when we've achieved some kind of balance between reacting and analyzing. And our checklists are only truly helpful, complete and reliable when they reflect that balance.

These ten "guerilla tactics" are geared to awaken you to not only how many more men there are "out there" for you—and how many more *appropriate* men you can find—but also to new capacities and possibilities in *yourself.* You may think that all you're changing is your idea of the "right man," but you're also, more deeply, changing your idea of who *you* are. As you learn to broaden what's acceptable to you, to be more receptive and trusting, you're allowing yourself to participate in the abundance the world has to offer you. Not only an abundance of men, but an abundance of new perspectives about yourself.

All of this can help you only if you feel *good* about yourself. As I've said before, problems with self-esteem underlie so many of our wrong choices in love. Because it's such a crucial concern, I want to offer you a little way station—an oasis—of self-esteem exercises to make sure that yours is as high as it can be. You won't *act* deserving if you don't *believe* you're deserving. Believe me, you *are*—as I will help you see in more concrete terms right now.

# Recognize Your Personal Power— Self-Esteem Exercises

A major theme of this book has to do with self-esteem—that's really what we've been trying to bolster in every exercise I've shown you, every self-freflective tool you've learned. The simple fact is that you won't take action to give yourself a happy life if you don't feel you deserve to be happy. And you certainly aren't in a position to find or enjoy love with a man if you don't feel good about yourself.

One of the most common resistances women feel about the idea of high self-esteem is that it sounds too much like selfishness. Women have been taught to *nurture* before all else, to sacrifice their own wants for the wants and needs of others. Isn't concerning yourself with "self love"— which *is* what I want you to do—paying too much attention to yourself? Wouldn't that be narcissism?

Self-love doesn't mean narcissism. It isn't obsessing about yourself in ways that block out the rest of the world. You need to love yourself openly and fully to *connect* to the rest of the world. When you have a low opinion of yourself, you withhold yourself from living fully—you *deprive* the world of all you could be. If you need an altruistic reason to bolster your self-love, you can't have a better one than this. Self-love is what allows you to be *available* to the world in the broadest and most fulfilling ways.

So give yourself permission to be "selfish"—in the sense of paying attention to yourself. Luckily, there are some very effective exercises for changing your inner messages and presenting yourself more positively to the world "out there"—the collective effect of which will be to improve your self-esteem, as well as to help you appreciate the *wonderful* gift you have in being you. You are your most precious asset. Learning to love that "asset" and present it in its best, most favorable light isn't narcissistic—it's crucial to happiness.

We'll jump right into something you may find a little frightening: your image in the mirror. Some of the following exercises will bring you face to face with yourself in a quite literal way, and give you helpful things to do and say to yourself. Just *do* it, don't "try" to do it! That's my maxim about all these exercises. As you'll see, from the moment you wake up in the morning to the moment you close your eyes at night, you can be working on a new relationship with yourself, one based on love, not fear; acceptance, not rejection.

## 1. CONDUCT A MORNING AND EVENING MIRROR PEP TALK

When you get up in the morning, say—and *mean*—"I love you. What can I do for you today to make you happy?" At night, still looking in the mirror, tell yourself what you did well that day and promise yourself, "I'll do something wonderful for you and with you tomorrow." Don't worry about feeling foolish—you probably will, at first. But do it anyway. You'll get used to being with yourself before long, and you'll find yourself becoming your own best lover.

## 2. BRAG ABOUT YOURSELF

Whenever you find yourself about to think or say something terrible about yourself—something in the least bit self-denigrating—call a halt, and do this exercise. *Purposefully* brag about yourself, either in your mind (if you're around other people and it would sound silly to suddenly spout it out!) or, perferably, aloud (if you're alone). *Exaggerate* your strengths and accomplishments. Congratulate yourself on your triumphs, of whatever kind. Believe it or not, you probably won't *be* exaggerating—you'll simply be reminding yourself of a truth about yourself you haven't faced lately.

### 3. Study the Face in the Mirror

Look at your face in the mirror, but for once don't accept this as an invitation to count what the beauty pages of magazines are so quick to call your "flaws." Look instead at your mouth, your lips. Are they curling upward, or are they set or sloping down? Do you look inviting to *yourself*? A smile is, of course, the most inviting sign of approachability and warmth—if you're not used to smiling, smile now. See the difference! Research even shows how changing the position of your body will change your mood. Looking up makes you feel "up." Remember throughout the day what you did for yourself merely by turning your lips up, not down.

### 4. Posture-Cize

We all know that other people's body language tells us much about who they are and how they feel, but we usually forget that our body language communicates just as much about us. Standing in front of a full-length mirror, pull yourself up tall. Stand straight, chin up, eyes straight ahead. It's interesting how pride seems to fall right along the spinal column. When people feel good about themselves, their heads are up. Feel pride straighten and strengthen you. Pull your tummy in. If all you're aware of is that there's a little too much fat around that tummy, imagine you've just lost weight and that you're as slim and compact as your ideal. You'll be amazed how standing up tall, "sucking in" and sticking out your chest can bring you closer to that ideal. Physiologically, you breathe easier by opening up your chest. And psychologically, that makes you feel less stressed and more powerful.

Now, let it all go. Hunch over and hang your head. Slump your shoulders, then peer up into the mirror again. Don't you feel as if you've lost energy? Could that be the same woman looking back at you, the same one who just stood tall and proclaimed how good she felt about herself by how she held herself erect? Transform again into that first woman—pull yourself up. You've already told yourself how *good* you can be! During the day, if you find yourself slumping over, remind yourself of what happened in the mirror that morning—and straighten up!

## 5. Practice Expressing Yourself

You may feel a little foolish about this, too, the first couple of times you try it, but (again) *do it anyway.* You can teach yourself so much in this exercise. Practice talking and smiling at yourself in the mirror. We rarely have an accurate idea of how we come across to other people for the simple reason that we're not seeing ourselves talk. So get some "real" data. See how you are when you respond conversationally to someone. Do you automatically frown or tense up? See what you can do to soften or warm up your appearance. Then remember how your face and body *feel* when you've done this, so you'll know how it *feels* to look your best even when you're not in front of a mirror.

## 6. State Affirmations

This is a little like the technique we learned about earlier in the chapter regarding your inner voice—and how you can change that self-talk when it's negative to something more positive. It's amazing how steadily repeated affirmations can reach you deep inside, like self-hypnosis. Some may seem like simple and undramatic assertions, but over time they can start to turn you completely around, if you let them. Make a list of affirmations based on traits you would like to have, but repeat them to yourself as if they were already true. Bring them into the *present*: affirm them as if they already existed. You'll find, sooner rather than later, that they *will* be a real part of you. Here are some examples:

I am a powerful person who draws people who love me.

I have friends who care about me and about whom I care.

I have a love partner who truly loves me.

I am completely supported in what I do.

I get up every morning pleased and excited to face the day.

I am attractive and I radiate wonderful energy that attracts others to me.

Notice that five of the six affirmations begin with "I am" or "I have." You might also begin one with "I feel"—rather than "*He* feels I am powerful, attractive, worthy. . . ." This is crucial because we have power only over what we do or feel about ourselves, and affirmations become "reality" only when they spring from our own selves. They are not, I stress, "wishful thinking"; they are statements of fact you can feel about yourself at the moment you say them. They are also statements of *intent*, implicitly telling yourself that this is who you are, and *will* be as well.

Another point about affirmations is that they are all stated positively. An effective affirmation will never begin with "I am *not* . . ." There is an important reason for this. The subconscious does not easily admit negatives: if you say "I am *not* criticized," it's likely that the inner you will erase the word "not" and hear "I am criticized." Therefore, make your affirmations *affirmative* in every sense, even the grammatical.

### 7. PRACTICE IMAGING

The first imaging exercise to help self-esteem is a simple and amazingly effective one, based on a fascinating principle. When you act "as if," you're *not* "fooling" your brain. Your brain doesn't know the difference between what you might call a "real" image and an "as if" image. So, when you visualize success for yourself, you're causing your brain to react *as if* you had succeeded. Which means you'll automatically be developing an *attitude* of success. Athletes have long used this technique: Fran Tarkenton used it to become a star quarterback; golfer Jack Nicklaus "images" where he will hit the golf ball; Olympic contenders began working with sports psychologists several years ago to visualize the perfect completion of their events. We can do the same thing. Get the image of who you want to be, what you want to look like, what you want your love life to be like. Tell yourself you have *achieved* it. See yourself in technicolor, living out the ideal you've proposed for yourself. Feel what it would feel like in your body to be doing, saying, being the ideal you.

The second imaging technique makes use of "flashback" instead of flash forward. Concentrate on a scene in your mind where you *were* at your best—what did you look like and sound like, what were the circumstances around you? Wallow in them, enjoy them, believe them to be part of who you are right *now*. This is especially useful if you forget you ever did anything well, if you tend to blank out the positive parts of your past. Remind yourself of real situations where you liked yourself—and keep that image fresh.

## 8. Do It—Yourself

You're crazy about him because he's so talented, smart and competent. But is what you're really feeling jealousy that you're not doing what he's doing? It's an extremely common tendency for women to confuse what attracts them in someone else with what they really, secretly yearn to do or be themselves. It's a tendency I once forgot in myself as well. I remember being obsessed with the fact that my man didn't listen to music, didn't have any interest in music groups or what was going on in the music world—and it really bothered me. For some reason, I couldn't just accept this about him, the fact that he had other interests. It rankled in me until I woke up to what was really bothering me. I was projecting my *own* desire to become more involved in music on him! I had a desire, which I'd kept secret from myself, to be a musician. Once I began to seriously play an instrument (and join a band), my resentment against him lifted—because I was *doing* something direct to satisfy my own desires, not deflecting those desires onto someone else and feeling an inappropriate resentment.

This points out something I've seen again and again with my clients: the more fulfilled *you* are, the fewer demands you place on others—and so the fewer disappointments you have. You are able to accept people as they are, instead of as fill-ins for your frustrated ambitions.

Make a list of what you want your ideal man to do. Then think about what's on that list. What would be more satisfying to you if you actually did it *yourself*? Don't stymie yourself with the usual old rationalizations (I don't have enough money, talent, time, energy). Just allow yourself to feel how satisfied you might be if you gave yourself a chance to fulfill some of these dreams. And now—do it! Take some definite action toward accomplishing what you want to accomplish. Enroll in a painting or drawing or sculpture class. Start waterskiing. Play the stock market. *Do it*. Self-esteem grows when you allow yourself to accomplish something meaningful to *you*. It's the most effective strategy I know for learning to feel good about yourself.

## 9. Make a Wish List

This is a three-pronged approach that can be wonderfully effective. First, make a list of *all the wants* you have in your life. Let your mind go free—put down every dream, every aspiration, every desire you're after. Don't stop because of practical restrictions like money or time or other circumstances you think you can't control. Just let 'er rip. Examples might be: "make more money," "buy a house in the country," "paint a masterpiece," "travel to Bali," or even more general goals like "be happier," "get a better job," etc. Whatever, fill your list with your dreams, following these three guidelines (that also apply to your affirmations):

*STATE WHAT YOU WANT IN THE PRESENT.* If you want to lose weight, don't say, "I *will* lose weight in the future." Say instead, "I *am* eating more sensibly today." Or if you fantasize about going to Bali, say, "I am making arrangements in my life so I can go to Bali." Bring your wishes into *today* in whatever ways you can—this will break down your resistance to change.

*STATE YOUR WANTS POSITIVELY.* This harks back to what I spoke of earlier: the unconscious admits no negatives. Remove the words "never," "not," "don't" and "can't" from your vocabulary. For example, instead of saying "I'm *not* eating a lot anymore," say "I am eating *smaller* portions every day."

*STATE YOUR WANTS SPECIFICALLY.* This will help you focus. It doesn't help as much to say something like "I want to be happy when I'm alone" as it does to enumerate specifically what makes you happy. Say something like "I like to sing out loud when I'm alone" or "I like to take long baths when I'm alone." Focus as precisely as you can on the positive *activity* you want to do—so you can feel it, do it, measure it and make it vivid.

## 10. Implement the Wish List—Making It Happen

Just as you let your imagination run wild in coming up with the entries on your wish list, now allow it to run wild coming up with ways to make those wishes come true. For example, Marilyn's wish list began with "I want to be rich." What I told her to do was brainstorm about ways to get rich, to not hold back just because any of those ways looked silly. So, at the top of a page, she wrote the heading "WANT:

To Make More Money," and the subhead "Brainstorm Solutions—Ways I Can Get More Money." Then she listed the following entries: "Marry a rich guy," "Change my career," "Do only things that I get paid for," "Gamble," "Take on more jobs," "Enter every lottery I can." In reviewing this list, she decided to cross out "Gamble" right away and to shelve marrying into money and the lottery at least for the moment. She began to concentrate on the remaining alternatives, the work aspects of her life, over which she could have control right now, *today*. Instantly, she could rephrase her wish "I want to have more money" as "I'm doing things today to get more money." She made an instantaneous decision to live *as if* she were already accomplishing her goal—which she's now proceeded to do!

The concept of living "as if" what you want is already true is a wonderful one. If you restate something *as if* it were happening now, it makes it more likely that you will begin to live that way. Tell your brain you're already doing something—and it will respond by making it more possible to accomplish what you want to do! This has been proven: the brain doesn't know the difference between what's imagined and what's real. So start now. Do it today. All dreams are worth having and nurturing. As my favorite phrase goes: "Whatever you can conceive and believe, you can achieve."

## DAILY PRACTICE

Your self-esteem begins to improve when you make these exercises a part of your daily life. Don't forget that you're attempting to change negative self-views you've spent a lifetime acquiring. Bad habits can be replaced by good habits. But the transition period from negative to positive takes some persistence—persistence that, I promise, will pay off. Make yourself a promise that you'll do these exercises for one week. At the end of that week, see how you feel—and make yourself a promise to do them another week. Keep repledging to yourself, one week at a time, and before long, you'll undergo an astonishing inner change. Your first impulse won't be, anymore, to tear yourself down. You'll start believing what I've been telling you all along: you are worthy of as much love and happiness in life as you want. Once you believe this, obstacles you once thought were insurmountable will begin to melt away—and the life you dream of having will start, bit by bit, becoming your reality.

## Step 7

## Discover a New View of Sex

I don't have to tell you that sex is powerful. I probably also don't have to say that positioning "sex" right after "self-esteem" in this book was no accident—in no area of our lives is the condition of our self-esteem more apparent than in sex. All the primal fears you've ever felt about acceptability, lovableness, attractiveness and competence come roaring into play— as well as all of the ache you feel for deep satisfaction, release and intimacy with another person. However rational you may otherwise be, you're not alone if you feel you lose all sense when you end up in bed with a man.

Making sense of the storm of passions and insecurities and needs and wants that accompany almost any sexual encounter may seem like a pretty tall order. But it's crucial that we make the attempt, because—as I'm sure I don't have to tell you—no aspect of our lives gets us into more trouble (and involved with more of the wrong men) than sex.

So let's go beyond the obvious —"sex is powerful"—to an exploration of some of the reasons *why* it is. The most basic physical experience of sex—orgasm—is more than just physically powerful. In my everyday clinical practice, I am impressed over and over again with how vulnerable women become once they go to bed with a man. And when they achieve *orgasm* with a man, feelings of vulnerability and dependence can become overwhelming! Much of this has to do with simple learning theory:

pleasure is a powerful reward, and we tend to do whatever we can to continue getting rewarded. If sex with a man is "good," it can become a powerful inducement to presume that we can get everything we want and need from that man, with no real thought about whether he's equipped to give it. When the pleasure is as intense as orgasm, the lure of the man who helped you achieve it can be nearly irresistible. Since, for most women, there's so much more to sex than the physical pleasure and release it can afford, you feel terribly vulnerable in lovemaking. You have opened yourself up in some of the most intimate ways imaginable—and it's no wonder the person to whom you open up can acquire an almost magical significance.

Magic is terrific, but it's also dangerous. We've seen what falling for *one* trait can do: it can blind you to so much else about that man and lead to some disastrous consequences if you hook up with him without allowing yourself to really see the rest of him. When a man's ability to please you sexually is the "trait" you fall for, you're on particularly dangerous ground. You may feel he's got the key to your *soul*. It's especially exasperating when you rationally know a man is wrong for you, and yet you're so sexually hooked you can't resist.

In this situation, some women fall hook, line and sinker for this one man—the "good lover." But some women, a little more wary, do what is called splitting: they maintain two relationships, one with a "good guy," who is loving and caring but may not turn her on, and another with a "bad guy," who may not love her but makes her weak in the knees. This split is so common it deserves more explanation.


## SPLITTING

Splitting happens when you unconsciously assume that *sex* is possible only with one kind of man and *love* with another. It can make sex seem like an infuriating urge! You get angry with yourself for not being able to turn on to a man you care about and who obviously cares about you; you feel weak in the head as well as the knees for sexually responding to a man who obviously doesn't care about you.

What's equally disturbing is the split you may feel in yourself —the sense that you can't be both "nice" and "sexual" with the same man. When a man has this problem, it's called the madonna/whore syndrome: once he marries a woman, she becomes pristine and virginal in his mind, so he seeks sex from another woman he can "allow" to be wild and erotic. Women have the same split. We'll devote a good deal of time to learning how to *repair* your split later on in this chapter, but for now let's explore the problem more closely.

It is immensely common for women to split between the man they suspect is good for them but doesn't turn them on and the man they know isn't good for them but does turn them on. You know the feeling when you keep falling for the "hot" guy who doesn't necessarily want you and ignoring the perfectly reasonable, kind, hardworking "nice guy" who does. In other words, your knees weaken for the "rich," "handsome" or "powerful" dream lover, while you overlook the less glamorous guy who might actually *care* about you. "Why do I keep ending up with the wrong man?" is often answered by "Because the wrong man always turns me on!" How can you resist a force as powerful as sexual attraction? All the reasonable advice in the world can't make up for that devastating moment when he looks into your eyes and you're a goner. The fact that he cares for you about as much as he does for a fun night out or a good meal in a restaurant doesn't, for the moment, faze you. Later, however, when you can't avoid the fact that he's incapable of satisfying you emotionally, you once again have to admit that you've again fallen for a dream lover and not a real love.

Good news. There's a way out of this cycle! First you need to be aware that what's turning you on sexually or romantically is blinding you to everything else in the relationship. Then you need to learn ways to help you turn off to the bad guy and respond to new input —to open yourself to a good guy. I've devised some simple tests and exercises to help you accomplish the ultimate goal of uniting sex and love—and of hooking up with a man who will be good for you both sexually and emotionally. These tests will further help you increase your awareness of what you really *want* in a relationship—which always turns out to be different from the self-destructive passion you repeatedly found with the bad guys in your life.

Remember the goal is not to change the guy, but to increase your sense of *self-caring* so you can also make new and better love choices. When you care about yourself enough, you'll take greater steps *not* to get hurt. I'm not saying any of this is easy, but it *is* doable. And it's *worth* doing, because it will open you up to a whole new world of possibilities with men. But first, once again, we've got to take a look at the dream lovers who get you into such sexual trouble in the first place. We've explored this in some depth already, but we've emphasized the *problem* end of it. Now let's look at some solutions.

## BURSTING THE DREAM LOVER BUBBLE

You'll recall that a major conclusion we reached in Step 3 of this program—the step about confronting your dream lovers—was simple: dream lovers are so often disappointing in the flesh because no actual human being can live up to that complete a fantasy. As obvious a truth as that is, and as many times as you may bang your head against it (thinking that *this* time the perfect Michael Douglas look-alike investment banker will be the One), fantasies are so powerful that we end up falling for the same icons all over again. Meet Julianne and Gary for a vivid example of how a fantasy can be unmasked— and drained of some of its dangerous power—so that the fantasizer is free to make those new love choices we're aiming for.

Julianne was sent by her company to a small town in the Midwest to scout around for a possible new location for the plant. She was met by one of the most charming men she ever expected to meet— too charming, she felt, to be the town's mayor, which was what he turned out to be. Julianne knew that Gary wanted to sell her on his town, but that didn't really explain the attention he lavished on her. He had an uncanny knack of doing and saying just the right thing —guiding her lightly by the arm through the streets and parks as if to protect her, anticipating her thoughts, laughing easily. He seemed so much more interested in *her* than in any business they were al- legedly there to discuss. She was baffled, flattered and more than a little swept away.

The real surprise was the lunch he had planned, a picnic on the still-wild grounds of the proposed location for the plant, complete with chilled white wine. Between sips, Julianne felt any lingering resistance melt away.

"I can tell you one thing about this location, right now," Gary whispered, smiling, his blue eyes seeming to embrace Julianne with warmth. "It's a whole lot better with *you* in it." He gently leaned forward and kissed her, just brushing her mouth. Julianne shivered. For a moment, she felt the distant sense that the world was swirling too soon—that maybe this was "crazy." Gary's embrace soon quieted her doubts, and she finally gave in to the pleasure of being in his arms.

Julianne felt this surpassed anything that had ever happened to her. It was phenomenal to feel such attentive *caring*—every touch felt "right," and thrilled her deeply. It wasn't only that Gary rated a perfect on all her checklist items—he was handsome, successful, in the limelight, smart—he also, judging by his looks and touches, seemed to know just what she wanted. She felt adored—*loved*—which made this encounter transcend any seduction she'd ever experienced before. Somehow with every touch, with every whispered word, she was convinced he found her *special*.

Julianne spent every succeeding night of her stay with Gary—meeting him at her hotel late at night so as not to be seen going in and out of his house. (Gary gently told her that he was concerned, not so much about his own reputation, but about what "they" might say about her and the business connection between them.) He'd hate for anybody to think someone was "bribing" someone else! Gary's sneaking into her bed each night gave an extra frisson to the affair, made it seem more illicit and thus, Julianne had to admit, more exciting. But Julianne began noticing something a little disturbing. Gary seemed to want to make love so that their reflections would be fully caught by the mirror across from her bed. At first she was a little titillated by the idea; then she became slowly aware that, throughout the proceedings, Gary's eyes were always darting back to the mirror. Why was he so interested in watching their lovemaking? And exactly *who* was he watching—Julianne or himself?

When Julianne finally had to leave, to go home and report on her "findings" ("Make sure you tell them *everything*!" Gary teased her on their last night together in bed), she was still glowing from how good lovemaking had been with Gary. But she couldn't dispel that note of disturbance—Gary looking in the mirror. Gary made her promise to call him every night—and she did—but their phone conversations were, frankly, something of a shock. Why did she feel used? Gary would relive their "nights of passion" in graphic detail, with an emphasis on his expertise. ("Didn't you love it when I . . . ?") What was he doing? Soon it was clear: Gary was in love with the idea of *himself* as a lover. This hurt Julianne. After all, she'd given herself so freely to him. But then she began to feel angry. The memory of sex with Gary began to seem a *lot* less idyllic. The "love" she thought she'd felt from him now seemed to be nothing but an act he'd put on to win her over—to get her to adore him. For all his attentions to her and his "self-effacing charm," Gary was turning out to be a typical narcissist and manipulator. He was simply swept away by his own need for praise and self-inflation, using Julianne to gratify himself.

The nail went into the coffin one night when Julianne called and Gary seemed particularly distant. "Is someone there with you?" she asked. Gary paused, cleared his throat. "Yes," he said, "a friend's over. I'll call you later." She knew the "friend" was a woman. And then Gary stopped calling. Julianne finally "got it." Gary had never loved Julianne for herself; he simply wanted a "fan," a flattering reflection of himself. Just like the typical narcissistic man, once he found a "better" reflection, he had no need for the previous conquest.

Julianne began to realize that it was her fantasy about Gary that had really made the sex so good. Not that he wasn't experienced, but the extra magic was something Julianne's own imagination had provided. When Julianne thought back to her actual time with Gary, she began to remember details that gave away his narcissism—stopping to comb his hair in front of store windows, subtly asking her opinion of how he looked—details Julianne had denied because her fantasy had been so strong. She began to see how she had hoodwinked herself by not allowing Gary's full *reality* to hit her.

Some women, once they realize this, become depressed or angry for being rejected; they feel used, deprived, or they blame themselves for being a fool. But you don't need to do that. I helped Julianne to stop berating herself for giving in to Gary, by helping her to realize her own role in "creating" Gary. Once she accepted this, she could even accept the sexual satisfaction she'd experienced with him. Knowing that she in large part created him, she could see that the power to create such intensity lay in *her*, not in him. She may have lost the real Gary, but she hasn't lost *her* ability to respond and give with intensity. Yes, she has to be more cautious in the future about whom she gives her heart to (and how quickly), but she also has gained (as Pat did in her relationship with Luke, back in the Dream Lovers chapter) a great deal from the experience.

This is an important point. By asking you to "burst the bubble" of your dream lovers, I'm not telling you to get rid of your sexual fantasies. Sexual fantasies are wonderful, and they can enrich your experience of sex with a man you love. Hold on to them! Just realize they *are* fantasies, so you can prevent them from clouding your vision or taking over your life. So if you are rejected by a dream lover, you won't feel devastated, but only a little sad and disappointed. Like Julianne, you will know you must take a closer, clearer look at the man who excites you before allowing yourself to give in to an intense intimacy.

You can learn to do what Julianne is learning to do, too. Remember that the goal isn't to rid yourself of your fantasies. They're very precious and can tell volumes about who you are; they also can add a lot of spice to your life! But learning to allow them to *remain* fantasies means developing a stronger self—a you that isn't totally at the mercy of the first rush of "Wow!" Developing that strength means learning to *tune into your sex life* in some new ways.

## SEX TESTS: ARE YOU GETTING WHAT *YOU* WANT?

The following tests are designed to help you tune into your sex life —to increase awareness of how satisfied you really are with your sex life so that you can change some of your "cues" if you need to.

### THE GIVE-AND-TAKE TEST

Julianne could have helped herself to see who Gary really was if she'd stopped to give herself the give-and-take test. The premise is simple: a good lover is a giver as well as a taker. A good lover is, in other words, a full *participant* in love, neither denying nor dominating with his or her own desires. A man who gives pleasure for the sake of pleasing you and who willingly accepts pleasure that you willingly give *him* sets up a dynamic that is a model not only of good lovemaking but also of relating in nonsexual ways.

The exercise is simply this. Keep a give/take sex journal. First write down exactly what happened in your last lovemaking experience. List what he said and what you said, what you both did. Then write the word "give" or "take" next to each, to see who was doing how much of both.

Now review what you wrote and ask yourself the following questions:

♥ Does he encourage you to ask for what you want?

♥ How good is he at responding to what you ask for?

♥ Does he make you feel like a "bad" or "inept" lover?

♥ Does he make you feel like a "good" and "exciting" lover?

♥ How does he react if you initiate any sexual activity?

♥ How much pleasure does he take in *your* pleasure?

♥ How much time does he spend pleasuring you?

♥ Does he insist that you have an orgasm—or does he not care at all whether you do?

♥ How much time do you spend pleasing him?

♥ What does he do if he reaches the peak of pleasure before you do?

If you don't already have a clear idea of the dynamics of lovemaking in your relationship, you will after keeping a give/take journal. The idea is to be clear about the kind of relationship you're in to see if it's part of a pattern of relationships you've been in before, and to see whether you tend to "give" or "take" more sexually. Ask yourself some simple, direct questions about who may be ignoring whom in lovemaking, and whose needs come first or aren't met. Check off what seem to be the usual answers as follows:

*Amount of Time*
*You Spend*
*Pleasing Him*
*When You Make*
*Love*            *Not much* ___ *Sometimes* ___ *Often* ___
*Amount of Time He*
*Spends Pleasing*
*You*             *Not much* ___ *Sometimes* ___ *Often* ___

The point is to give yourself *information* about your sex life. We'll talk about what to *do* with this information later. But it's not too soon to ask yourself some analytical questions about your findings now. For example, if you find out you spend all your time pleasing him sexually, is it something you resent? If so, you know there are complex issues in this relationship that eventually have to be faced. Why are you accepting so little satisfaction for yourself? If, on the other hand, he spends more of your lovemaking time pleasing *you*, you might ask yourself why this is so. Simply looking at your sexual behavior can tell you much more than what you do in bed—it begins to tell you what you feel about each other as well.

## THE LISTENING TEST

Good lovers are good listeners. They hear not only what you say, but your inner soul and your deepest needs.

Let's say that during lovemaking you say, "I feel wonderful about you." Beware if he ignores you or changes the subject—he may be afraid of intimacy or he may be a narcissistic dream lover. If he responds by criticizing you, what you do or say (even if it may be helpful to your lovemaking), he may be an overly controlling power monger dream lover who is interested only in being in control, not in what *you* really want.

It's a good sign of "real" love, on the other hand, if he acknowledges what you say—just registering that he hears you. Even better, if he asks you a question or invites you to "tell me more," getting you to explore, and enjoy, your feelings more. Better yet, if he follows up on what you say by sharing his own feelings and experiences.

## THE SEX-VERSUS-LOVE TEST

We've already touched on the phenomenon—and the dilemma—of splitting. We'll return to it later because it's so central to why so many of us are dissatisfied in love. But in its barest form, splitting often means separating sex from love. As liberated as men and women profess to be today, we'd be surprised to see how many recognizably Victorian notions of sex still plague us, even if not on a conscious level. Certainly the old idea that men use love to get sex and women use sex to get love seems awfully old-fashioned, but unfortunately it still has some truth today. Generally, men do have an easier time separating sex from love than women do. For most women sexuality is a very intimate and important experience that makes them feel vulnerable and emotionally exposed. In this exercise, you'll be looking at what the man you choose as a partner is after—how he feels about sex and how he feels about how *you* feel about sex.

You might do this test twice: first imagining what he'd answer; and later asking *him* what he thinks, so you can see how closely the answers match. (Be prepared for some surprises.) Then, just as important, write down your own answers to these questions, to see how differently or similarly you and your partner feel.

*Sex has to be linked to affection or love for you to do it at all:*
_____ *rarely*
_____ *most of the time*
_____ *always*
*You only* enjoy *sex when it's with someone you care about:*
_____ *true*
_____ *false*
*You enjoy sex for the "lust of it":*
_____ *rarely or never*
_____ *most of the time*
_____ *always*
*You can only have sex with someone when you assume there's a future to the relationship:*
_____ *true*
_____ *false*
*One-night stands are:*
_____ *unacceptable*
_____ *okay every once in a while*
_____ *fine*

These are only sample questions. If you have other questions you'd really like the answers to, please feel free to add them to the list. Obviously you don't have to keep them multiple choice! The object is to open up a dialogue in which you can be frank about each of your desires and assumptions about sex and love. One woman told her lover that she could only make love to him if she knew it meant something important between them. Her lover replied, "Can't you just like me, and love making love to me?"

This may seem like a perfectly reasonable answer, but it wasn't the answer she wanted. It was important, of course, to find out what he meant by his answer; for example, he could have meant that he wanted to go slowly, wanted them to get to know each other, and that he *could* separate sex and love. Still, she knew she was a very vulnerable person who made very strong attachments to men, especially after she went to bed with them. Although she liked this guy a lot, she decided not to get sexually involved, because it was putting her at too much emotional risk.

These are the kinds of decisions you need to make about your love life—although not all at once, and not all right *now*. Again, all I want you to do at this point is gather information. But realize that's where we're headed—to a reassessment of what your love and sex life is to be.

### THE "HOW DO YOU FEEL AFTER SEX?" TEST

You know how you'd *like* to feel after sex. Perhaps you've got an image out of a French art film, the two of you lying back on huge fluffy pillows, the early morning air softly blowing white curtains in an open window, your head on his chest, he kissing the top of your head—a picture of fulfillment, contentment, affection, love . . . Then you remember the reality. How he turned over and managed, it seemed to you miraculously, to begin snoring within two minutes. How you lay there in the dark, wondering "what it all meant."

What happens between you right after sex is as significant as what happened before or during sex. Check whatever following answers apply to you—and I'll meet you at the end for a roundup.

*I feel empty.*                                 _____
*I feel loved.*                                 _____
*I feel alone.*                                 _____
*I feel sad.*                                   _____
*I feel unfulfilled.*                           _____
*I feel content.*                               _____
*I feel happy.*                                 _____
*I feel rejected.*                              _____
*I feel beautiful.*                             _____
*I feel like I want to do it again.*            _____
*I feel like I'd like him to leave.*            _____
*I feel like leaving.*                          _____
*I feel exhausted.*                             _____
*I feel like I miss my last lover.*             _____
*I feel like I'd marry him if he asked me.*     _____
*I feel neutral.*                               _____

You may not feel terrific every time you have sex, but if you *usually* feel sad, empty, alone or unfulfilled, something's obviously wrong in the relationship. Perhaps you feel empty because there's no follow-up. The man who rolls over and falls asleep may be tired— and if he does this only now and then, it's not something to worry about. But if he does it continually, you could reasonably assume that he's pulling away or not capable of closeness and intimacy. You sense this—and you feel unfulfilled. Or perhaps *you* turn away— and need to face a similar inability to be intimate.

Perhaps now that you've taken these tests, it's clear that your current relationship—whether with a dream lover or not—is something you need to reconsider. But what if, even in the face of some obvious problems, you're still "stuck" to the guy because you continue to be incredibly turned on by him? Or what if you feel yourself falling for a type you know is bad for you—but one that you can't seem to resist?

## UNGLUING THE GLUE

The glue of sexual attraction might really be called "Crazy Glue"— it seems to endure beyond all reason, to hold you fast even when you know you're locked in a destructive embrace. Here are some quick pointers that can help "unstick" you when you find yourself weakening in face of an irresistible Mr. Wrong.

### 1. THOUGHT STOPPING

Every time the fantasy of being with him comes into your mind, picture a red light or a stop sign and immediately switch your mind to another *pleasurable* thought. Be sure to make the alternative thought pleasurable—you want not only to change your thinking but to reward yourself with an alternative you'll like. If you have trouble with this, try another variation: "listen" to his voice in your head, but then imagine playing a CD and turning the volume up until the sound drowns his voice out. Pick your favorite song and listen to that rather than to him. It works!

## 2. REFOCUSING

When you are overwhelmed with desire for him, give yourself another physical sensation—for example, massage your arms with a fragrant oil and enjoy the touch. But *do not imagine that it is him touching you.* The point is to retrain your body to accept pleasure that does not depend on him.

## 3. AVERSIVE CONDITIONING

Focus on what you didn't like about your lover—imagine him in the worst possible light. If you can't help imagining having sex, then focus on what he used to do that you hated. Repeat it. Remember—and experience—all his unattractive qualities. You can reprogram yourself away from him just as you programmed yourself toward him. If you can't imagine anything unattractive about him, then imagine a trait you can't stand in a man and then "give" that trait to your dream lover.

## 4. TELLING YOUR FRIENDS

I'm not asking you to gossip about the man, but tell a few trustworthy people why the man is bad for you and ask their help in reminding you that he's a mistake every time they see you weaken. Enlist their support!

## 5. OVERCOMING YOUR DENIAL

Every time you remember or think about an aspect of a dream lover you know was bad for you—that diminished or negated you—jot it down in a little notebook. Collect these details to remind yourself when you weaken *why* you need to stay away from him. It is so easy to blind yourself in the heat of passion—even the heat of passionate remembering. It is so easy to make excuses for him. Don't.

## IN SHORT—REPROGRAMMING!

Thinking is, to a large extent, a *habit*. You have much more control than you may realize over your habits of thought. If you get into destructive, self-denigrating thought habits—thinking, "Now that I don't have 'him' anymore, I'm not sexy, I'm not worthy, no one else will ever find me desirable"—you have the *choice* to affirm yourself, change the tape and replace it with something that builds you up. By continuing to tell yourself "I'm not good enough," you're actually prolonging your attachment to the man with whom you've broken up or are trying to break up. Practice the first of the directives—thought stopping. Replace negative thoughts with positive ones. It may seem contrived at first, but believe me it works. It works even in physical terms. By embracing the positive, you're redirecting neurons, affecting your body's chemistry. Remember you can't smile and frown at the same time. So choose to smile. Before long it will become a habit, and "he" will become a bad, distant memory.

## REPAIRING THE SPLIT

Remember our definition of splitting? We split because we become convinced that the sexual, sensual side of us can be satisfied only by one type of man—and the emotional, spiritual side can be satisfied only by another. The old madonna/whore ambivalence that has been thrust upon women for centuries—the idea that we are either saints or prostitutes—is an insidious one. However "liberated" we may be, few of us have escaped its most damaging effect—that women themselves often can't allow a man to be the source of both love *and* sex. You permit a man to be either nurturing and paternalistic, or an erotic "stud." Many women become convinced they cannot satisfy sexual urges and also share souls with one man—even while they nurture the hope that there must be, somewhere, a man who *can* embody both—a Mr. Right they just haven't met yet.

The hard truth is that when you're in the throes of this conflict, you haven't met him because you haven't let any man *be* Mr. Right. Many women refuse to seriously entertain the idea that one man might be both nurturing *and* sexual—that a "good guy" might also be satisfying in bed.

You may be shaking your head "No." "I don't separate sex and love!" you say, "and I've always looked for a man who could be my friend as well as lover. I just can't find one!" It's true that most women don't, as I've already suggested, make the kind of division between sex and love that men often do. But the way we unconsciously *respond* to men often indicates that we're almost as split as men are. For proof of this, just flash without thinking on a man you find a real turn-on. Don't judge yourself—just "see" him now. Is he someone you could imagine "bringing home to mother"? Is he someone you'd like to have see you when you're sick in bed with a cold? Is he someone you could tell your secrets to? Could you cry in front of him? Could you have an intellectual discussion—or share your doubts and fears and insecurities—with him? Could you marry him? Be realistic. Don't let the fantasy sweep away likely obstacles. Look at him not only as a dream lover but as a human being. Who is he now?

So many women (like men) have affairs outside of a monogamous relationship because they can't resolve the split in themselves between sex and love. They can't deeply *permit* one man to offer both because their assumptions won't let them. But you *can* allow yourself to find both in the same man. How? By learning to take responsibility for the fact that it's your assumptions which are holding you back, not the imagined or real inadequacies of the men in your life.

Priscilla had a classic case of splitting in her choice of two lovers. With Hank, a blue-collar construction worker, she had terrific sex. With Jim, a vice-president of an accounting firm, she had wonderful discussions about her career and her life, but very tepid sex. Whenever Hank, the blue-collar stud, tried to talk to her about anything deeper than the weather (or how terrific she looked that night), Priscilla would smile condescendingly and shush him—kissing him quiet so they could get down to what she knew he was "really" good at. And whenever Jim attempted to heat up their sexual relationship, Priscilla would suddenly tense—*that* wasn't what she was after, she'd tell him primly! Both men became dissatisfied with Priscilla, and she couldn't understand why. Hadn't she psyched them both out accurately? Wasn't she providing them with a good time appropriate to each? In fact, Hank wasn't just a stud; he was a feeling human being, and he resented being blocked out emotionally—a fact that astonished Priscilla once she woke up to it. And Jim very much wanted to express his love for Priscilla sexually; he resented being treated as a kind of talking head. The point is *both* men had resources and ranges of feeling and response to which Priscilla had blinded herself. Why? Again, because she couldn't accept that all of that potential could exist in one man.

I'm not suggesting that every man you meet is a potential combination Father Confessor/Don Juan. There *are* men who are limited emotionally and men who are blocked sexually—not every average Joe is a walking paragon of all human virtues. But so many men are capable of so much more than you may think. Waking up to this means realizing that *you* are capable of a great range of responses. When a nice guy doesn't turn you on, it's not always because he's unattractive or an obvious dud. Sometimes it's because you won't allow him to *be* a turn-on.

Luckily, there are practical ways in which you can learn to respond to new cues. Again, I'm not trying to take your sexual fantasies away from you—which is a good thing, because I couldn't even if I wanted to! I don't want sex to be any less pleasurable or exciting. I'd simply like you to *open up* the range of your responses so you have the chance of finding fulfilling sex with a man who can fulfill you in other areas of your life. How? Again, by retraining yourself to *respond to new cues.*

## WIDENING YOUR POTENTIAL—AWAKENING TO NEW SEXUAL CUES

You've got one important truth working for you right away. You can depend on the fact that the safety of being loved is a much stronger base from which to build consistent, lasting passion than the infatuation—however consuming—you might feel about a dream lover. I say this right off to prepare you for the fact that learning to respond to new cues *doesn't* mean depriving yourself of passion. Trust that passion will increase only when you allow yourself truly to connect it to love.

Spend some time thinking about the following suggestions. Let them spontaneously call up nice guys in your past or in your life right now; allow yourself to see them a bit differently. Imagine romantic possibilities with men with whom that once seemed unlikely. Keep an open mind—and heart—as you consider this list:

### 1. Realize the Difference

There is definitely a difference between an adrenaline high of furiously passionate love and the real intimacy of getting to know someone. Can you see where the two feelings might overlap? Can you see that you're after satisfaction in *each* type of love, not just one or the other? Imagine *talking* to your sexual fantasy; imagine *making love* with an understanding, but less glamorous man.

### 2. Don't Judge

One type of love isn't necessarily better or worse than the other. Accept your need for both. Consciously admit to yourself that you have sexual *and* emotional needs, and that it is all right to want to satisfy those needs. Neither is more or less acceptable than the other. This means giving sexual love its due, not guiltily pushing it away because it's not "deep" enough. But it also means giving emotional intimacy its due, not downing it as less exciting than highly charged romantic sex.

### 3. Look for Positives

Remember the techniques we talked about in the last chapter about concentrating on the nice guy's positive qualities. Allow yourself to see his wonderful eyes or a great profile, even if he's not as tall, dark and handsome as you thought your dream lover had to be. Allow yourself to see the new man's assets—don't dwell on his inadequacies.

### 4. Intensify Your Focus

Pick a quality that truly does turn you on to your nice guy and focus on that. Really enjoy that quality in your mind. Highlight and even exaggerate the color of his eyes, or the way he tilts his head when he listens to you. Lay back and listen to music and think of him in these ways: you'll be constructing a new romantic fantasy attached to a healthy man, which is a good part of your goal.

## 5. Switch the Fantasy

This proceeds from suggestions 3 and 4. Remember that you are the author, director and star of your own internal romantic scripts: you can change anything about the script you want to change! Do some creative rewriting and acting in these inner fantasies. Change the tired old rut of your usual type and substitute someone you may never have thought could play the part of lover. Give him a chance. You may find a new star is born! Give yourself new dialogue and cues—have fun with this new fantasy. Take yourself (mentally) out on a dinner date or walk along the beach with your nice guy; get to know him. What you'll find yourself doing is preparing for the real thing, for the actual date you can now engineer between the two of you. Have fun with your new fantasies—make them as pleasurable as possible.

If the face of your dream lover still keeps cropping up, try a few of these techniques:

- ♥ Let yourself fantasize about your dream lover, but at the crucial moment (at the moment you begin to make love) change his face—substitute the face of your nice guy.
- ♥ Whenever your dream lover appears in your mind, have the conversation you were about to have with your dream lover with the new nice guy—and let the conversation *change* to reflect his new personality.
- ♥ Try your new fantasies out on the *real* man. Part of your turn-on—a big part—is how *you* behave, not only how you fantasize your dream lover will behave. So try out some of your fantasy behavior with the nice guy. You may bring out those real qualities in him. Plan a romantic outing with him, be as attentive to him as you would be to your fantasy, and allow him to respond. You may find, as many people do, that he'll surprise you—he may turn out to be the fantasy lover you thought you wanted! When you communicate to a man that you want to make love, he very often responds with equal desire. You may discover heat you never knew was there.

## 6. Associate the Nice Guy with Pleasure

Remember I said sex is a powerful conditioning tool. Orgasm is even more so. If you allow yourself to experience great sex with a nice guy, you will see him afterward with different eyes. When you make love, allow your mind and body to flow. Don't rate him or yourself continually, don't compare this time to the best times of your past. Do everything you can to enhance the pleasure you're feeling *now*— and associate the pleasure you're feeling with the man you're with now. Soon, he will come to mean pleasure. You will find yourself surrendering to warm feelings for him even if your rational rating mind tells you he's not a god. Give your rating mind permission to turn off—and allow your instincts to take over.

## 7. Practice Reverse Affirmation

If your nice guy is short and you have always told yourself that you'd never go out with a short man, try taking out the "never." Rephrase the statement: "I rarely turn on to short men but it's not impossible." Then add, "But I *do* turn on to this man." Practice this mentally for a while until you can say, "Short men can turn me on!" Believe it or not, you can begin to change deeply rooted checklist items in this way—over time. Even if you never completely reverse the fantasy, you'll still be opening yourself to new possibilities—which is the point of all this.

## 8. Rehearse

Brain studies show that if nerve impulses pass along their selected pathway long enough they leave an indelible memory trace. It's like water running down a hill, cutting a channel and leaving a pattern in the earth. What it also means is that repetition makes you learn. That's why all of my switch and refocus techniques really do work in the long run—as contrived as they may seem at first reading. So repeat all of the conditioning techniques you've learned here. Let them lay new paths in your mind; let them open you to possibilities that are just as pleasurable as the ones that used to get you into trouble.

You do have the power to bring yourself closer to the goal of a complete relationship with a man. I hope that what we've explored in this chapter will have helped you on this path. I also hope you have opened up to the fact that there may be far more potential in men you once unthinkingly passed over. More deeply, there's far more to *learn* from men than you may have allowed yourself to experience. The bulk of this book has focused on how women feel and react, and how they can begin to *change* reactions in order to have more fulfilling love. But equally important is listening to the *men* with whom we're trying to connect. You can't appreciate the richness of what's possible between you and a man until you let him speak— and listen to him. And that's what the next step will do—give "him" his say.

# Step 8

# *Listen to Him: What Men Are Thinking*

The nice guy and the dream lover—we've talked *about* them. We've combed your motives about why you want them in your life. We've explored some of the family scripts and emotional traps that prompt you to choose the men you choose. We've done everything but let men speak for themselves. Now's the time to let them have that chance.

In this chapter I'm going to introduce you to a number of men who may surprise you. Don't think I had to dig to find extraordinary examples of the species. There are *many* men who fit the bill! In fact, you probably already know many of these men. You might even be about to meet a few new ones!

The good news is that men *have* changed in the past decade or two. They are more open to complexity, more willing to admit that life isn't a black-and-white proposition, less willing to clamp ironclad definitions on male and female roles. But the most important thing women need to realize is that men are just as complex and needy and interesting as women. Men must deal with conflicting societal messages that tell them, on the one hand, to be a "real man" and "macho," and on the other, to be "caring and sensitive" to women's needs. (It's as if Clint Eastwood were pulling one arm, Phil Donahue the other.) It's no wonder they are sometimes confused about what their "roles" are supposed to be.

More good news is that out of

this confusion are arising more and more men who manage to mix sensitivity with old notions of virility: a species I call the new man. Even better news is that he is everywhere. He is your neighbor, your co-worker; he stands next to you on the supermarket line. The new man isn't a *super* man. He is as human and fallible as you are. But he's at least grappling with what love means today, with the desires and needs of the women with whom he gets involved. And he's looking at his own checklist more critically. Sometimes this is because the women he meets won't have it any other way. Thank heavens feminism has made enough inroads in today's world to get all of us to question old, restrictive roles. But it's also because men want emotional support just as much as women do. They often feel *relief* that they're allowed to show more vulnerability now—that they're allowed to express feelings, hopes, dreams and desires in ways that would have been unthinkable a generation ago. Feminism hasn't led only to a greater liberation of spirit in women—it's helped men to open up, too.

Again, the real new man isn't someone dreamed up by women's magazines. I'm certainly not suggesting that there's a whole new miraculous generation of men who are completely free of the old sexism, of the old "Me Tarzan, you Jane" dynamics we labored under years ago. But men *are* different in some significant ways today, and the best way to prove that to you is to let you listen to a number of their own voices. This will introduce you to some nice guys—and also jog a few of your old assumptions about what men are "really after." It turns out what they're after isn't so far removed from what *you're* after.

Yet there *are* still emotional differences between men and women in how they handle their needs. We can point to some generic needs that the men I've interviewed all seem to be battling or attempting to accommodate in a variety of ways. Nearly every man alive today was a boy when "boy" meant acting tough and not crying, not expressing excessive emotion of any kind. Remember the nursery rhyme gender prescription limiting girls to "sugar, spice and everything nice" and making boys full of "spiders" and "toads"—with the implicit idea that a *real* boy wouldn't have anything to do with something soft or nice. It's no secret that our notions of masculinity and femininity are to a large degree culturally determined. Think about the extent to which that cultural mold has affected men. While men are changing, it's taken courage in many cases for them to modify the way they view themselves, not to mention how they view women. It's not easy to buck a cultural message as strong as the one they were forced to swallow, just as it hasn't been easy for women to get out from under their *own* cultural stereotypes. Many men have successfully transcended these culturally induced needs, but all men have had, in some way, to deal with them. What are those needs?

## THE NEED TO BE THE BOSS, THE CONTROLLER

Men have traditionally *been* bosses—at the office and at home. This idea is introduced very early in childhood in subtle but pervasive ways. Little boys have always been encouraged to be stronger, braver, more decisive and less emotionally open than little girls. By the time they reach the job market, there's no question that their sights are trained more on the board room than on the steno pool. The business world's definition of "macho" has to do with take-charge guys at the helm. Being the boss is therefore a powerful sign of virility, and men who are insecure about their masculinity often overcompensate by becoming especially overbearing "bosses"—and not only in the office. The need to control often stems from a need to prove masculine strength. Many men have a terrible fear of being out of control—it attacks a central view of themselves, one that equates control with manliness. Men who are especially insecure about their ability to control their lives may actually damage their health through the anxiety this causes (and the resultant ulcers or high blood pressure). It can be a dangerously tyrannical need.

## THE NEED TO BE THE MONEY-MAKER

It's undoubtedly no secret that many men have a hang-up about money. Until recently (the advent of the new man), it was almost unthinkable for a man to have a relationship with a woman who made more money than he did. This threatened every preconceived notion of manliness—notions we've already explored in the boss and controller needs mentioned above. But it's important to stress again that these notions arise from a societal assumption that—thank heavens —has begun to change.

## THE NEED TO BE STRONG

Any sign of "weakness" used to be thought of as unmanly, and it still is deeply inbred in little boys that men never show weakness. Weakness has a terrible variety of meanings to a little boy, including that men don't cry, complain, show any excess of joy, passion, hurt or grief. A man is not a "man" until he has, in some senses, shut down. What a terrible penalty to pay to be "masculine"! And what an inconsistency in the definition of "strong." To me, *real* strength means you *can* cry or stand any strong emotion.

## THE NEED TO BE MOTHERED

This is a need no "real man" wants to acknowledge, but as most women will tell you—and as you may well know from your own experience—it's one of the strongest needs men learn to feel regarding women. You know all the stories about what a baby he turns into when he gets a cold, how much he depends on you to cook, clean and in other ways take care of him. "Woman" to many men means, to a larger extent than they'd ever admit, "Mommy." Some amount of mothering—or parenting—is healthy in a love relationship (from whom do we learn about love and fulfilling needs if not from our mothers). The trick is not to turn your partner into a child or to overly mother him out of your own needs.

These needs have been characterized somewhat negatively, as if they're obstacles to be outgrown, surmounted. Certainly, when the need to be strong, to control, or be the boss means that a man insists on dominating everyone in his life, those needs do represent obstacles. But just as the need to be mothered has its positive side, so do the needs—which may also be read as *desires*—to take charge and take *care*. And just as men have much to learn about nurturing from women, women can benefit from looking at the "masculine" assumptions in men, assumptions that say you *can* deal with the world, you *can* triumph over the odds, you have a *right* to succeed. Taken to extremes, these needs add up to boorish domineering, but the *seeds* of these needs can flower in some very positive ways.

The key is to be able to express *all* sides of oneself. That's in fact what distinguishes the new man. It isn't that he doesn't feel the pressure of the old masculine needs society has bred into him; it's that he chooses to respond differently to them. It's not easy. In fact, it's just as hard for a man to work on changing his checklist, for example, as it is for a woman.

It's also as common for a man to split in the ways we discussed in our sex chapter, to seek sex with one type of woman and nurturing with another. (Indeed, it was once virtually the Victorian gentleman's prerogative to keep a mistress "on the side." The double standard has long historical roots.) But the new man is waking up to see that splitting really means being afraid of putting all emotions into one relationship. This is what learning to repair the split really amounts to—trusting that you can find more than one kind of love in another person.

All this leads to why it's important to listen to what men have to say. As you meet Brendan, Milo, Leo, Don and Paul—and the women with whom they're working toward having happy, healthy relationships—keep in mind they're making changes in their self-views and views of what's possible between men and women. The point in listening to "him" is to gain a wider appreciation of the fears and blocks men are up against, as well as of the potential they possess to overcome them.

An equally important goal is to allow yourself to see men as full human beings. Watching these men make contact may make you a little more compassionate about the struggle—and a little more willing to withhold quick judgment the next time you meet a new guy. He may well turn out to be a "*new* new man." The species is out there in greater and greater numbers! Meeting the men here may make you a little more disposed to give that new man a real chance.

## BRENDAN: "I'M LEARNING AS FAST AS I CAN!"

Brendan, a thirty-four-year-old partner in a lucrative discount sporting goods business, doesn't lack for money. But, as he freely admits, he's not the most sophisticated man in the world. "I grew up in a small town in New Jersey—real working class—and I'd have gotten beaten up by my brothers if I'd ever expressed any interest in art or books or classical music." Brendan smiles. "Boy, if they could see me *now* . . ."

Brendan says he always wanted to "better" himself, even back then as a kid, and what that meant to him was work hard and make money. While the rest of his friends goofed off after school, Brendan took on part-time jobs—paperboy in the morning, working at a sporting goods store in the afternoon. His boss at the sports store quickly took an interest in Brendan. He could see how important it was for Brendan to make something of himself, and he regarded him as a kind of son. When Brendan graduated from high school, he decided to stay on at the store. He quickly became the manager, and when his boss retired, he bought him out at a rock-bottom price. In the next ten years, Brendan turned one store into a string of stores, and he was becoming a well-off, well-respected "player." "Respected in business circles, anyway," Brendan emends. "Now that I was making money, I was getting invited to classier parties—charity balls and things—and it was clear to me I had a lot to learn."

Brendan realized he had a lot to learn when he met Chris, "an incredibly classy woman." They met at a business conference about improving employee productivity by improving employee morale. Chris, a consultant with a background in psychology, was one of the speakers.

"She wasn't, I guess, a knockout," Brendan recalls, describing Chris. "I mean, most of the women I'd taken out before this were very beautiful in obvious ways—I always felt like if I had a gorgeous blonde model-type on my arm, *I'd* look better. Chris dressed sort of plain, but she was so damned *smart*. She had this incredible competence. It was like there wasn't anything she didn't know. I don't know why I felt so attracted to her—I've always been a little afraid of smart women—but I was so tired of the brainless beauties I'd been hanging out with before that I guess I just wanted to see what it would be like to have an actual *conversation* with a woman. So I walked up to Chris one evening after this brilliant talk she gave, told her how impressed I was, and wondered if we could meet for a drink. I had sweaty palms—here I was, this big successful businessman, quaking in front of a woman. I'd never felt like that before. When she said yes, I felt like a kid getting the date he wanted for his senior prom! She made me so happy just by agreeing to have a drink with me."

Brendan felt from the start that Chris and he were an odd couple—she was so much more educated than he. "The only thing

I knew about were different makes of tennis rackets and basketballs and running gear. Chris knew about everything *except* that. And yet we hit it off. It was like we each were some strange new creature to the other. It was an adventure—the sparks flew. There was a lot of chemistry." Brendan remembers how much Chris opened up for him: "I knew nothing about art or music or any of that stuff. I still don't know all that much, but what I *do* know I owe to Chris. She'd always get so excited over something cultural. It was contagious. I found myself really interested in Picasso—we actually went to museums on our dates!" Brendan laughs. "But it was good. It was good until"—Brendan sighs—"until one day when Chris said that, for a relationship to work, we had to be completely honest. We had to say *everything* we felt about each other. I guess it was her background in psychology coming out or something. Anyway, I thought things were fine just the way they were. I told her she was perfect just like she was. She got annoyed—she didn't like being put on a pedestal, she said. She kept nagging at me to come up with something I didn't like about her. Finally I felt driven into a corner. The only thing I could think of was that she didn't dress up for our dates like the other women I'd gone out with. She was more casual—she didn't put on a lot of makeup and wear fancy clothes and stuff. I guess I missed that a little. So I said something like, 'I wish you'd dress up a little more when we go out.' " Brendan rubs his forehead for a moment. "It was like I slapped her in the face."

Brendan says Chris completely froze, and then spat back, "You don't like what I *wear*? That's the only thing you can think of to say?" "She said she couldn't believe how superficial I was. What did I think she was, some bimbo who dressed up to be attractive to men? I kept trying to tell her it really didn't bother me—it's just that women I'd gone out with before had always tried to look glamorous. . . . I'd really put my foot in it this time. Now she said she knew I didn't find her attractive, and she frankly didn't know why *she* bothered spending time with me. Suddenly it was open season on *me*. She said I embarrassed her whenever we went any place because I didn't know anything. Like once she and I went to a concert and I said after the first half how much I liked the orchestra. She blew up at me. 'It's a *quartet*,' she says. 'Don't you know chamber music from symphonic music?' It really steamed me. Okay, I didn't know what she knew, but I was willing to learn, wasn't I?"

There was another problem. When Chris lost her most lucrative consulting account (because of some stiff company cutbacks) and Brendan began to pay for a lot of their times together instead of them sharing, Chris began to accuse him of trying to *control* her. "She said I didn't own her just because I paid for everything," Brendan said. "That didn't give me the right to make comments about how she *looked*."

Obviously Brendan had pressed a painful button for Chris, where she equated money with control. But Chris had pressed some painful buttons for Brendan, too, in reaction. "I wondered if maybe I was compromising. Maybe I really *did* want a glamorous woman like I used to date. I was angry at Chris, I guess because she got me where it hurt. When she said we should stop seeing each other, I sulked a little, then said okay—if that's how she wanted it, fine. We left each other really angry."

Brendan couldn't get Chris out of his mind, even after he started to date other women, the flashy blondes he'd hung out with before. But none of them had Chris's vitality, wit or intelligence. He missed her terribly. "I didn't care how Chris dressed—she was a fine-looking woman just as she was. But she'd said such awful stuff about me. How much could I change to become more like the man *she* wanted? She'd made it crystal-clear that I didn't measure up. I didn't know what to do." Somehow, however, Brendan drummed up the courage to call Chris. He had no idea what to say to her, except that he was sorry and he missed her. He'd never met anyone like her before, and he didn't want to lose her *friendship*. "I thought I'd soft-pedal it," Brendan says. "I was afraid I'd scare her off."

Chris amazed him by apologizing to *him*. She said she'd been under such pressure because of work. She'd always been in such awe of his success, his incredible business mind, that she'd reacted "defensively." "She was in awe of *me*?" Brendan exclaims today. "Here I was feeling like a brainless worm, so much less than Chris. . . . I broke up laughing in the middle of the phone call. Chris asked me what was so funny. I told her I thought we both had a few screws loose. Then I said I was hungry for a hamburger and her opinion of Picasso's 'blue period' and could I see her immediately since I didn't think either hunger could wait."

Chris and Brendan have learned to be with each other much less warily than before. The road to accepting someone else has to begin first with self-acceptance. As Brendan learned to frankly acknowledge his lack of education and his desire to learn more, and as Chris overcame seeing money as a means of controlling a relationship, they were free to see how much they truly cared for each other. "Maybe we're as different as apples and oranges," Brendan says, "but mix the two and you've got a nice dessert. What makes us want to be with each other is that we *like* each other—our different backgrounds don't matter anymore. And who says each of us can't learn what the other knows?"

Brendan isn't the only man who's been able to overcome the constraints of his background and conditioning; I know so many other men who've been able to buck what society told them they were "supposed" to do. Brendan was fortunate to have felt as open as he did to learning from a woman—and to want to explore other realms (like the arts) even though he'd been taught they weren't masculine when he was growing up. Not all men are as willing to be this receptive. Certainly there are men who continue to buckle under the weight of society's myth of manliness. Milo, the next man you'll meet, had a hard time getting out from under this particular yoke. But even he—a self-described "macho man"—was able to make some breakthroughs.

## MILO: IRRESISTIBLE PLAYBOY MEETS IMMOVABLE WORKING MOTHER

Milo is, on the face of it, perhaps the least average man you'll meet here. He is, in fact, what seems to be the rarest of phenomena: handsome, sexy, funny, smart, rich, forty-two and single. (He is also, not to put too fine a point on it, a terrific dancer!) The mid-seventies were Milo's heyday—in his early thirties, he had his pick of women, and he picked an inordinate number of willing partners. In those pre-AIDS days, promiscuity was almost a badge of honor for a man like Milo—and there wasn't a singles scene he didn't know about. Of the common needs we talked about at the outset, the need to be strong was Milo's great motivator. He saw himself as *invincible*. At twenty-eight he'd already gotten his own seat on the stock exchange and was regarded as a financial wunderkind, which just added fuel to that belief of invincibility. The *world* was Milo's.

If Milo developed a pretty good opinion of himself, it's perhaps no wonder. He "had everything." He began to *expect* women to fall in love with him, since it happened so often. That, for a long time, was his only problem. Women kept wanting to get serious when Milo kept wanting to have fun.

As the seventies turned into the eighties and Milo drew nearer to forty, he had to admit to being a little bored. AIDS wasn't yet the specter it's become today, but Milo had had so much sex with so many women that when he first heard about STDs (sexually transmitted diseases) he began wondering if he was really at risk. Milo also drank a good amount—it was hard not to at all the singles bars over which he reigned—and had a hefty cocaine habit when cocaine was fashionable. The party life was beginning to affect him. He began showing some strain. His complexion was a little sallow, crow's-feet began to deepen around his eyes. He was still enormously attractive to women, but there were times, in the morning, when he groggily looked into the bathroom mirror and tried to remember the name of the woman he'd left sleeping in his bed. And there were times when he looked into his reflection and wondered who was looking back. Milo was discovering something amazing: he was no longer happy.

"The turning point for me was the October crash of 1987," Milo says. "A lot of people recovered from that crash—but I lost everything. It really shook my confidence in myself as a stock market genius! It also happened just as I was about to hit forty. Something in me screeched to a halt. After a couple of decades of feeling like Superman, suddenly I felt like Elmer Fudd. I'd crashed not only financially but, I guess, emotionally too." What Milo discovered when he took a new look at his life—a life he could no longer afford now that he was suddenly poor—was that he was sick of the sex and booze and drug party his life had become. "When I look back on it now, losing all my money was one of the best things that happened to me. For one thing, it opened me up to meeting Trudy."

Trudy was a real estate agent Milo turned to in his quest for a cheaper apartment. "I'd sold my co-op through this place and gotten a fair amount for it—at least it would tide me over until I got another job, I thought. And it would allow me to rent something smaller. Trudy was the agent I worked with, and she was totally different from any woman I'd ever had anything to do with before." A single, divorced mother with two young girls, Trudy struggled to make ends meet in a small house in the suburbs; she worked twelve-hour days on a regular basis; she was as far from a "party girl" as any woman could be. "But something fascinated me," Milo says. "She was so *competent*. It was like she'd really decided what was important in life and she was going for it. What was important to her wasn't glitz and glamour and having a good time. It was making a good home for her kids. It was doing something she liked doing and was good at."

Milo asked her out to lunch to discuss some new apartment possibilities—Trudy said yes. "That was another thing that attracted me," Milo says. "She wasn't falling over in a dead faint over me. I know it sounds conceited, but frankly that's what I was used to—women fawning over me. Trudy wasn't like that. I couldn't tell whether she even *liked* me, much less whether she was infatuated! She was all business." Milo realized that he'd never learned to talk to a woman like Trudy, a woman who hadn't made romance her primary goal. "It was like I didn't have the vocabulary to talk to her. I realized how split I'd always been. I mean, I talked one way to guys, usually business or sports, and another way to women—anything to get them into *bed*, basically."

Trudy wasn't responding to any of Milo's usual bait. So Milo, at a loss (he'd really made Trudy a challenge by now, and he was determined to win her), dropped his usual "subtle hints" and went for the direct approach. "I mean, she was so businesslike about everything. I thought maybe she'd respond to something a little more, well . . . *frontal*. So I told her I really found her attractive. I told her I'd love to make love to her. Boy, did *that* not go over."

Milo heaves a long sigh. "She really let me have it. She said she knew all about my rep as a ladies' man, and what the hell did I think she was, another bimbo I could just take to bed when I felt like it? She said she'd always wondered if I was the big baby she thought I'd be, the spoiled brat who'd always gotten what he wanted, and now she said she'd gotten proof that's just what I was. She said she wasn't working twelve-hour days and struggling to bring her kids up so she'd get the chance to meet a self-centered bastard like me, and who did I think I *was* anyway. . . . Whew!

"It hurt," he continues, "because I was starting to believe a lot of that stuff about myself already. Even before I lost all my money, I was starting to wonder what my life was all about. And now, here was this hardworking lady—this *grown-up* woman, as I realized I'd started to see her—telling me where to get off. It hurt, but it also made me angry. What right did she have to say all that about me anyway? I mean, all I'd done was tell her I found her attractive!"

Milo went from hurt to defensive anger and said if Trudy were

going to be that uptight about a simple proposition, he wasn't sure
he wanted to have anything to do with her—in or out of bed. "I can't
believe how coarse I sounded. It was just that I was angry. Anyway
I guess I got what I deserved. She slapped me. And she left the table.
I felt roughly two inches tall."

We could leave the story here as a simple fable about what not
to say to a hardworking single mother. But, as you've probably guessed,
there was more to it. Milo called her office the next day in an attempt
to apologize. He knew he'd acted like a fool. But the receptionist
who answered the phone said Trudy had had to rush home—something about an emergency, one of her daughters had had an accident.
Milo was amazed to discover he felt real concern, even shock. He
had a sudden inspiration. "Look," he said to the receptionist, "I'm
an old friend, but I've lost Trudy's home address. Could you give it
to me? Maybe I can go out there and give her some help." The
receptionist was wary, but Milo had not lost all of his charm, and
she finally relented. He jumped in his car and sped out to the address
in the suburbs, consulting a large foldout map he hadn't looked at
in years, nearly getting into an accident himself trying to read it and
drive at the same time. But he finally found the house. It was a small
development bungalow, a simple, plain house like hundreds of others
around it—a far cry from the luxurious surroundings Milo had known
for most of his life. But he approached it as if it were Buckingham
Palace. He was so afraid he'd be turned away. He'd thought at the
last minute of bringing something—an apple pie, he thought. That
was what neighbors out in places like these brought each other, wasn't
it? Luckily he found a bakery at the last minute, an expensive French
place, but the pie looked good. Underneath all his anxiety about
whether Trudy would open the door when she saw him was a genuine
concern that amazed him. It was so unfamiliar for him to really care
about anyone. He really hoped Trudy's kid was all right.

"I got out of the car, with the pie in one hand, and went up to
ring the bell. Nobody answered. I wondered if they were at the hospital
or something—I really was worried about her! I decided I'd just camp
out on the front stoop and wait for someone to show up." No one did
for one hour—then two hours.

"I don't know why I stayed. But I was determined to wait for
Trudy. I'm amazed none of the neighbors came out to ask me why I
was waiting around. But no one did." Finally a station wagon rounded
the corner and pulled into the driveway. It was Trudy—and two

girls—one with her arm in a sling. Milo said Trudy's reaction was simple and quick: " 'What the hell are you doing here?' she spat at me. I got up from the stoop to hand her the pie, but for some reason—graceful me, never missed a beat on the dance floor—my feet flew out in front of me. I slid on the doormat! I went flying—and so did the pie. I fell hard on my rump, and the pie splattered all over my lap. Trudy's kids—even the one with her arm in a sling—burst out laughing. So did Trudy, which pleased me most, at least when I thought back on it later. At that moment I was in more than a little pain. Trudy said it looked like we had another accident on our hands and walked up to me, asking me if I was all right. I told her I guessed I was. I apologized about the pie. Then I burst out laughing too."

The laughter helped, even though Milo's rump still hurt. And when it sank in that Milo had come because he was actually concerned about Trudy and her daughter, Trudy softened. She asked him to stay to dinner. She said she thought it might be a good education to see how people lived in the suburbs. Milo stayed, and hugely enjoyed himself. After a little awkwardness, with Trudy's girls at first too shy to do anything but stare at this large man who'd thrown a pie all over himself, things warmed up. The little girl who'd fallen off the swing decided she'd confide all the gory details to Milo. Milo discovered he was good with kids, something he'd never had the opportunity to find out before. Trudy began looking at him differently. They both became a little more human to each other.

Over time Milo's "consciousness" began to raise, and he and Trudy began to bridge what each of them had once thought were unbridgable gaps. What happened in both of their cases is that their old checklists spontaneously changed. New realities made certain priorities shift, and even disappear altogether. Milo was learning not only about responsibility but about how to talk to a woman like a human being, not just a bed partner. Trudy was also learning that men were whole beings—with flaws, issues and a past just as complicated as her own. She was also learning that a man can *change*, that she didn't have to wait for some fully formed perfect Mr. Right to come in and complete her life. Trudy and Milo are a good example of what can happen when you allow your checklists to change. It's amazing what—and who—you can end up with!

## LEO, DON AND PAUL: A ROUNDUP OF OTHER NEW MEN

As we've seen with Brendan and Milo, a large part of the problem men have with women is learning how to speak the same language, to find a vocabulary that doesn't trap both men and women in confining stereotypes. But there are other obstacles men feel keenly, and other triumphs men have been able to make that we haven't explored yet. The following trio of men should give us a much broader idea of how men are reaching women in more satisfying ways. And they can tell us how they're allowing themselves to be reached.

Leo, a big friendly bear of a man, is a fireman. In fact, the guys he works with call him "Smokey." He's well liked by a large number of people and has a good sense of humor. But he describes himself as a "down-home country boy"—making it even more surprising that he got involved with Melissa. She is a high-powered corporate executive whom he met in what might be thought of as a classic fireman-meets-lady-in-distress way. Melissa's cat was caught up in 'her tree, and in their small town it was the fire department's job to come to this kind of rescue. Leo was sent to do the job.

"Melissa was dressed in overalls," he remembers, "but they didn't look like they'd seen much work—they were too clean. This wasn't a woman who did much manual labor, I thought to myself. And yet she was pretty good at climbing trees! She'd obviously decided I hadn't come quick enough, so she'd gotten up the tree and was out on a very unsteady branch grabbing at her cat, who wasn't having any of it. I brought a ladder to everybody's rescue, and she asked me in for coffee." Something about this "city woman," with her manicured hands and beautifully done hair, struck him right off.

"I could tell she wasn't spoiled, even if she did seem well-off. She was a real adventurer." This was borne out when, after they'd taken a sip of coffee, Leo asked Melissa where all the strange masks and foreign-looking doodads hanging on the walls had come from. "It turned out she'd traveled a lot—to places I'd always dreamed of going—and when I asked her to tell me about some of those trips, she lit up like a little kid. She told me stories about almost getting capsized in storms, lost on mountains—this was one amazing woman!"

Melissa was now a successful businesswoman who'd just bought this little house because she was sick of the city. She wanted to "settle down." Leo told her it didn't look like that would be easy, after all her exploits. She smiled.

"She said it would be nice to have a friend to show her another side of life. I can't tell you the chemistry between us then! I knew I wanted to be that 'friend.' In fact, suddenly I was head-over-heels. Amazingly, she seemed to return the feeling, especially over the next few weeks, when we started to go out on dates. She said she was so sick of the guys she usually met in her 'sphere'—guys after a buck, guys who didn't know themselves or what was really important. I think she knew I really didn't care how much money she made, which was true."

When Leo's fellow firemen got wind of Leo's "catch," they wouldn't let him alone. "Looks like a damned nice situation to me," one of them said. "Let the ol' lady work. Way to go, Leo!" Leo, who'd never been known to raise his voice, found himself getting angry. Partially, he now realizes, it was because there was some secret part of him that wondered if falling for a woman like Melissa meant he was somehow less of a man, if her greater success reversed the "natural order" of things. The guys at the firehouse were really getting to him.

Melissa sensed Leo's discomfort, and wondered why he seemed to be withdrawing. "She always took the direct line with me, which I loved about her," Leo says. "She asked me why I was shutting down. I couldn't deny that I was. But I didn't have the guts to tell her what I was feeling. I finally mumbled something about the guys at the firehouse. And she said, 'It's my money, isn't it?' And I said, 'Yeah, sort of.' I said the guys were saying I was 'Mr. Melissa.' She laughed. I asked her what was so funny. I thought she didn't realize how hurt I was. She told me that the thing she loved about me was how I'd always accepted her for who she was, not what she did or how much she made. And I had to wonder to myself if that were true. But then I looked at her, looking at me so trustingly. And I realized I loved this lady more than anything or anyone else. Nobody else mattered. That's when I asked her to marry me."

Now, Leo says, he's learned to take all the ribbing his cohorts want to dish out—he'll even go along with the joke. "Sometimes I'll tell them what a good deal I have, being Mr. Melissa. Now that they see they can't get a rise out of me, they've quit bothering me. And, who knows, maybe some of them are impressed. I mean, most of those guys couldn't conceive of being with a woman who made more than they did. And they see it working for me."

Leo's inner self-confidence is what allowed him to get over the outside pressure he felt from his co-workers. A lot of men desperately want to feel like one of the guys. When they face doing something that they're told is unmanly, they'll run scared. But men are learning to meet women in some new ways that have more to do with the particular man and woman than with reacting to outside opinion about whether or not they make a good match. The new man is able to trust that, between the two of you, you can come up with all the strength and love and solutions needed to combat the "outside world."

Don is an example of a man who has learned to change his checklist, to let go of his stereotypes about what types are right for him. "I knew when I met Margaret that I probably wasn't her type. I mean, she had a glamorous career in the fashion world—she was a buyer for a big department store. I was an aspiring painter, but to pay bills I was working in the gift store of an art museum. Actually, I liked it; I was always around a lot of art, and it inspired ideas for my own painting. But I didn't have any burning ambition to 'make it' the way I knew Margaret did." Don met Margaret at a fancy fashion benefit dinner that was held at the museum—he was moonlighting as a bartender at the open bar. He vividly remembers Margaret's first words to him: "Damn it!" Margaret had walked up to the bar to get a glass of white wine, but the glass slipped out of her hands and the wine poured all over the front of what Don imagined was a very expensive dress.

"She looked terrific in it—it was dark blue velvet. I shoved a bunch of napkins at her, and said something to commiserate. She looked up at me, as if noticing me for the first time, and she smiled. 'Perfect!' she said, 'Just as I'm about to land the biggest account of my life, I'm going to smell like a wino.' We both laughed. She was terrific—way out of my league but, at that moment, I would have done anything to see her again. She seemed to linger at the bar for a moment—which got my hopes up—but then she excused herself to go to the ladies' room. I was a goner."

Don never quite had his eyes off Margaret the whole rest of the long evening, and he could swear her eyes kept darting back to him. He was overjoyed when she came up to him at the end of the party, when he was starting to clean up. "Look," Don says she told him, "I'm not in the habit of picking up strange bartenders, but would you mind going someplace for coffee? You're the first *human being* I've seen here all night. I'm so damned *sick* of clothes people right now, I could . . ."

Don couldn't believe his luck. This coffee date led to others. At first, Don couldn't understand what his appeal could possibly have been. Finally, he says, Margaret told him.

"She said she'd never felt so understood by a man before. By this time, we'd talked about everything—about our backgrounds. She was from a small town in the South, she grew up virtually a farm girl, and she disliked pretentious people more than anything else, which meant she'd had a real hard time getting along with people in the fashion world. I told her about growing up near Chicago, that I came from a huge, poor, but pretty happy family, where everyone was encouraged to do what he wanted to do. I told her about my interest in art—and my interest in *her.* I knew she wasn't really into the la-di-da stuff she had to put up with in her job. I guess I *did* feel I knew her, like we'd met somewhere long before, like we could almost see *into* each other."

It was this "soul communion" that each responded to, and respected rather than dismissed because of other objective facts that didn't immediately spell out a perfect pairing. "I'm starting to feel like maybe Margaret loving me isn't such a freak anymore," Don says. "I've always had a pretty strong sense of myself—and I can accept that things are possible between two people that have nothing to do with money or status. It's not that we don't have some rough moments. I know Margaret feels, sometimes, she has to explain me when she introduces me to some of her high-powered friends. But we can usually make a joke out of it. And sometimes it's a little hard not to feel inadequate around her. It's not just that she makes more than I do, but her whole world can seem so intimidating. But, again, we usually can get back to *ourselves*—and I really don't feel threatened. What we've got is something so much more precious than status. And we know it."

When a man "knows who he is," he's gone a long way to preparing himself for a wide range of possibilities with women. That, of course, applies equally to women. We are selves *beyond* our gender, beyond our society's expectations of what we're supposed to be or do. As we'll see in our next chapter, it's not that societal and self-imposed expectations are always so easily ignored, shed or dealt with. They can be real obstacles. But they are *surmountable*. Let me introduce you to one more man who's surmounted them—Paul. He brings this whole idea of self confidence into especially clear focus.


Paul is an airline attendant, a job he loves, not only because it allows him to travel, but because he genuinely likes dealing with a lot of people. "What other job lets you see so many different kinds of people—all over the world? I feel, sometimes, like an airplane is a flying sociology laboratory. The stories I could tell!"

One of these stories has to do with Joan, a lawyer he met in the first-class cabin of a London to New York flight—a woman who looked, every inch of her, like she *belonged* in first class.

"We were grounded for a long time on the runway—the weather was pretty bad, and the backup of planes was worse than usual. We served our first-class passengers drinks, and I noticed Joan, not only because she looked so great, but because she was the only passenger not complaining about the delay. She had a real sense of calm about her. She ordered a club soda, and when I brought it to her, she got this real mischievous look in her eyes—totally at odds with the Professional Demeanor she'd conveyed up till then. She said, 'What I wouldn't do for a nice game of poker!' I couldn't imagine a woman who looked like Joan even knowing how to *play* poker, and I laughed. She'd set the tone for the whole flight. She was really terrible. She kept trying to crack me up with strange faces whenever she heard me trying to placate some passenger about the food or how long the flight would take. She was obviously enjoying the heck out of teasing me, and I enjoyed being teased. She said she loved the way I laughed—like a kid. Something made me believe her. In her strange way, Joan was telling me I interested *her* as much as she did me."

Joan's unexpected playfulness was followed up by something even less expected. "She handed me her business card when we got into Kennedy. That's how I found out she was an attorney—at one of the biggest firms in New York, too. But she'd written on the back of it, 'One nut deserves another. Call me.' And so, because I had a week off in New York, I did."

Initially, Joan and Paul had what felt, to Paul, like a somewhat confusing relationship. "At first I thought, okay, I wasn't born yesterday. Maybe this high-powered woman just wants a nice young man to have sex with. A no-strings little affair—when I'm in town, we get together. I tried to make myself happy about that thought, but to tell the truth, I hoped I was wrong. There was something about Joan that was special to me—I didn't just want to be a fling."

When he met Joan the first few times, he felt a little tense, as if waiting to be asked up to her apartment. When she didn't ask, he was almost relieved. But emphasize *almost.* "I was glad she didn't just want to see me for sex, but then I started to wonder if she found me attractive! She joked with me—she said she really liked being with me—but she made no real romantic move toward me. I was confused. What did she really want?"

On a warm spring night, Paul walked Joan back to her apartment building and decided he'd take a risk. He felt silly, like a sixteen-year-old on a first date, but before Joan walked into the lobby, he tapped her on the shoulder. And then drew her into his arms. It was the first time they'd kissed—after five or six dates.

It turns out Joan was a little shy with Paul. She didn't feel as if she could make the first romantic move. She covered up a lot of her shyness with banter, but she really did want more. Paul says she was wrestling, privately, with her own doubts about whether a female lawyer could find happiness with a male flight attendant—but then she said, what if the sexes were reversed? "Would I hesitate if I were a man?" Paul, miraculously, felt no such qualms. All he knew was he liked Joan. He really didn't care what she did for a living. "Joan is a funny, marvelous, smart lady—and I think I love her. That's all I need to know. I think that gives Joan strength to love me back, not to worry about what her mother, boss or doorman will think."

These "new men" may sound a little too good to be true—and I don't have to stress that love can sometimes be a very uphill battle when you're going against the societal grain. Again, we'll learn more about fighting that battle in our next chapter on navigating through real life. But if I've stressed the positive in this chapter, it's because there *is* so much "positive" in men who are available to you. The happiest news is that men are human beings, too, and many of them are waking up to the fact that *women* are human beings as well.

Now—on to making this relationship work in "real life." But remember, part of life's reality is that men and women have more in common than we have been brought up to think. Men aren't the enemy, purposefully out to deprive women. The men with whom you want to get involved are struggling to find love just as much as you are.

These men who share your quest—these nice guys of the world—what qualities do they share? They seem to be the following:

1.  The nice guy has self-confidence. He believes he is a valued, worthy, lovable and loving person beyond the checklist score he may get from a woman. He knows he is desirable—"eligible" —for the *person* he is, not for what he does for a living, earns or looks like.

2.  He is open to select from a wide range of partners. That is, his checklist is not rigid. He has overcome sex-role stereotypes and is comfortable enough with who he is—and has resolved his own fears and negative scripts enough—so that he has no rigid expectations of what a man and woman "ought" to be and do. He has broad definitions of what's appropriate for men and women and is not frightened by a woman who bucks old male/female conventions.

3.  He is comfortable with his own personal power. He doesn't need to intimidate others or make other people feel "less than" in order to feel adequate himself. He's comfortable with his sexuality, his masculinity, and doesn't feel he has to prove himself as a man.

4.  He is careful he doesn't fall into the opposite trap of dependency, of relishing a woman's power over *him* too much. He doesn't look to a woman to improve his status, support him or take care of him. He strives for balance, so that the care-taking is reciprocal, mutual and fairly equal.

5.  He is capable of commitment, of devotion to *you*. This doesn't mean he's obsessed or possessive. It means he's open to sharing his deeper self with you and knows that becoming truly intimate takes time and trust—time and trust he's willing to invest in you.

When you pick the nice guy, you are really going for what I call the GOLD. The G stands for being good to you; the O means he's open; L says he loves you; D means he's devoted to making your relationship work—and last.

Once you know he wants a relationship as much as you do—

that he has examined his attractions, understood his past, adjusted his checklist and overcome his emotional blocks—you're *both* ready to make it work and to face the problems not just inside you, but in the outside "real world." In the next chapter we'll see how the new man—or nice guy—can be in specific situations that come up for most couples. You'll meet a number of men and women who may seem somewhat unconventional as couples, but who are struggling with the realities of everyday life in a way that will make you realize unconventionality doesn't have to be an obstacle. Facing realities like money, sex, children, friends and time, these couples will teach an important lesson: they'll show you how to navigate the sometimes rough waters of "real life"—and hang on to love.

You know a lot about yourself now that you probably didn't know before. But you may still be wondering how your new insights and, more specifically, how the new techniques are actually going to *work* in your life. "This is a book," I can hear you say. "You can make it all seem so do-able here, but what happens when I'm out *there*—in the real world? Not all the men I meet are going to be what you call new men—not everything goes according to plan." Believe me, the tactics I've been teaching you not only work in the case histories I've chosen as illustrations—they'll work in your real life, too.

The real life problems you'll read about next are problems I've taken from situations that people have brought up on my radio and TV shows, at seminars, or in response to my magazine and newspaper columns (with names and identifying details changed, of course). The answers I've offered to them show you just how workable this program is—and illustrate how "impossibility" can turn into "possibility." There is always a way to turn the prism on a problem. No matter how backed against a wall you feel, you can always shift perspective to move forward.

You may have to give yourself *time* to gain that new perspective. Much of what gets us into trouble in love and in the rest of life is the urge to react instantly to a problem—to follow our first knee-jerk reaction and "fix" things as fast as we can. But

*Step 9*

# *Navigate Through Real Life*

when you find yourself in "fixes" as a result—when you continually end up with the wrong man or without a man at all—the evidence proves that those knee-jerk reactions aren't working. Thus you should have all the inducement you need to pull in the reins, calm down and allow yourself to look at where you are, what you're feeling and what your real range of options is.

This whole book has been designed to show you your options, and that's the premise behind the solutions you'll read about next, no matter how difficult the situations that gave rise to them. So get ready, and don't worry if the problems you read about here remind you of similar problems in your own life that you're convinced can't be fixed. Pay attention to the *solutions* you'll read about here, and see what you can apply to your own life. I guarantee that you have the power to take back control in many areas, to feel as if you're something more than a victim of Fate. Look at these problems and solutions for clues about what you might do constructively to make your relationship work. At the end of each situation, you'll find a summary of the steps from this book to which the solutions apply. Go back and reread those sections to remind you of what you might do in your *own* life.

## SITUATION 1: CHOOSING DAN OVER DADDY

Meg is a woman whose parents disapproved of her choice.

"I've been married for two years now," Meg told me, "and I love my husband, Dan. He's done really well for himself. He's a building contractor and makes a nice living, so we don't hurt for money. But my father can't stand him. It's like putting two male lions in a room whenever we get together. Dad puts Dan down every chance he gets, and Dan just withdraws.

"At least he did until the last time we got together. Dan had had it with my father's digs about how he wasn't educated or smart enough for me—and he stood up to him. He said he was sick of Dad's put-downs and he wasn't going to take it anymore. He dragged me away from the dinner table—we were right in the middle of eating—and I'll never forget the look on my mother's face. She was so embarrassed, and I was, too. Then Dad said something awful—

he shouted at me, 'I *told* you he was a bum. If you had any brains you'd get a divorce. I'll pay the legal bill.'

"It was a horrible scene, but what makes me feel terrible isn't only that Dan and Dad finally blew up at one another, but that I can't help feeling Dad might be right about me not having married someone more educated. Dad is a very successful attorney—went to Harvard—and expected me to marry someone who came from a better background than Dan. Now Dan is pulling this macho thing on me where he doesn't want me to work. He wants me to be the 'little woman' who stays home taking care of the house. I wonder if I've been trapped into something I can't get out of. I mean, I still love Dan, but I hate the way it's torn my family apart, and I wonder if I made a mistake marrying him. I'm just so confused. Dan wants us to have kids, but I'm holding off. . . ."

## MY ADVICE TO MEG

Don't be surprised if part of you agrees with your father. He holds a lot of power over you, and you may not forgive yourself for not marrying someone more like him—so you feel vulnerable. Anyone who levels criticism at Dan hits you in a sore spot. It can feel like a risk to marry someone from a different background, and you may have to accept that it *was* a risk before you can see whether or not it's one you're glad you took. What you need to do now is take some time to sort out what *you* feel. Maybe you married Dan in rebellion against your father. If that's the only reason you married him, you obviously don't have much to build a marriage on. But you do say that you love him, so take some time to remind yourself what you mean by that. What do you really love about Dan? Write down a list, making it as complete as you can. What don't you like about Dan? Make that list complete, too. Out of this, you should begin to see what is really important to you and what you may just be responding to because you know how your father feels about him. If it turns out you really *do* love Dan—that your choice to be with him isn't out of rebellion but because you do want to be with him—let yourself enjoy that. And let Dan know it, too! Soon you'll be strong enough to say to your father, "Look, I know you don't approve, but this is my choice, and I'm happy with it. I love you, and I don't want to hurt you, but I ask you to respect the fact that I also love my husband."

See Dan as your ally in this—let him be your friend. It sounds as if Dan may be getting angry because he senses you're secretly on your father's side, and so he's lashing out because he feels abandoned. That may be why he wants to keep you home, so he can "control" you and reassert his masculinity, too. Let Dan know you love him, and that he comes first in your life, and you'll probably find he'll want you to do what you want to do—because he won't be threatened by the idea of you going away or disapproving of him.

### Applicable Techniques

Reassess checklist, page 43. Employ three-step process to get over your need for approval, page 141. Value-load with your husband to concentrate on his assets, page 145. Awaken to family script, in this case where the little girl wants to please and maybe "marry" daddy, page 116.

## SITUATION 2: COPING WITH OTHERS' CRITICISM

Ellen's problem illuminates another aspect of dealing with parental disapproval.

"I married Abe because I love him," she told me, "though my mother wished I had picked a rich, WASPy guy instead. My mother never comes right out and says anything nasty, but she's a master at the subtle dig. For example, one day when she came over, she noticed that our refrigerator was broken, and she looked at me with these long sad eyes and said, 'I hate to see my little girl suffer so.' I asked her what she meant, and she said that in her day husbands made sure they could provide adequately for their wives, but . . . She often implies that I married a man who doesn't make enough money. She looks for every opportunity to push my nose into the fact that Abe isn't rich enough to suit me—or, more important, *her.* I get angry at her eventually and yell, and she looks at me with these great hurt eyes again, as if she can't understand *what* she could possibly have said to annoy me. How can I keep from going crazy—and how can

I get her to change? I love my mother, and we're very close, so this is really tearing me apart."

Like Meg, Ellen is upset by her mother's digs because they trigger her own hidden feelings—that she really *might* be happier if Abe made more money. She gets angry at her mother for bringing this up because she doesn't want to acknowledge feeling the same way herself.

## My Advice to Ellen

Resolve that your choice is right for you, that you accept Abe for what he is, even if it means making some compromises. Separate your checklist from your mother's. But if money really *is* a problem for you, don't be afraid to bring up the issue with Abe. Don't nag him. Approach the problem as something you might be able to solve jointly, as a cooperative venture. How can you help to save money? What might you both do to earn more?

As for your mother, first of all, you have the choice to ignore what she says. If you don't respond to a comment, eventually she may not repeat it. If you blow up, what you're telling her is that she's succeeded—she's gotten to you. But if her comments continue anyway, you can also say—calmly—'I don't appreciate hearing things like that. We clearly disagree.' That says how you feel without insisting she do or think what *you* want. The true test of maturity and security is letting others disagree and feeling okay about it.

To help you even further reaffirm that you are different from her—and to help you get over your own inner doubts about your choice of a man—you can even say, 'Mother, I get upset when you don't approve of my choice. Maybe it's *my* problem. But it would help me if you wouldn't trigger these feelings so strongly by your criticisms.' If the conflict and criticism reach an intense stage despite your efforts, you always have the right to request that the topic be off-limits. And, finally, if parents or friends get abusive—which doesn't look like it will happen with your mother, who seems to bend over backward not to appear offensive—your last resort is to avoid seeing them. Why put yourself and your love through that pain? You have the choice not to.

## Applicable Techniques

Value-load to reinforce your sense of Abe's powerful qualities, page 145. Awaken to family scripts and roots of the tremendous dependence on parental opinions and needs. In particular, review stopping escalation, page 141. Recognize your own abilities to get what you feel you want, page 154.

## SITUATION 3: WHEN MONEY MEANS POWER

Connie's problem illustrates the increasingly common dilemma of what happens when the woman earns more than the man. She is an executive at a major film company earning six figures, while her live-in lover, Jim, is a talented, but struggling, set designer.

"I met him on a movie we were producing," she explained, "and I loved how creative and spontaneous he was—it was really refreshing to be around someone who felt so much joy in everything he did. It's very different from how I normally am. I'm very organized—and a lot of my success comes from the fact that I'm good at paying attention to details and keeping things straight. Now I'm starting to lose my temper with Jim. He's always losing things; he's always changing his mind. He gets very mad at me when I don't just drop everything and do what he wants, like take an overnight trip in the middle of a work week. I *can't* just pick up and go like that. Now I'm starting to think he's irresponsible. He doesn't make nearly as much money as I do, but that never seemed to bother me or him. But now I'm wondering if I shouldn't have hooked up with someone who's more like me. I have to admit it's starting to bother *me* that he's not more successful. But I still love him—even though I'm getting more and more exasperated by him. What do you think?"

## My Advice to Connie

The tension you're talking about is very common between a man and a woman when she makes more money than he does. It sounds like

Jim may be stepping up his "irresponsible" act because he's having a difficult time with what he imagines to be your "superiority." He may very well feel scared that he is inferior or less mature, and his "spontaneity" may be a bid for independence, a bid to be noticed more or a way to assert himself by rebelling—choosing to do "whatever he wants." He may feel that, by playing along with your rules, he'll become so submissive he'll "lose" himself. I doubt that much of this is conscious, but that doesn't mean *you* shouldn't be conscious of it!

Here's what I'd suggest doing. First of all, let him know as lovingly as possible what you like about him (always emphasize what you like). Recall the times he behaved as you liked. Also, tell him that you need to feel loved, too, and when he flies off the handle, it hurts you; remind him that it's not your temperament to be too "loose." But most important, focus on the areas in which there is real, concrete, specific disagreement. Don't just say "I can't stand it when you're irresponsible"—let him know what happened that week or that day that really upset you. Invite him to do the same thing. See what specific behavior you might be able to change—don't just hurl accusations at one another. Don't worry if this is rocky going at first. It probably will be, because you're dealing with some highly charged emotions. But stick to the specifics; allow him to see how one particular action hurt or disappointed you. And, again, ask him to do that with you, too. Out of all this will come a deeper more workable understanding of what triggers each of you have, and should give you a better idea of what to avoid doing around each other.

The deeper level may take some time—and therapy—to reach. A man and woman with a problem very much like yours came to me not long ago. Through a number of sessions of therapy, they began to see the deeper family-script dynamics that were holding them back. He saw he was responding to her as if she were his mother—rebelling against her, and striving for "independence." She was buying into this and unconsciously treating him like a misbehaving child—as, ironically, her own father had been treated by her mother. It takes courage to wake up to the fact that we may be following our own scripts, but it sounds as if you and Jim could do with a little couples therapy to reveal the scripts that may be unconsciously trapping both of you. One wonderful thing about couples therapy is that it often "tells" partners that they're serious about their commitment. That in itself can be healing.

APPLICABLE TECHNIQUES

Awaken to family scripts, page 106. For him: do self-esteem exercises, page 148. For you: face the real issues and write the real screenplay to show the real, unspoken dialogue between you two, so that you're clear what the trigger is, page 136. Confront any emotional traps, pages 90–105.

## SITUATION 4: FOR LOVE OR MONEY

Barbara's situation concerns money, too, but with a different twist.

Barbara enjoys being able to "treat" Paul, who makes ten dollars an hour to her two hundred. She pays for all their dates and even extras for his family. It's usually not a problem, except, as she says, "When my friends get me alone, they slip in something like 'Boy, he's got a good deal,' or 'Don't you think he's taking you for a free ride?' I *love* Paul, but this makes me wonder if I am buying his love. Does he love me for me or for the comforts I buy him?"

Barbara needs to listen to herself, not others. But she also needs to explore what money means to her.

### MY ADVICE TO BARBARA

I hear that you want and need love so much, and I agree that, if Paul gives it to you, the price you pay seems very small. But don't let this convince you that love can be bought. If you feel love—and if you feel love coming back from Paul—it's real. Only *you* can tell if his caring is genuine. And make some rules about managing your finances together, so that the position of each is respected.

Why worry that you pay for more than he does? What about all those years men worked and brought home the money—did they worry that women loved them only for the support they received? In a way, you may need to acknowledge that supporting him *may* be part of his attraction to you. But as the wise man Teiresias answered when Oedipus asked, "Do I love the Queen because of her, or because she is a queen?"—"You cannot separate the two. She *is* the Queen." In other words, if he loved her, he loved a queen. He had to accept everything about her. Similarly, if you love Paul, you must accept the disparity in your incomes—and the fact that you can afford more than he can.

Men today are often turned on by powerful, successful women. Successful women are usually more independent and feel good about themselves, which takes pressure off a man and allows him to value her as much as she values herself. He doesn't have to provide her with self-worth, because she's already got it in abundance. If that's the case between you and Paul, enjoy yourselves—you're accepting each other as you are.

However, if ultimately you *do* feel used, you must learn to value yourself so that you won't gravitate to situations in which you allow yourself to be used. If you're in a relationship with a man who earns less than you do, ask yourself some questions about what you like about earning what you do: Does it make you feel you can control the relationship? Does it make you feel good about your abilities, about yourself? Or does it make you feel "adequate"—as if, now you can *buy* what you wouldn't be able to attract in any other way?

Then talk to the man you're with about what money means to each of you.

### APPLICABLE TECHNIQUES

Do self-esteem exercises, page 148. Listen carefully to your man's views and issues in relation to power and money, pages 178–79. Separate fantasy from reality to assess what's really going on between you and write the real screenplay, page 136. Dispel Dream Lover (the Operator) fears, pages 63–89. Overcome emotional blocks, pages 90–105.

## SITUATION 5: DIFFERENT SOCIAL STYLES

Andrea's dilemma was as follows. In her words:

"I'm a commercial artist, and I'm engaged to a 'fine artist.' Tim and I have been up-front with each other about what each of us wants out of life. And he accepts that I'm happy doing a 'craft.' I accept that he wants to paint, not for the masses, but for the select few.

He's very unconventional, and I learned to love this in him, but now it's posing a problem.

"My problem sounds silly, but it's really been bothering me. I was invited to a really high-level fancy party, full of advertising executives and art directors from top agencies. There was a good chance of my getting a top-level art director job, and part of the politics meant meeting the right people. I wanted Tim to go because I hate going to those things unescorted, and anyway this was so important to me that I wanted him to be part of it. Tim hates these parties but he agreed to go. What he did not agree to do was wear a tuxedo. The party was black tie, and I pleaded with him, just this once, couldn't he compromise his standards and conform? But he wouldn't. Finally I said he might as well not go if he wasn't going to wear a tux, but now he'd got it into his head that he *wanted* to go. So we went. He wore a brown velvet jacket and this sort of scarf around his neck like an ascot. He looked like something out of the last century—elegant, but way out of place. When I introduced him around, every man gave him the coldest reception you can imagine. I hate to say it, but I started to feel embarrassed to tell any of the male executives we hadn't met yet that he was my fiancé! Tim ended up standing by himself in a corner for most of the evening—looking unspeakably 'superior' to everyone else. I felt like killing him!

"I don't know what to do. Tim thinks I've 'sold out,' and he wants nothing to do with my world. Why is it so hard for him to accept what I want to do? And why am I so mad at him all of a sudden for not being part of the 'normal' world?"

## MY ADVICE TO ANDREA

You say that you and Tim once accepted what each of you did in your work—that he understood the importance you attach to your craft—and you support his desire to do fine art. But you've set yourself a very difficult task. You're both in the same field, and Tim probably feels more competitive with you than he'll acknowledge. Pretending he's superior could well be a defensive tactic. It's often difficult when a couple work in the same field, even if you're in two distant parts of it.

The first thing to do is talk over with him how he feels about what he's doing—and about what you're doing. You may find that he has doubts about the direction of his own career, and feels threatened by your success. You need to talk about your own feelings, too. Tell him that you feel hurt when he puts down what you do, and reassure him that what you're doing in your career doesn't mean you value him or his work any less. You need to open up a much more meaningful dialogue so you learn to trust each other with your doubts and fears. Try to be Tim's friend—and let him be yours.

The other thing you might consider is fairly obvious: you and Tim may have very different styles. Don't expect him to react to things the way you do. Maybe leave him out of fancy parties if you don't think he'd enjoy them or if you're too uncomfortable. But, if you do invite him, let him be himself! The idea is, be conscious that you're two different people and that you can't control each other's reactions. Discuss your differences without blowing up or being "shocked" by something you would have been able to anticipate if you'd given it a little clear thought. But above all, let each other know you *value* each other—the way you are now.

### APPLICABLE TECHNIQUES

Rewrite the screenplay to see what you're really telling each other, page 136. Do the drawing exercise in Step 5 and answer questions ("How close were you on the page?" etc., pages 124–25). Pay attention to his needs, as in Step 8, page 176.

## SITUATION 6: FROM EMBARRASSMENT TO ACCEPTANCE

Lillian was distressed over a similar dilemma—where love works behind closed doors, but not in front of her friends.

"I've been lovers with Jack for over five years, and he's terribly devoted to me. When we're alone, I love being with him. He seems to understand me intuitively like nobody else—and our lovemaking is wonderful. My problem is that my friends don't like Jack. Jack comes from a poor background, and he's worked himself up so that he's got a good job managing a small hardware store. He's really done well for himself. But he can't carry on a conversation with any of my friends. He gets shy and tongue-tied, and my friends are terrible. They think he's a typical 'deese, dem, dose' lunk, even though I know he's smarter than he ever lets on in public. But my friends are impossible. They say things like, 'We know it's hard to find a man these days, Lillian, but that doesn't mean you have to give up *all* your standards. . . .' Or, 'Boy, sex with Jack must be *unbelievable*.' 'Some friends,' you might say, but they're all pretty good people. They all went to college, and they're all, like I am, pursuing careers. (I'm a financial consultant.) It's just that they're all from a different *planet* than Jack is.

"I feel bad for Jack. Whenever we go anywhere, he shuts down completely. It's like he speaks a different language from anyone else. And then when we get home, he feels so defeated he expects me to tell him to *leave* because he thinks I don't think he's good enough. The problem is, sometimes I wonder if I *did* choose the right man. When we're alone, we share beautifully—at least we used to before the strain of my friends started to get too much. Maybe two different backgrounds don't mix after all. I hate to admit this, but sometimes I make sure Jack won't come somewhere I think he'd embarrass me, like to an art opening or a concert. I'm starting to lie to him, sometimes, about where I'm going and what I'm doing. I hate myself, but I can't help feeling this way. What should I do?"

## MY ADVICE TO LILLIAN

So many couples enjoy their time together when they are alone, but don't mesh well socially. So, you might feel your first bit of relief just knowing that your dilemma is a common one—you're not alone.

What you have to do, first, is get clear about who each of you is, what each of you is capable of contributing in a social situation and then, if necessary, compromise. You need to accept responsibility for the fact that you chose Jack with all of his qualities—the qualities you love and the qualities you don't. Accept his strong points as well as his weak points. Don't let your energy be drained by being angry at something you don't have the power to change. Then, instead of just assuming you know what's going on when he's with you and your sophisticated friends, *ask him* what he feels when he's in that group. What particularly makes him feel "shut down"? *Who* makes him feel particularly uncomfortable? You may find that not all of your friends intimidate him—there may be only one or two that make him turn into a "lunk." Perhaps you could plan some gatherings *without* those people. Think about Jack's comfort to some degree—maybe invite only one or two of your friends over for a small dinner, and let Jack get comfortable with being around them. It's important to find friends you have in common. Perhaps you might show more interest in people he knows, or knew from his past. Don't feel it's all a task of dragging him into *your* world. You might try to enter his, as well. Perhaps he knows some people from work, or relatives he loves but hasn't seen for a long time because he's been afraid you'd disapprove or they wouldn't "fit in."

What about going out for a pizza, or to a movie, or to the beach? Pick shared activities that won't make Jack feel like a fish out of water. Also, accept the fact that it's perfectly okay for you to do things on your own, to have friendships and attend social gatherings that *don't* include Jack. This is a particularly important point for so many couples—so many men and women think they've got to do *everything* together. It's all right if your interests are a bit different; that just adds variety to your life. Once you've accepted each other for who each of you is, you can begin to accept the possibility that you don't have to agree on everything or spend every minute of your lives together.

### APPLICABLE TECHNIQUES

To help accept your man for who he is, you might make sure you're operating from your own checklist—not from friends' idea of who you ought to be with, page 138. Self-esteem exercises for Jack will help him, page 148. Bottom-line what you love about him, page 144.

## SITUATION 7: GETTING OVER NAGGING DOUBTS AND FEARS OF THE FUTURE

Sally was torn between her feelings and vestiges of thoughts of what she *should* have and be.

"I've worked very hard to get where I am. My family couldn't afford to put me through college, but I managed to pay my way through for two years, and then, when it got too hard, I dropped out and took secretarial courses. Now I'm an executive secretary, and there's a good chance I might rise higher in the company because my boss is so pleased with my work. I already earn a very good salary, and I expect I'll be earning more pretty soon. I want to make it clear I'm not afraid to work for a living and get what I want through my own efforts, not just by marrying 'rich.'

"My problem is I've fallen in love with a man I promised myself I wouldn't fall in love with. I always thought I would end up with a man who was as ambitious as I was, and hopefully one who was from a better background than I. I've worked too hard to get out of the 'lower middle class' to want to get tied to a man who's still part of that. It may sound conceited, but I want the best for myself—and I think I deserve a rich, Harvard-grad CEO just as much as any other woman! However, the man I've fallen for, Leonard, manages a couple of video stores, and he's from a background and neighborhood very much like mine. The main difference is he's not ambitious at all. He's perfectly happy doing what he's doing, and he says as long as he makes enough 'to live on,' he'll be fine. That's not enough for me! I wish I didn't love him—but I do. Now he's asked me to marry him, and I don't think I can bring myself to say yes. I just hate the thought of being dragged down by anybody! But I've never met a man who cared about me more, or a man who made me feel so good in so many ways. I'm completely torn about what to do, whether to say yes or no. What do you think?"

Like many women, Sally needs to become what she wants, rather than expect to live vicariously through a man.

## My Advice to Sally

You've got every reason to feel proud of yourself for accomplishing what you have in your job, and there's no reason you can't continue to succeed and make as much money as you want. Not even if you marry Leonard! Why let Leonard's lack of ambition hold you back? Why can't you love him *and* succeed on your own terms?

I know that when you have a fierce desire to get away from a background you feel held you back, you often want to cut off all contact with anything that reminds you of that background. But what you may really be expressing here is a lack of self-esteem. You need to see that you've got all the power you need, right now, to succeed on your own with or without Leonard's (or any other man's) help. Maybe you have a secret desire to be taken care of—perhaps what really bothers you about Leonard's lack of ambition is that it seems to indicate he doesn't want to take care of you as completely and "richly" as you feel you deserve. But, if Leonard loves you as much as you say he does, you have to accept that his lack of ambition has nothing to do with not wanting to take care of you. That's pure projection on your part.

I do think you have to let Leonard know how important your career and desire to be wealthy are—you'll have to gauge for yourself whether he could accept a wife who is more successful than he. But, again, if he really loves you, he'll find a way to accept everything about you. And, if you really love him, you'll discover ways to accept even his lack of ambition (which, remember, may change in the future). Be sensitive to the fact that your Harvard-grad-CEO dream lover may only be your dream created out of rebellion against your background, not one you've created out of free, unfettered *desire* for it. Take another look at Leonard—he may be exactly what you need.

## APPLICABLE TECHNIQUES

Examine dream lover traits and see if they're unrealistic and/or not what you *really* want, Step 3 (pages 63–89). Similarly, rewrite your checklist, page 142. Recognize your personal power and become what you want instead of expecting *him* to be it, page 148. Given your strong desire to escape your background, examine family scripts. In particular, do the Seeing the Family Picture exercise, pages 124–25.

## SITUATION 8: GETTING AN EX OUT OF YOUR MIND

Joanne's problem was similar to Sally's, but she had the specter of an old dream lover to deal with.

"Five years ago I had an affair with a guy I was crazy about, but ended up getting dumped by," she told me. "It turned out he was seeing my best friend without my knowing it. It was really a horrible situation, and I haven't talked to either of them in all that time. I'm still really hurt by it. In the meantime I've gotten involved with a really sweet guy, Peter, whom I love and who I know loves me. He is everything my ex wasn't: attentive, caring, devoted, sensitive. He isn't especially ambitious, but he's got a good job with the phone company, full benefits, and he gets raises every year. His prospects are good, and he's on his way up. He's asked me to marry him, and I want to say yes. Or I did, anyway, until I opened up the paper yesterday and saw a wedding announcement—my ex-lover and my ex–best friend got married! I thought I was over this guy, but all the old feelings came back. It was on the society page, and they gave it the full treatment. He's from a very good family and went to classy schools—so did she. He's now a vice-president of a bank; she's a broker. They were honeymooning in Switzerland.

"It's a wonder that my eyes didn't burn a hole in the paper! I was furious! All the pain and resentment came back full force—and something much worse. I was terribly jealous! I really loved that awful guy—and something I didn't want to admit to myself was that I was really turned on by him, too, in a way that Peter never turned me on. That's what really made me feel ashamed. Here he was, getting married and being rich and beautiful and getting my ex–best friend in the bargain—and I felt like nothing. Suddenly the very thought of Peter made me freeze. He could never measure up to what I really want.

"I know I'm being awful, but I haven't been able to see Peter for days—I've been putting him off ever since I saw that announcement in the paper. He wants an answer to his proposal, and I just can't talk to him now. I can't help the way I feel. What should I do?"

Joanne needed to know that her reaction was normal, and that she could transfer those erotic feelings about her dream lover to her nice guy.

## MY ADVICE TO JOANNE

I appreciate the misery you're going through. It's hard to regain clarity about something this painful, but there are things you can do to get perspective on the problem, even during the heat of it. First, it is natural to have fears before facing a marriage! All kinds of doubts come up! Thoughts of ex-lovers are only one such doubt.

You also need to use this opportunity to examine your attractions. It sounds as if your love antennae drew you to men who tested your "worth." Your feeling of betrayal is completely understandable. Your ex took away your best friend! Even more to the point, your best friend took him away from *you*! (Of course, neither happened; they are equally responsible for meeting behind your back.) You need to shift your focus from them back to you. Do your best to see your ex-lover for who he really *is*. Remember his insensitivity, his betrayal —concentrate on what was truly bad for you in the relationship. Make this as vivid as possible. Every time the picture turns "romantic," remember how he hurt you. Now, every time he pops up in your mind, replace him with Peter. Concentrate on Peter's kindness, on his sensitivity, on his genuine caring for you. Practice this "replacement tactic" over and over, until the man before your mind's eye is Peter.

If you do love Peter, your deeper self will draw you back to him—that love will be able to combat the terrible ambivalence you feel about your cad of an ex-lover. You may also have to take a look at your past to see if there is a pattern in which your ex-lover played a part. Did you find yourself attracted to destructive men before this? What part does Peter play in this pattern, if any? In any event, congratulate yourself on having found someone who truly loves you —Peter. Make him your dream lover, which you have the power to do by continually changing the picture and emphasizing what you love about Peter.

This is a slow process, and you may find disturbing thoughts cropping up every so often in the future—that nagging "if only" about your ex-lover. But, again, you always have the power to change your focus and remind yourself of the destructive reality of that relationship. You can always "come back" to Peter, and to your life today. As for the wealthy lifestyle that your ex-lover may now represent, if that's important to you, there's nothing to keep you from increasing your *own* wealth through your *own* power. Remember that what attracts us to others is often what we wish we had ourselves—and often what we have the power to *give* ourselves.

APPLICABLE TECHNIQUES

All of Step 6, especially the tips on changing your self-talk, pages 127–47 and Step 7 (a new view of sex), pages 156–75. Pay attention to the urge to "split," which is covered in Step 7, page 156. The Give-and-Take Test and the Sex-Versus-Love Test are especially applicable, pages 162–65. So are all the tips under Ungluing the Glue, page 167.

## SITUATION 9: A STRANGLEHOLD ON LOVE . . .

Meryl was concerned about how much togetherness she can expect or have.

"I already know what you're going to tell me—I'm too 'possessive'—so I don't even know why I'm asking your opinion! But, who knows, maybe you'll surprise me. If I am too possessive, I certainly don't know what to do about it. John is my second husband, and I'm his second wife—we really want this marriage to work. But we're having some real problems, not so much between us, but because of his friends. John works at the post office, and in the town we live in, the postal workers stick together. They go out to bars, go bowling, play cards; it's like a big club.

"I know John's friends don't much like me. It's obvious they think I'm stuck up—a 'city' woman. (I run a business in the city, and I commute back and forth between there and home; I know they give John a hard time about it.) But what bothers me is that John seems to want to spend so much time with them, even when he knows I don't like them. I can't stand their small town-ness, and I really don't know what John sees in them. I've tried to get John to meet new people from the city so we could have some friends in common, but he doesn't feel comfortable with my friends either. I resent the fact that he spends nights away from me having fun with people I can't stand and who I know don't like me—even if he doesn't do it all that often. I just don't know why he'd want to be with people who don't like his wife! What do you suggest we do?"

## My Advice to Meryl

It's hard to accept that the man you love sometimes wants to be away from you, even while he loves you every bit as much as you love him. If you're "possessive," join a very large group—a lot of women suffer from these feelings of abandonment. However, from what you tell me, John's absences aren't all that excessive. He seems to need the camaraderie of his postal-worker cohorts, and I think you'd find that if you deprived him of this outlet, you'd have a very unhappy husband and an even less happy marriage.

Learning to give each other space can be hard. It may be that you're used to being threatened with abandonment. That may have happened with your first husband, or at least it may be what you feel, despite what really happened. You may want to look back to your childhood to see what pattern, if any, may be inhibiting you now. You may benefit from some therapy, which will allow you to see that John is John and not some stand-in for your father or mother or someone else you depended on who let you down. I'm just speculating, but usually "possessiveness" has these kinds of roots.

But there are some things you can do now. Why not make more of an effort to get to know John's friends, maybe not all in a group, but by asking a few of them over to dinner? They may think you're "stuck up" because you haven't given them a chance to know you. Similarly, you might make more of an effort to invite your city friends out to your house, to have them meet John on his "turf" so he gets the chance to get to know them. Friends are more important than many of us realize, and the ability to develop and sustain friendships is a precious one. Enjoy the fact that John is good at it, and accept that it's part of the way he takes care of himself. You may find yourself feeling a little more kindly toward his friends when you accept his need for them. You might also open yourself up to new friends.

## Applicable Techniques

See if the emotional trap of dependency is holding you back (Step 4), page 94. Awaken to family scripts if they apply, page 106. Try some self-esteem exercises to make sure you feel as good as possible about yourself, page 148. Develop a new view of sex, page 156.

## SITUATION 10: "IF I'M SO SUCCESSFUL, WHY DO I FEEL LIKE A FAILURE?"

Eileen is a woman confused by the link between sex and power.

"I'm in a real mess—and I really don't know why. I've just been promoted to bank vice-president. I'm the first woman in the history of this branch to be so appointed, and I have every reason to feel terrific. My boyfriend, Mike, is proud of me, and he doesn't seem to feel threatened by my new success. He brags about me to his friends. I know I'm lucky, because I know so many other women whose boyfriends or husbands would feel emasculated by or competitive with my success.

"But what I don't understand is that suddenly, in the wake of this great success, I feel an almost total loss of sexual interest in him. The only time this has ever happened before was once when I was going through a very deep depression! Now that I'm supposed to be happy, I suddenly feel the same way—no interest in making love. But that's a part of the problem I haven't yet mentioned: actually I *do* want to make love, but not with Mike. For some reason I've been fantasizing about the head of my division, Hank, who's fifteen years older than I and married for twenty years. Why these fantasies? And why my loss of interest in Mike?"

### My Advice to Eileen

Both men and women can feel a great deal of pressure when they suddenly succeed. They are told they should be happy, that they should enjoy their new power, that all is now terrific! But if you haven't made some inner adjustments, success can be very frightening. It's not at all uncommon for women who suddenly become successful to lose sexual interest in their men. As much as your conscious mind may tell you otherwise, you may feel your man is less powerful now that you've made your own rise in status. It's no secret why the head of your division is suddenly so attractive—he's the one man in your life who seems more powerful than you! Of course you'd be attracted to him.

You sound as if you have a pretty extraordinary boyfriend—he doesn't seem to be bothered by your success at all. This makes me think he'd be sensitive and aware enough to talk to. You might simply want to tell him a little about how being successful this abruptly makes you feel. It's okay to admit that you're afraid. It's okay to admit some doubts about how this will affect your relationship—even to admit the ways it already has! Give him the opportunity to respond to you, to show you *his* strength and understanding, so that you can begin to see he's powerful emotionally—that he has the strength you're really after. Recall the times you used to enjoy making love; concentrate on what you've always loved about him, especially on what turned you on about him. There are different kinds of power. Not all power comes from the size of your paycheck or what office you occupy. See his strength, and enjoy it. But don't hold your doubts and fears in—let him know what you feel so you don't build up a resentment against him that really isn't warranted.

### Applicable Techniques

Self-talk—to reprogram how you feel about your husband, page 136. Value loading—to reinforce your sense of his assets, page 145. Ungluing the glue—to help you get over new fantasy lover, page 167. Self-esteem exercises—to allow you to see that you deserve success, page 148. Reread all of Step 7, on discovering a new view of sex, pages 156–75.

## SITUATION 11: NOW HE'S AT HOME WITH THE KIDS . . .

Jackie was having some problems with accepting role reversals and relinquishing her stereotypes.

"My husband Andrew and I used to pride ourselves on being 'evenly matched.' We both had similar dreams and ambitions—we met in college and we both wanted to teach music. We fell in love and hoped we could get married and land some dream double job teaching in a school system somewhere—I'd teach choral music; he'd conduct the band. It was such a lovely dream! Unfortunately, there was a real crunch on teaching jobs, and he won out—he got the only one available. I was thrilled for him, but I knew we couldn't exist just on his teacher's salary, so I tried to pick up some freelance work.

I'd always written a little music—rock songs and short tunes—really just for fun. Then a former teacher of mine suggested I try to get work writing advertising jingles. I never thought I could do it, but —you guessed it—I could. I ended up getting hired by some top agencies, and I finally went into full-time business for myself. I was making terrific money, and Andrew loved his teaching job because he loved kids so much. We had a great life. Then I got pregnant. Not that that wasn't great, too, but it meant taking time off my work and a sudden drop in income. We had twins—wouldn't you know it!—and I knew I'd have to get back to work as soon as I could to help pay all the added expenses. But who'd take care of the babies?

"It was Andrew's idea. He said, 'Why not me?' He loved kids so much, and he knew that my salary would more than take care of expenses. He also knew how much I loved my work. Couldn't he just be the house-husband for a while? At first I thought it was a great idea. And Andrew is terrific with the babies. But now I have to admit that, with all the high-powered people I'm working with, I'm a little embarrassed to have to admit that my husband is 'home taking care of the kids.' Andrew is happy, but I'm really not. I can't get over feeling *he* should be the one making money, not me. Am I crazy?"

## MY ADVICE TO JACKIE

You are not crazy—if there's any stereotype more ingrained than the one about "men should make more money than women," it's that "women should take care of the kids." Don't hate yourself for falling prey to it—we've all been indoctrinated by the idea.

Entertain the idea that you might be *proud* of Andrew. Every time you start to feel that "embarrassment," think about the work it takes to mind twin babies and imagine Andrew accomplishing that feat. Visualize it as vividly as you can. (Watch him change both their diapers at once; watch him feed one, then the other; watch him play with one while trying to calm the other one's cries; watch him warm the milk and answer the phone and keep the babies from crawling out the front door . . . you get the picture!) It's also possible that you feel guilty for not spending enough time with your babies. Although you don't mention that, I wouldn't be surprised if that's your feeling. But do you feel guilty because you think you "ought" to be doing what Andrew's doing, or because you really *want* to? If you love your work and that's what you want to spend your time doing, thank your lucky stars for a husband who's willing to support you in it! But if you feel a real pull to take care of the babies yourself, then sit down with Andrew and discuss dividing the labor more satisfyingly. Remember, also, that how things are *now* isn't the way they always have to be. You can always change roles—you can always share and shift responsibilities and priorities. It sounds as if you've got a husband with whom that will be especially possible!

### Applicable Techniques

Value loading and self-talk are especially useful here to remind you of how proud you deserve to feel about your husband, pages 145 and 136. Also try on dependency and power emotional traps for size, pages 94 and 97, to see how you may be holding yourself back. Examine your definitions and stereotypes about what a man and a woman are and what they do.

These situations suggest the range of ways in which you may end up bumping heads with a man when he's not what society or mother or your friends and co-workers tell you he should be. But they should also give you an idea that, as long as there is love, the problems are surmountable. A common thread throughout the situations is that, when you open up to a partner, when you allow him to be what he is rather than a picture of what he should be, you instantly widen the range of what is possible between you. Sometimes the only thing you need to change in a relationship is your perspective. Don't hate yourself if you find that you're bound by strong prejudices or stereotypes. We all are. But know there's something you can do about them! We've explored a tapestry of ways you can combat negative thinking and destructive assumptions and experiences. Take a quick look back over the applicable techniques to remind yourself of some of them. Remember you have access to these tools whenever you need them. And the more you use them, the better you get at it.

"Successful" couples are successful because they've learned to make their lives positive in exactly the ways we've learned. We've concentrated on the problems in this chapter. Now let's look at some of the rich, even immeasurable, rewards of learning to love someone for who he is, not what he is, does, or makes. Let's look at some real success stories. And then let's watch you add your own story to the list!

So much of our focus so far has been on changing your checklist. In fact, when you refocus your goals into a new checklist, you're really translating what you once thought was important into something that genuinely *is* important to you! With every new step you've taken toward clarity of your motives, true feelings, wants and needs, you've been opening yourself to a whole new realm of *conscious choice*—a realm in which you're more fully awake to what you really want in a man. You may have thought at the beginning of this journey that your task would be to give up your dreams, to settle for something less than the best. Now I hope you see that's not the goal at all. I want you to have nothing *but* the best love you can get. Second best isn't good enough—and there's no reason to settle for it. The task is to find out what first best really *is*. I want you to "select, not settle."

Success in love means satisfying your desires. I've stressed this all the way through. I'm not out to keep you from getting what you want; I'm out to help you awaken to what you truly want, so you'll be able to take steps to get it. As you've already seen in the experience of numerous women in this book, happiness in love is possible only when you learn to stop reacting to old, unconscious messages that hold you *back*.

An exhilarating sense of freedom comes from responding differently to situations that used to elicit the same old knee-jerk reactions.

## Learn From Success Stories

Facing every day as a new adventure—with open heart, mind and eyes—not only prepares you for happier relationships, but defines an attitude that makes *all* of life more rewarding. Certainly that's what women who've succeeded in their relationships tell me. "Success" in their terms is light years away from what most of them once thought it would be.

Let's look at some of these women—and the men they've consciously chosen to share their lives. As you'll see, each story gives a clear sense of before and after. You'll be able to see how each woman uses—either intuitively or because she's learned them in therapy—many of the tools you've learned in this book. Following each story are before-and-after checklists, too, showing you at a glance what each woman was able to translate from old assumptions to new insights. *Not one woman here had to give up anything.* In fact, each woman ended up with far more than she ever dreamed. See for yourself.

## CHARLOTTE AND DON: FROM "HE'S NOT MY TYPE" TO "HOW COULD I HAVE BEEN SO BLIND?"

Charlotte, an attractive thirty-five-year-old editor of a folk art magazine, says the loudest sound ticking away in her head was the notorious biological clock. "I really wanted to have kids," she says, "and I couldn't help mentally rating every man I met as a potential father. I'd compute height, weight, eye and hair color, straightness of nose, intelligence, health—all those data—as if I were some avid genetic engineer. I didn't even care all that much whether I was head-over-heels in love with the guy—he had to be a great potential *father*. I know I was nuts, but you don't know the pressure a woman feels when she enters her mid and late thirties and she really wants children. I couldn't help myself!"

Charlotte says she was always pretty clear about the kind of man she wanted for herself. "Despite the sort of arty crowd I hung around with because of my work, I was a pretty conservative, conventional person—organized, got things in on time, took care of myself, paid my bills. I wanted a man like me, I guess. I didn't want the life I'd carefully built for myself to be 'rocked.' I met some nice guys and dated, but something was always a little wrong with each of them. I

see now that no man could have lived up to the fine-tooth combing
I mentally put him through, but I didn't know that then. I kept
hoping—expecting—that the right man would come through the door
and I'd know it and we'd live happily ever after. But here I was,
thirty-five, and Prince Charming had continued to make himself scarce."

The man who ended up walking through the door (in this case,
the door of the rustic seafood restaurant in which Charlotte was having
lunch with two girlfriends) couldn't have been *less* like Charlotte's
imagined perfect suitor. "Don was incredible. I've never seen such
brilliant light-blue eyes—startling against his tanned face. It wasn't
the kind of tan that came from lolling around on the beach, either.
Don was a lean working-man type—he looked like someone who
worked on the boats. He was a little short, and there was something
sort of rough about his features, but I've never seen a guy with more
vitality. The room *crackled* when he walked in."

Charlotte's two girlfriends noticed the electricity immediately.
One of them, Ann, quickly sized Don up and came to a succint
conclusion. "Eyes 10, marriageability 3. He's *not* your type, Charlotte. Stop gaping." But Charlotte couldn't help it. She'd never felt
attracted to someone like this man before. She certainly wasn't in the
habit of picking up *anyone*, even if he looked like an Ivy-grad banker,
in a bar. But something about this guy flustered her—totally. When
the women paid their check and rose to leave, Charlotte kept dropping
things. She was terribly nervous. Ann pushed her out the door. "I'm
going to save you from yourself if it's the last thing I do!" she said.
Charlotte laughed. "I'm not attracted to him. Is that what you think?
Don't be silly. I'm not into longshoremen. He's just—interesting-
looking, that's all."

Charlotte had left her scarf in the restaurant—it was one of the
things she'd dropped in her nervousness—and she turned back to
get it. It wasn't under their table; she looked around for the waitress
to see if it had been picked up. Her eyes caught the "longshoreman's"
eyes, and she froze in her tracks. He smiled broadly and waved a
scarf at her. "You know," he said slowly, "you wouldn't keep losing
things if you had more confidence in yourself." Charlotte stammered
thanks-for-the-scarf and turned to leave. "Meet for a beer after work?"
Charlotte turned back toward him. "What? Oh, no—I couldn't, really
. . ." "Six o'clock okay?" Charlotte was amazed by how sure he
seemed she'd be there. She was more amazed to find herself nodding
okay.

Taking this kind of risk was very strange for Charlotte. Again, no one was more controlled in her choices than she; no one left things less to chance. But this man—who'd introduced himself as Don— "By the way, my name is . . . ," he'd said as she left the restaurant, "what's yours?" and she'd mumbled her first name back—made her feel as if, for once, abandonment might be okay. But then she got scared—what had she done? All that afternoon she told herself what a fool she'd been, and she was thankful she hadn't given her full name or told him where she worked. She certainly wasn't going to meet him—what could she have been thinking of? But as the end of the day drew near, the memory of his eyes suddenly became vivid —and her feeling of unthinking trust in him came flooding back. She decided to meet him after all. What harm could it do?

Charlotte's "adventure"—which is how she thought of her first few dates with Don—completely threw her. Don, it turned out, was a guide for hiking expeditions, and his work took him to every exotic corner of the globe. He was about to leave for Fiji in a few days, and she found herself uncharacteristically dazzled by the fantasy of what it must be like to live such a rootless life. The first feeling she had about him—that she could trust him—only deepened. "He totally lacked artifice," Charlotte says. "He said exactly what he thought and felt—he never beat around the bush. But he wasn't rude. He was genuinely kind, sensitive, understanding. I felt like I was talking to an old friend within minutes. I'd never met anyone like him. I gave myself permission in these early days just to have a 'romantic adventure,' telling myself this wasn't a guy I'd marry in a million years, but why not enjoy someone a little different? What I didn't bank on was that I'd fall in love with him."

When Don left for Fiji, Charlotte resigned herself to the end of their "friendship." We are so different, what is the point of trying to keep it going, she thought. She also imagined that he probably had "a girl in every port." "Why should I think I was the only woman he got involved with? It was madness to think any more about him." But, to her astonishment, Don wrote her a letter. "I was as nervous as a sixteen-year-old when I got the envelope with the Fiji postmark. I couldn't believe it! And yet the letter was pure Don—neat printed block letters—even his handwriting was pared down to essentials. And the message was simple, too: 'I love you,' he wrote. 'Don't think it's too soon to tell. I know myself very well, and I want to be with you. See you when I get back in three weeks.' What was I to make of that? I mean, a part of me was thrilled. But a part of me was scared out of my head. Don wasn't the man I thought I'd end up marrying. I felt swept out of myself, taken to someplace new and strange and uncomfortable. His eyes kept coming back to me—the feeling of trust kept returning—but then what I thought of as my rational side took over. What kind of absentee father would he make? Think of how often his job will take him away from you! You can't marry him. And so, against everything my heart was telling me, I steeled myself to tell him we really couldn't see each other again."

When Don came back, Charlotte was afraid to look into his eyes—she was so afraid she'd lose her resolve. But she wasn't the first one to speak. "I figure," Don said, "that if we're going to be with one another, I can't keep running off to Fiji and places like that. I guess I'll have to get a steady job somewhere." He smiled. She looked into his eyes after all. She knew, in that moment, that she loved him, that all of her careful plans about "genetic engineering" and the "perfect man" she'd envisioned for herself didn't amount to anything. "We've both got a little adjusting to do," Don said, "don't we?" He *knew* he wasn't the type Charlotte had been looking for, but he also knew something Charlotte was only just learning. That what connects two people is rarely what you imagine. You can't predict love—it will happen where it will.

Charlotte and Don have had some rocky times. Charlotte remembers once when, with all her art-crowd friends, Don made a comment about a Monet poster up on the wall—how that "Monette" really knew what he was doing. Charlotte was mortified, and then hated herself for feeling embarrassed. When she told him (icily enough so that Don knew he'd embarrassed her) that the artist's name was pronounced "Mō-nay," Don bristled at first, then relaxed and gave a little laugh. "You can dress me up," he said, "but you can't take me anywhere, huh?" Charlotte laughed, too. Who cared how he pronounced "Monet," she thought. He had a better natural eye for art than two dozen other "art critics" she could think of. She learned at this time and many other times to value who Don *was*, not just what he sometimes sounded like. And Don learned to soften his sometimes *too* direct approach a little, too. He'd lived alone for so long that he almost lacked tact; he'd never seen any reason not to say exactly what he felt about anything. Now that he had a "respectable" job (he began managing a thriving bar/restaurant on the wharf after doing some bartending and waiting to start off), he realized he had to hold back his opinions if he wanted to succeed. It's been a learning experience for both Charlotte and Don.

They've just had their first child—a boy. "He's got Don's eyes," says Charlotte. "I've never loved anybody as much as I love Don and my son. Whatever it was I 'gave up' to have this life doesn't matter now. I can barely remember what it was I thought I was after!"

Charlotte had to use many of the techniques we've talked about to make the transition from her old rigid views to the more open perspective she now has. Everything from self-talk and value loading to balancing her brain (allowing the "feeling" and the "analytical" halves of her brain to coexist) confirmed her decision to stay with Don. As I told her about each of these tools, she kept saying "That's exactly what I did!" after each one. Intuitively, she knew that Don was right for her and out of a healthy sense of self-protection, she bolstered her positive opinion of Don until she felt the strength to say yes to his proposal of marriage. She understands the notion of a checklist very vividly. In fact, she drew up the following translation columns—before-and-after checklists—which we'll use as a model in the rest of the success stories I tell you about here.

| **What She Thought She Wanted** | **What She Got That Made Her Happy** |
|---|---|
| *An Ivy League guy* | *A guy who has common sense and an equally fascinating background* |
| *A guy who dressed elegantly* | *A guy who has his own sense of style and looks great to* me |
| *A good conversationalist, well versed in the arts* | *A guy who's got a greater* nat-ural *appreciation of "art" than anyone I've ever met—and a guy who says what he feels* |
| *Sophisticated* | *Worldly* |

The most important and revealing thing about these two lists is that they indicate what I promised at the beginning: Charlotte didn't have to give up anything (except an outdated fantasy) to get what she wanted. In fact, had she gotten a man who reflected the traits in her first list, she wouldn't have been happy! Her new checklist—the translation she was able to come up with after knowing Don—told her what would really make her happy. She came up with that checklist by allowing herself to become honest about what was truly making her happy—not what she'd fantasized about before out of fear and reflex.

## SUNNY AND BRADLEY: FROM "LIVING MY LIFE THROUGH HIM" TO "BEING MYSELF—EVEN WITH HIM"

"Boy," Sunny said to me between sips of tea, "when I think of the men I put up with before Bradley! When I think of how *perfect* I thought they were!" Sunny gave me a quick rundown. "First, there was Marty, the TV game-show director. He was a live wire—the quickest, most verbal man I ever met—a natural 'showman.' I often wondered why he wasn't in front of the camera instead of behind it. He was thought of as some kind of media whiz kid, and I was entranced. He knew everyone in the business and was winning all kinds of praise for innovations he kept bringing to game-show formats. I thought I was in love with him, but really I was *jealous*. I was trying to break into TV work myself, and what I didn't realize then is that I fell for Marty—hard—out of a misplaced desire to do what *he* was doing. When I realized I didn't care all that strongly for Marty, I thought I'd awakened to my tendency to fall for men I really envied and I'd never make *that* mistake again. But then I met Lance—at an acting class I was taking because I hoped I might find some work as an actress if I couldn't find it on the production end of things. Lance was already a success—he'd done a lot of soaps, had just landed an important movie role and was 'brushing up' in this acting class—and I fell for him like a ton of bricks. I completely ignored the fact that he was a totally self-absorbed narcissist. I was doing exactly what I'd done before. I was attracted by his success, and I was jealous of it. It was exhausting to keep doing this with men. I began to wonder if I was capable of loving any man."

Sunny said she rationally knew what her problem was, but she couldn't make herself change. She kept being attracted to men for the old wrong reasons—she wanted to do what *they* were doing. When she met Bradley, she hardly noticed him. "Bradley was about five-six and losing his hair. Everyone had told me what a great guy he was—witty and smart—but at first I couldn't get past how unprepossessing he *looked*. He also wasn't driven by ambition the way I was. The only thing he seemed to have was a real interest in *me*. This *threw* me," Sunny said with a long sigh. "I was so unused to a man being interested in *me*. It had always been me running after *him*, tailing the great master like a puppy dog. I couldn't relate to a man who actually seemed to care about me!"

Bradley's persistence began to pay off a little, however. "I'd worked my way up to television producer by this point, finally beginning to succeed in ways that I thought only *men* could succeed. Bradley was a script writer, one of many we called on to help doctor ailing scripts. We were working on a particularly difficult show and, at Bradley's urging, I agreed to a long meeting after work at a nearby restaurant to talk things over. I'd had a long, frustrating day. A man I'd been seeing—a high-level executive at a major network, who was just one more example of a self-absorbed guy I was attracted to because he was powerful in the business—abruptly phoned me and said he wanted to stop seeing me. Things, he said, were getting too 'intense.' Several business deals I was working on fell through. I was tired and vulnerable. The prospect of spending hours with Bradley didn't thrill me. But he picked me up right on time, and I went through with it."

Sunny isn't sure what began to turn things around. She only knows that by "the middle of our appetizers, I lost it. I was depressed and exhausted and for some reason I just started to cry! I was so embarrassed, but Bradley quickly made it clear I didn't have to be. He responded so simply—so beautifully. He took my hand in his and said he understood. He said it was good to cry. He said he knew how much I'd been holding in. He knew how much pain I'd been in. He seemed to know everything about me—everything about my feelings! Here was this short, sweet, quiet man—so different from all the high-powered media execs I'd been pursuing all my adult life— giving me something no other human being, no matter how powerful, had ever given me. Understanding. Caring. Love."

This is what broke the ice between them—or rather *in* Sunny. "I started to look at Bradley differently, because I started to look at what I had done to myself for all this time. I knew what my problem with men was. I was always drawn to men I could compete with, or men who were what I wanted to be. But never until this moment had I realized that what I really wanted was a full life myself. Then I could choose a man who loves and appreciates me."

Sunny's checklist changed because of her inner transformation.

The more she allowed herself to become what she had been seeking to be *for* her, the more she wanted to be with Bradley.

Sunny and Bradley are now a couple—they've come, through the years, to value each other for who they really are. Sunny is amazed to find herself doing the very things that caused her to envy men. And she can further appreciate her life through Bradley's eyes: "It's like Bradley allowed me to see a whole new part of myself. That *my* life is fun and fulfilling. So I can value him for the love he offers me—not the vicarious life."

In therapy, Sunny went through the whole process we learned in Step 6 in this book about facing the fantasy, and ended up using her own judgment. This, importantly, meant learning to separate fantasy from reality. She accepted not only intellectually, but emotionally, that the fantasies she'd had about "ideal" men were really displaced desires to become as competent and powerful as those men—a tendency we've seen in other women in this book. When she could truly allow herself to accept this about herself, she could open herself to someone who actually loved her for who she is—Bradley. Here's how her before-and-after checklists shaped up as a result:

| **What She Thought She Wanted** | **What She Got That Made Her Happy** |
|---|---|
| *Dazzlingly handsome* | *Attractive "inside" as a loving human being* |
| *Powerful* | *A man who helps me feel my own power* |
| *Wildly successful* | *Happy in what he does* |
| *Rich* | *Responsible* |
| | *Plus: A man who increases my self-confidence and who loves me for myself* |

## SARAH AND VITO: FROM "FEELING EMPTY WITH MR. RIGHT" TO "FULFILLMENT WITH A MAN I CAN RELY ON"

Sarah took some time to learn the truth of something I told her very early in therapy. She'd come to me after she'd met Vito—a "brilliant but strange" man who, for some reason, "adored" her. She'd just broken up with Bill, who she thought was the real Mr. Right, the dream lover she'd waited all her life to meet and who now had left her. What did I tell her? Through our love antennae we draw to us those from whom we need to learn something.

Sarah looked at me blankly at first. This didn't explain either Bill, the man that ran away, or Vito, the man who wouldn't leave. Then she thought a little more carefully. "Bill had it all," she said. "He was gorgeous, a Yale graduate, a genius with money—*Forbes* had written him up by the time he was thirty-two as one of Wall Street's leading lights. He even dressed right. He had it all: steel-gray Porsche, house in the country, high-rise condo, weekend escapes to Paris. He was so *smooth*. When I was with him, it was as if I were the only woman in the world—he focused in on me like radar—I felt *full* of him. Bill had the most amazing ability to become fully absorbed in whomever he was with, whatever he was doing. I've never seen such powers of concentration. When we made love, it was like making love was the most thrilling, most important thing he'd ever done. And I tried so hard to please him. Playing tennis, I was so set on winning his approval that I even thrived on his criticism. While he never told me I played well, sometimes—after I returned a serve using the exact form he told me to use—he'd give me a brief nod that said, 'You got it.' It wasn't much, but I lived for those nods—and I played harder."

Bill seemed to offer a dream life. "When we were with one another, he couldn't come up with enough plans for us! We were going to take off for Monte Carlo for the weekend. We were going to rent a yacht to take us to the Virgin Islands. We were going to the cottage in the Vermont woods he owned. It was so romantic!"

Unfortunately, things never panned out. Sarah's face darkened as she continued. "The problem is, we rarely *did* any of it. Bill would promise to call—and then disappear for two weeks. When he'd surface again, he'd be so apologetic that I couldn't help forgiving him. It was always some terrible crisis at work, or some crucial meeting he had to fly overseas to attend." It never occurred to Sarah that the crucial meeting might have been with another woman. Not, anyway, until, in the society pages of a glossy magazine that reported such things, she saw the unmistakable glamorous figure of Bill, resplendent in black tie, next to an equally beautiful Englishwoman listed in the caption as his "fiancée."

Sarah tried to be philosophical, but all she could feel was devastated. Then angry. "How dare he? I suddenly didn't care that he was the most perfect man I'd ever known. How dare he treat me that way?"

It was in this mood that she met Vito. "I was at my desk at the legal firm where I work—I'm an executive legal secretary—fuming. Vito, a legal assistant—not even a lawyer—suddenly appeared in front of me. It was lunchtime. I'd just slammed the magazine down, and I glared at him. He stammered out something like, 'Uh, I was just going out for a pizza. Wanna come?' I spat out, 'Yes, dammit!' He turned several shades paler—I think I scared him to death!"

Vito, it turned out, was tall, gangly, endearing in a kind of clumsy way. "He seemed to bump into doors a lot," Sarah said. But he had the most amazing mind.

"Vito knows the oddest things. Like details about the Mesopotamian War. Or what *really* happened to Troy. He wasn't only interested in ancient history, though. He loved talking about today's politics and had the most interesting and unexpected opinions about what was going on in the Senate, what was really being discussed behind closed doors in the Oval Office—it was like ideas just sparked out of him! Despite myself, I was fascinated. What a strange duck, I thought. And, amazingly, he wasn't boring. He wasn't like some idiot savant, spouting arcane knowledge and boring the heck out of everyone. He was really *fascinated* by the quirks of history and politics, and his enthusiasm was contagious. As much as I was prepared to sulk through lunch, I found myself laughing—and even a little entranced."

What is a bright guy like Vito doing in this job? Sarah thought. He explained he'd once owned restaurants, but they went bankrupt when his partner got into bad trouble. Vito obviously had more than a passing interest in Sarah—he shyly admitted he'd wanted to ask her out for a long time—and Sarah, intrigued, started to encourage him. "Part of it was I was so sick of 'smooth' men like Bill had been. There was something raw about Vito—refreshing. I never took him exactly seriously, but I thought, back then, that he'd be good for a diversion." What Sarah didn't realize was that Vito saw her as much more than a diversion. He was in love with her. At first this didn't sink in with Sarah. "I thought the fact that Vito called me to see how I was, that he always followed through on any plans we made, was just simply because he was 'conscientious' . . . like, I don't know, he'd been brought up to be a good little boy and so he couldn't help being polite. But it turned out to be more than that."

Sarah realized this when she got a bad case of flu and had to stay home for a week. "Vito called me every day. He insisted on bringing over chicken soup and fresh fruit, which I did *not* want him to do because I looked like death warmed over, and I've never allowed a man—even one as goofy as Vito—to see me in that bad a state. But he was really concerned and, frankly, I was glad for the help. So I gave in."

When Sarah recovered from the flu, Vito was still there. She began to see him differently—he seemed a little less goofy. She just wasn't used to a man reaching out to her this way—it was so different from Bill. One day she found herself in a free-floating fantasy and was amazed that *Vito* was the center of it. She softened toward him, which he clued onto in a moment. Suddenly their dates became romantic dinners. Finally, she realized that she wanted to make love with him. How had she changed so much? Was she just learning to settle for less? Was it just because she was on the rebound from Bill and needed *someone*—it didn't really matter who—to turn to?

"I was full of so many doubts. Vito was *not* the man of my dreams—at least of my old dreams. But he started to enter my new dreams. It was baffling—and, to tell the truth, I didn't like the idea that what I was really doing was settling for less. I began to convince myself that Vito wasn't really good enough for me. I stopped my romantic fantasies about him. I tried to tell myself that I really deserved someone as 'good' as Bill, and I shouldn't give up before I found him. So—I hate myself when I think of it now—I stopped seeing Vito. I made up every excuse I could whenever he called. I buried my head in work whenever he passed my desk at work. I struggled to ignore him." Sarah knows now that she hurt him a lot. He was really confused. "Once he left a short note on my desk. 'What's wrong?' was all it said. I didn't answer it. I just couldn't go back to Vito. It would be like admitting defeat."

Sarah forced herself to go out with other men—rising, young, handsome, Ivy-educated lawyers at the firm. She found herself increasingly bored by all of them. They turned out to be, she realized, empty suits. Most were just as self-absorbed as Bill had been, and the rest, for some reason, just didn't appeal to her. "I couldn't understand it. How could so many 'perfect' men be so awful? Then it hit me. Maybe they weren't 'perfect.' Maybe they weren't what I really wanted after all. I thought of Vito—and how I'd dumped him so cruelly. I felt terrible."

Sarah walked up to Vito's desk the next day and leaned on it. "I'm sorry," she said simply. "I'm a fool." Vito seemed to understand. He got up from his messy desk, wrapped his long arms around her and kissed her. She felt she'd come home. This was the man she loved after all.

A lot has come out in therapy for Sarah. She began to see that her dream lover, personified by Bill, was a fantasy she'd created because she wanted to feel glamorous and powerful and "smooth" herself. And, even more important, she wanted to win the unattainable man and his approval, to prove her "worth" (just as she had sought her daddy's love as a child). Once confident that she was lovable, she could choose Vito, who approved of her!

As we've seen in our previous success stories, the experience of love—when it's given to us freely, unconditionally, abundantly— can be a real shock when we don't think we deserve it. We tend to suspect it, undermine it, mistrust it. Sarah felt the need to withdraw from Vito, to demean his love as something second best, to try to see him at best as a diversion, because she was so deeply terrified of extending herself to someone as open as Vito. Out of her own fear of intimacy, she was attracted to unavailable men like Bill. Even if they appeared to be temporarily available, they were so self-absorbed that they weren't capable of anything longer than brief affairs. We've seen a number of women react similarly in this book. But what allowed Sarah to make a breakthrough was her willingness to accept that her old dream wasn't working anymore. Self-absorbed men simply weren't going to satisfy her—she fully woke up to the fact that they weren't going to make her happy.

Now when Sarah thinks how the love antennae work, how we draw to us those from whom we need to learn something, she can apply it in many ways to her experience with both Bill and Vito. "I see now that I had to hit bottom with men like Bill. What I needed to learn from 'perfect' men like Bill was that they wouldn't really satisfy me. And what Vito allowed me to learn is that I've got many more resources than I thought I did. I can accept being myself—I don't need to 'fill myself up' with someone more powerful or glamorous or successful than I am. When I accept that about myself, I actually have room in my life for love—both giving it and receiving it."

Sarah's before-and-after checklists reflect her new insights.

| What She Thought She Wanted | What She Got That Made Her Happy |
|---|---|
| Perfect looks | Looks that express individuality |
| Wild and fancy lifestyle | Can create fun experiences together even at home |
| Smooth and sophisticated | Sincere and enthusiastic |
| Terrific in bed | Caring in bed |
| Top education | Knowledgeable, curious and interested in what I think |
| Rich | Willing to work with me for what we both want materially |

## LUCY AND DIETRICH: FROM "HE'S TOO YOUNG— DON'T BE RIDICULOUS" TO "WE CAN DECIDE WHAT'S RIGHT FOR OURSELVES"

"I've read so much about older women and younger men," said Lucy, forty-seven, a lovely woman who is a highly regarded publicist in a major textbook publishing company, "and until I met Dietrich, I have to say I found the whole idea a little—distasteful. I never wanted to be one of those women like, I don't know, Vivien Leigh once played in some movie—the aging, needy, 'fading beauty' who depends upon some gigolo for false assurances that she's still 'desirable.' What an awful thought! As much as everybody's consciousness is supposed to be raised about how it's all right for older women and younger men to have relationships, there was something deeply resistant in me. I really couldn't help thinking that a woman made a fool of herself when she got into something like that. And as for the man—either he was out for her money or he had some neurotic mother fixation." Lucy laughs. "Look at how prejudiced I was! God, it's amazing how things can turn out. . . ."

Lucy, who was forty-five when she met Dietrich, a thirty-year-old editor whom her firm had just hired, liked him immediately. "He was the first man I ever regarded as a *friend*," she says. But, although she felt the beginnings of a romantic "tug," she quickly banished all such thoughts as "foolish." "I always had known what I was after," Lucy explains. "My first husband, to whom I was married for fifteen years—before he suddenly ran off with a younger woman" (Lucy laughs again and comments on the irony of that today) "was pretty much everything I had on my checklist. Steady, secure, settled in his life, mature—at least he seemed to be those things until he had his little mid-life crisis. I was devastated when he left, but my checklist still hadn't changed. I wanted a man, an *older* man if anything, who'd take care of me. My first husband obviously wasn't quite the one, but it still hadn't occurred to me to look for someone very different from my husband. I just wanted a better *version* of him." Lucy sighs. "It all seemed like a pipe dream to want someone 'perfect,' though. I mean, I was already in my middle forties. Who was I going to find? I'd really pretty much resigned myself to being alone. I felt my day had passed."

Lucy was so depressed after her divorce that she sought therapy. It was clear to me that she had very little confidence in herself. Her self-esteem was low and as a result she had little awareness of what she really needed. But she had to wake up to this herself before she could do anything about it. Dietrich helped her immeasurably. "Dietrich kept finding reasons to write memos to me and then to have little coffee-date meetings, which I realized weren't really necessary. I mean, textbook editors rarely have an urgent reason to meet with publicists—but I have to admire his ingenuity! He said he just wanted to 'pick my brain' because he was so impressed by my work. But I could tell, even then, there was more. I just didn't want to believe it. It so much went against the grain—not only society's grain, but my own! I knew he was attracted to me, but I couldn't deal with it. It just wasn't a part of my script."

Dietrich was persistent, however. He finally asked her out on a real date, not just a trumped-up business meeting, and Lucy hesitated. "I felt suddenly shy. I wanted to tell him that I really didn't think it was *appropriate*. But he seemed to anticipate this wariness, and he took over very charmingly and with great powers of persuasion—he had a couple of tickets to an out-of-town play and he said he knew I'd enjoy it. Anyway, I went." Lucy says she entirely forgot any age difference during this date—they had such a good time and had such an easy back-and-forth conversation, all she could feel was *good*. What an extraordinary person he is, Lucy thought to herself. By increments, she began giving herself permission to "like" Dietrich. It would never turn into anything serious, she promised herself, but why not have a good time with him? She slowly forgot to wonder what other people thought when they went out together. "In fact, I knew I was in pretty good shape—nobody was going to think I was his mother!—but something deeper in me began to let go. I just didn't care so much what the world might think. I was enjoying Dietrich too much!"

Dietrich began to open her up to a lot of new thoughts and experiences. "He was really unconventional. He had rented an apartment with three women—none of whom he dated—simply to save on rent and because he liked the women as friends. That did make me wonder a little at first. But it seemed to be a great arrangement for him, and it opened me up to the idea that men could be friends with women, which anyway Dietrich was demonstrating wonderfully with *me*." Lucy continued to enjoy being with Dietrich, but she refused to see anything permanent about the relationship. "If I allowed myself to think about it at all, I vaguely imagined we'd eventually drift apart and he'd find someone closer to his age. But I really didn't want that to happen, so I just didn't think about the future much."

What got Lucy to "think" about her relationship was something she still cringes to recall. "We had a general meeting at my company that both Dietrich and I had to attend. Quite naturally, we sat next to each other—it must have seemed obvious to other people that we knew and liked each other well. At the end of the meeting, Dietrich impulsively leaned over and gave me a small kiss. I blushed—and suddenly I realized I was ashamed! I really didn't want anyone to know I was 'seeing' Dietrich, and I felt suddenly mortified. He could see me push him away, turn suddenly cold. To make matters worse, as I was leaving the conference room, another publicist, Betty, walked up to me and winked. She said something awful like, 'I never took you for a cradle robber, Lucy!' I could have *died*."

This abruptly changed things. "What had I been *doing*? I mean, I was just about old enough to be Dietrich's *mother*. Suddenly I imagined everyone laughing behind my back. I felt like such a fool. I realize now that I had managed to ignore my deep fears about Dietrich; I'd never really dealt with them. But now they all came tumbling in. I really raked myself over the coals. On a good day I look maybe forty-two—I've got olive skin from my Italian forebears, the kind that doesn't show age too soon—but in no way did I look thirty! I just couldn't believe the fool I was making of myself. I knew then and there I had to regain some kind of . . . dignity. Act like the mature woman I was supposed to be. And I knew I'd have to talk to Dietrich."

Lucy summoned up her courage and phoned Dietrich that night, asked him to come over for coffee. There was "something" she wanted to tell him. Dietrich bounded over within the half-hour. "He looked like this eager, hurt puppy!" Lucy said. He started, "Look, about this afternoon, I know I made you uncomfortable when I kissed you, and I'm really sorry—" Lucy interrupted him. No, she said, it was good it happened. It had brought things to a head. Lucy took a deep breath and then sounded as "mature" as she knew how: "I told him that I thought it was inappropriate for us to continue seeing each other. There was an unbridgable gap between our ages, and I didn't want to keep him from meeting a woman he really ought to be meeting, someone he could get serious with. I went on like this for about ten minutes. Dietrich just sat there, this slight smile on his face. He looked like some obedient but slightly mischievous student sitting through a teacher's monologue. When I was done, he asked 'permission' to speak. I remember laughing a little nervously. Of course he could speak, I said. 'There's one thing you've left out,' he began. 'I love you. And, whether or not you know it, you love me.' "

It's been two years since that confrontation, and Lucy says that, although she resisted the truth Dietrich laid out that night for a long time, the strength of that love—Dietrich's certainty that Lucy was the woman he wanted to marry—has slowly pulled her through. "We've talked everything through. I've said, what about in twenty years time—when you're still young and I'm not? He's not worried. I'm convinced of his love. And I'm convinced now of something just as important. That I *deserve* his love! That despite the difference in our ages, I'm worthy and desirable and *sufficient*—my self-esteem has grown immeasurably. I don't think it could vanish now, even if for some reason Dietrich did. I know so much more about myself now—about what I really want. And I'm willing to accept Dietrich's love, just as I'm willing, now, to give my love freely to him."

It hasn't all been easy. Some of Lucy's old friends can't accept what she's done. Both sets of parents had a hard time with the decision, too. Sometimes her own old fears come up—and Lucy tenses, wonders if she's done the right thing. "But it's incredible," she says. "What Dietrich and I have together, just the two of us, has become so strong that it's able to weather any assault from outside. The longer I'm with him, the more I know we've done the right thing. A part of why my self-esteem is so much better now is that I accept this as a decision I've made for myself—I've taken responsibility for it. What I've created is *mine*—that's a very new feeling for me. I'm not reacting to what a 'woman my age' is *supposed* to do." Now, when Lucy looks into the mirror, she doesn't see an "older woman—a middle-aged lady whose time has passed." "I see a new serenity in myself—a self-acceptance which, ironically, makes me look *younger* than I did before!"

Lucy's before-and-after checklists tell the story in a nutshell.

| What She Thought She Wanted | What She Got That Made Her Happy |
|---|---|
| *Settled* | *Committed* |
| *A man who'll always be able to take care of me financially and emotionally* | *A man with whom I can build a life equally, since I can care for myself already* |
| *Older* | *Age doesn't matter—the man does* |
| *Conservative* | *Alive—interested—enthusiastic about the world* |

I said before how exhilarating it is to experience the *freedom* that comes from breaking through old assumptions—to an idea of what *you* really want for yourself. I hope you've started to feel a little of that freedom yourself. The most exciting thing about all of the women you've met here—women who've made the leap into trusting themselves to come up with the real answers to what they want in love and in life—is the freedom and joy they feel. Taking responsibility for your own choices is the key: trusting that you know what's better for you than anybody else is what allows you, ultimately, the courage to take that responsibility.

Remember how the love antennae work: we draw to us those from whom we need to learn something. When you develop this perspective about your life and your relationships, you can start to let up on yourself for making "mistakes," for continually getting into the "wrong" relationships. You can begin to look at the romantic and family and emotional patterns in your life and see why you needed those people in your life and what it is you've really learned from the people with whom you've gotten involved. Then you are free to make new choices—for example, the nice guy that will bring you happiness.

The notion of choice and responsibility is very important. When you accept that you've chosen to be with someone—that out of all the millions of possibilities, you've centered on this one human being—you can't help but realize there must be some pretty powerful forces at work, and some pretty important lessons to be learned.

The most resonant lesson of all, I hope, is that you don't have to give up any of your true desires for love and intimacy and happiness with a man to make a relationship work. Select, don't settle. The range of options available to you is virtually infinite. Your only task is to get clear about which of those options will please you the most. What a different view this is from what you probably once thought! You may have believed that, since love hadn't happened, it never would, or that you were chained to a dream that never brought you lasting joy. You likely thought you'd have to "settle" if you'd ever have a man. I hope you now see yourself as that proverbial kid in a candy store. Look at all those options! And then begin your process of choice. I promise you that you have the power to look into yourself and find what can really make you happy. Luckily, you don't have to do that alone. You've got the help of this book—and of the hundreds of women whose experiences gave rise to it.

You deserve all the love you can get—and you have the power to get it. Good men are out there, and many are those proverbial nice guys you overlooked. Once you've gone through the steps of this book, examining and changing your love choices and becoming the "you" you want to be, you won't have to put that smile on your face as you open yourself up and look around. It'll be there naturally. Your checklist will be in good working order, and your love antennae will vibrate to bring to you the nice guy with whom you can have it all.

## ABOUT THE AUTHOR

Dr. Judy Kuriansky is a highly respected clinical psychologist and popular TV and radio personality. She is the host of "Money & Emotions" on NBC's Consumer News and Business Channel and fill-in host on ABC's "Talk Radio." A recognized expert on relationships, stress, and trends, she has appeared on "The Oprah Winfrey Show" and "Donahue," among others. She is a consultant for businesses and films and her many articles appear in magazines and newspapers in the United States and abroad. A psychology professor at New York University, she is in private practice at the Center for Marital and Family Therapy in New York.

**BOOKMARK**

The text of this book was set in the typeface Bodoni Book
by Crane Typesetting Service Inc.,
West Barnstable, Massachusetts.

It was printed and bound by
Berryville Graphics, Berryville, Virginia

*Designed by Bonni Leon*